The Tree Hunters

Also by Thomas Pakenham

The Company of Trees
Meetings with Remarkable Trees
Remarkable Trees of the World
In Search of Remarkable Trees

The Tree Hunters

How the Cult of the Arboretum
Transformed Our Landscape

THOMAS PAKENHAM

WEIDENFELD & NICOLSON

First published in Great Britain in 2024 by Weidenfeld & Nicolson
an imprint of The Orion Publishing Group Ltd
Carmelite House, 50 Victoria Embankment
London EC4Y 0DZ

An Hachette UK Company

The authorised representative in the EEA is Hachette Ireland,
8 Castlecourt Centre, Dublin 15, D15 XTP3, Ireland (email: info@hbgi.ie)

3 5 7 9 10 8 6 4 2

A CIP catalogue record for this book is
available from the British Library.

ISBN (Hardback) 978 1 4746 1190 9
ISBN (eBook) 978 1 4746 1192 3
ISBN (Audio) 978 1 4091 8950 3

Typeset at The Spartan Press Ltd,
Lymington, Hants

Printed in Great Britain by Clays Ltd,
Elcograf S.p.A.

MIX
Paper | Supporting
responsible forestry
FSC® C104740

www.weidenfeldandnicolson.co.uk
www.orionbooks.co.uk

In memory of my wife Valerie

CONTENTS

.

INTRODUCTION

Living Dangerously

Twenty years ago I stumbled into making an arboretum at my home in Ireland. I called it the 'New Grove' and had little idea where it was leading me.

My choice of a site was unusual: an eighteenth-century shelter belt of beech and oak and sycamore planted to shield the house from the worst of the north-easterly gales. Already half the shelter belt had succumbed to these storms and the surviving beech were living on borrowed time. Should we restore the shelter belt by planting young beech and oak and sycamore? Of course that was the sensible plan – and the preference of my wife, Valerie. But I yearned for something more exotic. Why not live dangerously?

I could plant a hundred young trees I had recently collected as seeds in China and Tibet. The contrast would be irresistible: maples, canary-yellow in autumn and a foil for purple magnolias, leathery cork oaks beside silver-coated firs, and all these newcomers at the feet of the giants of the forest. So the New Grove led me, step by step, to the New Arboretum.

And it encouraged me to embark on a new journey by writing this history of arboretums and their origins.

Today there are several hundred collections of trees actively managed in Britain. The most ambitious is the giant arboretum founded by the Holford family at Westonbirt in the early nineteenth century. Now the jewel in the crown of the Forestry Commission, its coat of many colours in autumn draws in tens of thousands of visitors every year. At the other extreme there are numerous small collections of trees hidden away in back yards by passionate but secretive collectors.

How many of these collections deserve the sonorous name of 'arboretum'? There is no consensus for a definition. The one I prefer is this: 'a documented collection of trees planted for scientific study or enjoyment'. Unlike the trees in a woodland garden these are *specimen* trees. They do not merge – or are not supposed to merge – with their companions. You can study them and enjoy them in the round.

* * *

When were the first arboretums planted in Britain and Ireland? In the opening section of this book, Roots, I have traced their shadowy history. The pioneer in the early seventeenth century was a daring tree hunter, the elder John Tradescant. His collections included apricots from the Barbary coast of North Africa and fir trees from the wilds of Arctic Russia. His son of the same name took ship for Virginia and returned with seeds of many American trees that would soon be famous. These included the red maple, the swamp cypress and the tulip tree.

In 1664 John Evelyn launched his book *Sylva* – perhaps the most influential book on trees ever published – and it appears that his own collection was rich in exotics. The majority of the trees portrayed in *Sylva* had been introduced from Europe, Asia or America. Evelyn was followed by Henry Compton, Bishop of London, who also revelled in exotic trees. To add to his collection, he sent out a young clergyman, John Banister, briefed to hunt for trees in Virginia and the other colonies of eastern America. Banister was killed in a shooting accident, but before he died he had sent back seeds enough to make a dazzling collection of new trees and shrubs. These included the liquidambar or sweetgum, the scarlet oak and the first of the magnolias to reach Britain, the sweet bay.

By the mid-eighteenth century we come, for the first time, to a collection described in print as an arboretum. Originally the word was simply the Latin for a 'grove of trees'. By 1763 it was being used, in the modern sense, to describe the small collection of trees planted for Princess Augusta in the royal estate at Kew. After her death in 1772 the gardens at Kew were dramatically enlarged by her son, George III, trusting to the advice of Sir Joseph Banks, a distinguished amateur botanist and former plant hunter on Cook's first expedition. Meanwhile the fashion for rich landowners to create arboretums was slowly spreading.

In the second section of this book, Trunks, I have followed the trail of these landowners – from the Duke of Argyll to his nephew, the Earl of Bute – and to the men they commissioned to scour the world in the hunt for trees.

Many of these pioneering tree hunters – like Archibald Menzies and David Douglas – became famous. As the fashion for arboretums spread to smaller landowners and professional men, the numbers of tree hunters swelled. So did the number of nurserymen selling trees and shrubs. By the early nineteenth century the best known arboretum in the world was the Horticultural Society's 30-acre garden at Chiswick.

It was this society (now the RHS with more than half a million members) which commissioned David Douglas to risk his life in the wilds of what are now Oregon and California. Douglas sent back the seeds of many of the trees that now dominate British arboretums (and British forestry): the noble fir, the Sitka spruce, the Monterey pine and the eponymous Douglas fir. Douglas himself died miserably in Hawaii, gored to death by a wild bull.

The third section of the book, Branches, is dominated by a trio of dukes and a young Scotsman of genius. From each came a new sort of arboretum. The Duke of Marlborough arranged his huge collection at Whiteknights in a series of theatrical settings. But he was beggared by the cost, and soon went bankrupt. The Duke of Bedford arranged his collection of trees at Woburn in a two-mile-long twisting circuit around the pleasure ground. It was the Duke of Devonshire at Chatsworth who created the most scientific and up-to-date version of an arboretum. There were no fewer than fifty genera of trees and more than five hundred individual specimen trees arranged in a botanical sequence. The trees had been selected and arranged by his brilliant young gardener, Joseph Paxton, and received the blessing of the young Scotsman of genius. This was John Claudius Loudon, the owner and editor of the *Gardener's Magazine*, and the high priest of the new cult of the arboretum.

In 1833 Loudon launched his campaign to make Britain what he called a 'paradise'. He was intoxicated by arboretums. Gone would be the monotonous mixture of trees and shrubs now planted by public authorities. Instead the great London parks – Hyde Park, Regent's Park and Greenwich Park – would be replanted as arboretums. The cornucopia of exotic shapes and colours would delight the public – and educate them in the new science of botany. This was his vision and he struggled to make it a reality. By the end of the decade he had completed only one arboretum of his own: a pioneering design for a public arboretum in the town of Derby. He also risked going bankrupt by publishing a hugely expensive eight-volume work, *Arboretum et Fruticetum Britannicum*, before dying exhausted in 1843.

For the rest of the nineteenth century, and the first decades of the twentieth, it was Loudon's ideas that dominated the design of arboretums. Sheffield and Nottingham followed the example set

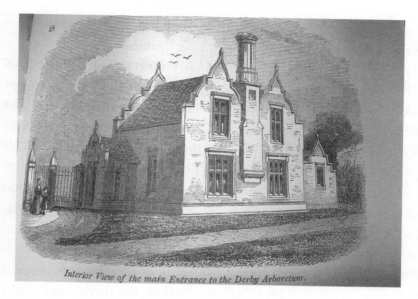

Interior View of the main Entrance to the Derby Arboretum.

Entrance at the Derby arboretum

by Derby. There were also many private collections of trees. The most ambitious by far was Robert Holford's private arboretum at Westonbirt in Gloucestershire, begun in 1839. Holford was a little-known squire, but he had two enormous advantages. He had just inherited a cool million pounds from a bachelor uncle. And the nineteenth century was proving a golden age for millionaires eager to employ tree hunters.

So I have concentrated in this book on Westonbirt's astonishing collection. It has turned out to be the most complete and comprehensive in Europe. Many of the rarest trees are now giants. And what giants were the tree hunters who risked their lives to supply Westonbirt! It would be hard to do justice to these long-suffering explorers. In North America the heroes were Archibald Menzies, David Douglas and William Lobb; in China William Kerr and Robert Fortune; in Japan Philip von Siebold and James Veitch; in China again Ernest Wilson and George

Forrest. I have documented their triumphs and their numerous misfortunes.

In the epilogue, Twigs, I have revisited some of the most important collections. A few are still intact – like Westonbirt – and even expanding. Bishop Compton's garden at Fulham has been lovingly restored. But many have been lost, or found a new role as a public park or a woodland garden. And they have had few modern successors on any scale.

Why has the fashion for arboretums slowly ebbed and died? For the same reason, perhaps, as the fashion for building large country houses. Large landowners now choose other sources of study and enjoyment – and other ways to impress their friends. And trees grow more slowly than buildings. To create a great new arboretum will cost enthusiasts half a lifetime, and that is not for them.

There's another reason for the decline of this cult. What made the nineteenth century a golden age for arboretums was the drama that *followed* the tree hunt. New trees arrived in Britain with every post, dispatched by the tree hunters from the wilds of America and the East. Would the trees rejoice in Britain's wayward climate – or fade like the consumptives in so many Victorian homes? No one knew. But tree hunters were not the only ones at the cutting edge. Tree collectors, too, shared the delirium of success and disaster.

In my own small arboretum in Ireland, I have shared some of that excitement. I have added more than fifty new specimen trees from seed I collected in China and the Himalayas. Some are already more than thirty feet tall – maples, oaks, magnolias, silver firs. But six more of the giant beech trees have now succumbed to winter storms, crushing a few frail newcomers. Perhaps my wife Valerie was right. Was it sensible to create an arboretum under the shadow of beech trees living on borrowed time?

ROOTS

CHAPTER I

The Storm

The storm hit London soon after midnight on 26 November 1703. His red-brick house shook in the blast as forty-year-old Daniel Defoe waited ready at hand with his notebook. One day in the future his creation, Robinson Crusoe, would make Defoe famous throughout the world. But in November 1703 he was a little-known pamphleteer, bankrupt brick-maker and jailbird. He had been recently released from Newgate prison. Earlier he had spent four months on the run with a price on his head. In due course he had been caught, and convicted for criminal libel. His crime was to write a pamphlet attacking the High Church Tories in favour with the new government that followed the recent accession of Queen Anne.

Ironically it was the storm that gave him a new start. This was to be Defoe's first full-scale book: *The Storm*, published in 1704. It's a work of reportage, based on eye-witness accounts he had collected himself after advertising in the newspapers, and it reads like a piece of modern journalism. After three hundred years, it still has the power to shock.

The City was a strange Spectacle [he began] the Morning after the Storm, as soon as the People could put their Heads out of Doors: though I believe every Body expected the Destruction was bad enough; yet I question very much, if any Body believed the Hundredth Part of what they saw.[1]

There had been a run of wild nights throughout that week in November. The gales broke some windows and peppered the streets with tiles and slates. But this storm was different: ferocious, apocalyptic. For four hours it raged, blocking the streets with fallen trees and bringing whole houses to the ground. Defoe himself had a narrow escape when the house next door in Newington Green collapsed, shaking his own red-brick house to its foundations. Outside, the air was full of smashed tiles flying like bullets from a gun. No one could remember a storm of such demonic power. And Defoe, it appears, didn't exaggerate. Meteorologists have recently confirmed that it was the most violent tropical cyclone to attack southern England in 300 years.

When daylight came London looked like a city that had been bombed. The elms in St James's Park, said to have been planted by Cardinal Wolsey, had been squashed flat. There were gaps in the streets where chimneys had fallen and reduced a four-storey house to a pile of red bricks. Many churches, and Westminster Abbey itself, had been stripped naked by the storm, losing ogees and battlements.

Trees lay in the streets like fallen warriors. Many of the rare species planted at Fulham Palace were crippled or stricken. They had been planted by one of the new breed of tree collectors – the Bishop of London, Dr Henry Compton. He said it was God's judgement on the city.

Outside London the same pattern repeated itself. Churches seemed especially vulnerable to God's judgement. Church spires were brought down all over the south of England. Some fell harmlessly into the adjoining graveyards. Others, like the 70-foot spire of Stowmarket near Ipswich, crashed through the roof, destroying the pews and monuments.

Yet the storm had one redeeming feature. As people picked their way through the rubble in towns and villages next morning, exchanging stories of miraculous escapes, it was clear that astonishingly few people had died – in southern England at any rate. Only twenty-one people were reported to have been killed in the capital – apart from a handful drowned in a ferry crossing the Thames. About a hundred more had been killed by fallen chimneys in southern England. Others, mainly small farmers, were drowned in the low-lying marshes beside the Severn, when the tide rose to an unprecedented height and the river overflowed its banks.

One bizarre casualty was the much admired, newly built, 130-foot-tall Eddystone Lighthouse. To prove it was safe, its eccentric designer, Henry Winstanley, chose to visit his creation on the night of the storm. The lighthouse disintegrated, taking Winstanley with it. The only other celebrated victims of the storm were the Bishop of Bath and Wells and his wife. They lived in the oldest part of the Bishop's Palace and both were killed when the main chimney crashed through their bedroom.

Otherwise the majority of casualties were at sea – and their number was hard to believe. A single night's storm had crippled the British navy, and left a dangerous breach in the famous 'wooden walls' that kept Britain safe from invasion.

With hindsight it's easy to see the disaster might have been avoided. Sir Cloudesley Shovell, the accident-prone admiral in charge of the main fleet, had returned from an expedition to Russia, carelessly leaving many of the ships anchored near the mouth of the Thames. The storm snapped their cables, scattered the fleet and drove many ships onto the Goodwin Sands. One of the doomed ships was the *Mary*, commanded by Rear-Admiral

Beaumont. She was lost with all but one of her crew of 273. Other ships that foundered that night were the *Reserve* with 247 men, the *Restoration* and the *Northumberland* with a total of 639 men, all of whom drowned. The *Sterling Castle* sank with the loss of 280 men. And the storm seemed insatiable. For it soon proved that the first list of casualties was a mere fraction of the losses that night.

No doubt there were many acts of heroism – and the reverse. Defoe published a report of the way 'an abundance of poor Wretches' were left to die, 'who having hung upon the Masts and Rigging of the Ships, or floated upon the broken Pieces of Wrecks, had gotten a Shore upon the *Goodwin Sands* when the Tide was out.

Boats sailed out, 'coming very near them in quest of Booty, and in search of Plunder, and to carry off what they could get, but no Body concerned themselves for the Lives of these miserable Creatures'.[2]

One solitary hero emerges from Defoe's pages: Thomas Powell, the mayor of Deal, in Kent. Realising the sailors would be drowned at the next high tide, he tried to persuade the local customs officials to go to the rescue. They refused, claiming they had no authority to rescue anyone. So the mayor took their boats by force and persuaded some local fishermen to man them, offering 5 shillings from his own pocket for each sailor they could save. The fishermen agreed to the deal, and 'above 200' sailors were duly snatched from the sands before the tide rose and drowned the rest.[3]

Today naval historians reckon that a fifth of the seamen of the British fleet were drowned that night or in the days and nights that followed. Add the crews lost in merchant ships, and a total of over eight thousand men are believed to have been drowned or crushed or died of exposure. So the storm inflicted a worse defeat on Britain than any foreign enemy had ever achieved. And it was in a sense a double defeat. Apart from the loss of ships and men, there was the loss of millions of trees. These were the trees that were needed for naval timber: for filling the gaps in those wooden walls.

It was *trees* – timber trees and trees planted for ornament – that, on land at least, were the most numerous and most visible casualties of the great storm. In one part alone of the Forest of Dean three thousand oaks were uprooted. Four thousand oaks were lost in the New Forest, which looked like a battlefield after a defeat. Defoe made a tour of the fields of Kent in the weeks after the storm, and claimed he had counted fifteen thousand fallen trees – before losing count. And the trees that would be most missed were not fruit trees but the giants of the English landscape: the oaks and beech and pines and walnuts and sweet chestnuts newly planted both for timber and ornament. In a single medium-sized estate south of London – John Evelyn's in Surrey – two thousand oaks were smashed to the ground. It was reckoned that the total losses in country estates numbered millions.

If there was one man who had helped create that treasure trove of new trees in the previous century it was that eighty-three-year-old country gentleman, John Evelyn, who lived at the family estate, Wotton. His red-brick, gabled house, hidden in the Surrey hills between Guildford and Dorking, looked modest enough. Evelyn's grandfather had bought it after making a small fortune in the gunpowder trade.

But his grandson, John Evelyn, was cast in a different mould. He personified the kind of modest, well-educated, middling country gentleman not rich enough for a baronetcy, nor poor enough to need a job in the army or Church. But, unlike most men of this class, he had the right connections to make him an insider at court. He had married the daughter (and heiress) of the British Resident at the French court, Sir Richard Browne. Evelyn was a leading member of the council of the Royal Society, rubbing shoulders with many of the movers and shakers in the newly liberated world of Charles II. His personal friends included architects like Christopher Wren, civil servants like Samuel Pepys, and scientists like Henry Newton and Robert Boyle.

John Evelyn

Soon after the monarchy was restored in 1660 the King's Commissioners for the navy had become alarmed at the lack of home-grown trees suitable for building ships for the fleet. Everyone knew that oak timber was the key for this strategic task. But why was no one planting the trees? The newly created Royal Society commissioned John Evelyn to write a report on the subject. This was duly presented to the society in October 1662 with the sonorous title of *Sylva or a Discourse of Forest-trees and the Propagation of Timber in His Majesty's Dominions*. In due course it was published to great acclaim – and republished many times in his lifetime and beyond.

In *Sylva* John Evelyn introduces himself with disarming modesty. 'I speak only here', he tells us, 'as a plain husband-man and a simple forester'.[4] In reality Evelyn was a polymath, a virtuoso in both the arts and the sciences, a hands-on gardener as well as a scholar with a dozen books to his credit. With *Sylva* he broke entirely new ground in the overlapping worlds of forestry, botany, horticulture, economics and landscape design. It served as a 600-page manual for people anxious to plant trees for timber or pleasure, or for both combined. The practical advice was spiced with weighty passages of history and classical mythology. Evelyn had travelled widely in France and Italy as a young man, anxious to keep out of trouble with the Cromwellian authorities at home.

With *Sylva* he took his readers on an extended tour of the great trees of antiquity, 'like some great oaks of the Hercynian Forest which Pliny tells us ... were thought coevous with the world itself', and the Ruminal figtree in Rome under which 'the bitch wolf suckled the founder of Rome and his brother, lasting (as Tacitus calculated) eight hundred and forty years'.[5] Much of this information was clearly fabulous.

The book also struck a practical note exactly right for the times. Evelyn pointed the finger at some of the more remarkable trees in Britain that had survived for hundreds of years, like the great chestnut of Tamworth (now Tortworth) in Gloucestershire and the ancient yew of Crowhurst in Surrey. (And both of these ancient trees, *mirabile dictu*, are still going strong today, 350 years later.)

But *Sylva* is a great deal more than a travelogue. Here was an eloquent summons, a clarion call to the country gentlemen of Britain. Plant a forest, they were told, as part of your patriotic duty to defend the country. Enjoy the new Garden of Eden you will create. And rejoice in the thought that this investment will make a fortune for your grandchildren!

For Evelyn himself this was a labour of love. He had spent his boyhood roaming the wooded hills of Wotton – 'Wood-town', as he named it. It was here that he had developed his fascination with trees. He never tired of celebrating the mystery by which the tiny grain 'which lately a single Ant would easily have born to his little Cavern' would ascend 'by little by little... into an hard erect stem of comely dimensions, into a solid Tower as it were'.[6] Evelyn himself was deeply religious. And his love of trees chimed with his love of God. Trees were an embodiment of the higher nature and spiritual aspiration of man. A single tree was a 'Sacred Shade', a grove a place for prayer and meditation.

One might well ask how many other country gentlemen shared these exalted sentiments. In practical terms, at any rate, Evelyn's clarion call was astonishingly successful. By the end of the seventeenth century thousands of new plantations of oak and other forest trees enriched the landscape. And *Sylva* did so much more.

It was the first book to focus successfully on the need to import *exotic* trees: maples and pines from the American colonies, cypresses and cedars from Europe and the Lebanon. In fact two thirds of the species of trees described in detail in the pages of *Sylva* (and elegantly engraved in later editions) were exotic new-comers to Britain. Many, like the maples, were collectors' trees for the garden, not forest trees for timber or fruit trees for the orchard. Others, like the oriental plane from Greece and Turkey, were suited to the woods, and they carried the romantic associations of the classics – of Plato's Academy and Xerxes' obsession with the tree.

So *Sylva* had an important lesson, apart from the need to plant oaks for the navy. Collecting trees was now in fashion. This was an exciting novelty. For centuries there had been country gentlemen who collected exotic pictures for their saloons and rare books for their libraries. Now they had begun to turn to planting nurseries which could offer exotic introductions of trees. To popularise this fashion was certainly not the least of Evelyn's many achievements, and it helped to transform gardens in Britain and Ireland in the coming centuries.

* * *

But we must return to the immediate aftermath of the great storm of November 1703.

Out on the hillside above his beloved estate at Wotton, John Evelyn surveyed the wreckage of his young plantations. He wouldn't have been human if he hadn't felt something close to despair. He had devoted his life to these trees at Wotton and their counterparts at his wife's estate, Sayes Court. Now look at them. As he put it, eloquently, in the closing pages of the fourth edition of *Sylva*, published three years after the great storm:

> methinks I still hear, sure I am that I still feel, the dismal groans of our forests; that late dreadful hurricane... having subverted so many thousands of goodly Oaks, prostrating the trees, laying them in ghastly postures, like whole regiments fallen in battle by the sword of the Conqueror, and crushing all that grew beneath them.[7]

The dismal groans of the forests. But Evelyn, now eighty-six, could display an extraordinary resilience in the face of disaster. No doubt the dazzling success of *Sylva* gave him comfort and strength – coupled with his deep-rooted religious faith. And one thing was obvious to anyone, like Evelyn, who had read Daniel Defoe's shocking book on the storm. The lesson of *Sylva* – to plant trees as a patriotic duty – was never more relevant than in the aftermath of the great storm. Millions of fallen oak trees must be replaced by new plantations for naval timber. It was a debt that England owed the eight thousand seamen drowned in the storm. And alongside these new forests a new landscape of exotics would surely flourish, transforming a land of barren moors and heaths to a version of paradise.

Evelyn's spirits rebounded at the prospect. His final edition of *Sylva* concludes like a peal of bells or the crash of trumpets:

> *Haec scripsi octogenarius* [I have written these words in my eighties], and shall, if God protract my years, and continue my health, be continually planting, till it shall please him to *transplant* me into those glorious regions above, the celestial Paradise, planted with Perennial Groves and Trees, bearing immortal fruit . . .[8]

CHAPTER 2

Bishop Compton's Antidote

In the summer of 1713, Bishop Henry Compton, aged eighty-three, and once famous as the 'rebel bishop' who had helped to precipitate the 'Glorious Revolution', was buried under the east window of his parish church at Fulham. He was not short of company. All around him lay the tombs of his brother bishops, some late-medieval with crumbling Gothic stonework, others more recent, ponderous slabs of baroque design. Compton had

Bishop Henry Compton

been bishop for forty years – far longer than any other Bishop of London. But ostentation was not one of his vices, at least in his old age, and his tomb is one of the plainest.

It's an unromantic spot, though shaded by oaks and sycamores, as only an iron railing separates it from the hurly-burly of Fulham High Street. But a world away, down a winding, grassy path through the churchyard, you can glimpse the bishop's old home: the sumptuous, red-brick Tudor courtyard of Fulham Palace, where the Bishops of London lived and worked. And between the courtyard and the churchyard is the walled garden, and the ghosts of the astonishing collection of trees to which Bishop Compton devoted so many years of his long life.

*Bishop Henry Compton's modest tomb (centre)
in Fulham churchyard*

What makes a man a collector of trees? In Compton's case, and no doubt that of many others, trees were the antidote for disappointment. He had aimed to win the top job in his profession – and he had failed.

Compton came from a Royalist family known for its energy and often reckless courage. He was the sixth son of Spencer Compton, Earl of Northampton, who had been killed leading his cavalry in the Civil War. (Captured by the Parliamentary infantry, Lord Northampton was offered mercy. He replied that 'he scorned to take quarter from such base rogues and rebels as they were'.[1] He was soon dispatched with a blow to the head.) Of course the Compton family welcomed the return of the Stuarts. In 1675, after several years wandering abroad and a spell as a soldier, young Henry Compton took holy orders. He had powerful friends, and by the age of forty-three was made Bishop of London. He was hard-working and generous and very much liked by most members of the Anglican Church. People began to speak of him as the next Archbishop of Canterbury. He was the clear favourite for the job in 1677 after the death of the current archbishop, Gilbert Sheldon. But he had made two fatal errors in his career as a bishop.

He had alienated Charles II by harping, in his addresses to the clergy, on the lax morality of the court. Worse still, he had made a personal enemy of the king's brother and heir, the Duke of York, the future James II. Compton was a militant Protestant and passionately hostile to Catholic claims for tolerance. James had now declared himself a Catholic, and was hell-bent, according to Compton, on the conversion of England to that faith. So there was little chance of compromise. In the event Compton was humiliated to find that William Sancroft, a mere Dean of St Pauls, was chosen as archbishop.

A decade later, in 1691, Compton suffered an even more humiliating rebuff, when a later Dean of St Paul's, John Tillotson, was chosen to replace Sancroft as archbishop. William and Mary were now joint monarchs, and both owed a personal debt to Compton. Perhaps he was too high-handed and too flamboyant for William and Mary's taste. But he had risked his own neck in their cause. He was one of the 'Immortal Seven' of the 'Glorious Revolution': the only bishop among the grandees who had committed treason by signing the famous coded letter which invited William (then Prince of Orange) to set sail for England. He had then played a daredevil role as soldier-bishop, rescuing Princess Anne from the clutches of her father, King James. In full military uniform, with pistols in his holsters, he had escorted the princess to safety.

After the success of the coup, it was Compton who had acted as archbishop by placing the crowns on the heads of the new monarchs, William and Mary. (This was because the current Archbishop of Canterbury, William Sancroft, refused the job out of loyalty to James II.) And now, in 1691, Compton was to be passed over in favour of another Dean of St Paul's. Compton felt the bitterness of a man betrayed by his friends. Only time could heal these wounds – time and his collection of trees.

In fact his professional disappointments gave him a great deal of extra time for his hobbies. In 1687 he had defied James II by siding with the Anglican clergymen who refused to read the king's Declaration of Indulgence for Catholics. His punishment: to be suspended from his work as a privy councillor and in effect to be frozen out of politics. The timing was good – at least for collecting trees. As we saw, John Evelyn had made tree planting fashionable. And in due course half a dozen small nurseries had emerged ready to provide exotic trees for new clients.

Already two daredevil plantsmen and plant explorers, John Tradescant and his son of the same name, had assembled pioneering collections in their garden in south Lambeth. During their lifetimes – spanning the thirty years between the reign of

Charles I, the Civil War and the Restoration – this garden was a commercial venture on view to the public. And no wonder enthusiasts, like John Evelyn, drove the few miles south of the Thames to inspect these novelties.

Adjoining the garden was an extraordinary second collection, the 'Ark', an incongruous collection of several hundred oddities arranged in the form of a small museum. The Tradescants could congratulate themselves that this was the first museum open to the public in Britain. Most of the exhibits had been collected by the family on their travels abroad, or donated by well-wishers (including Charles I himself). One twenty-four-year-old German tourist, greatly impressed, listed some of the exhibits:

> we saw a salamander, a chameleon, a pelican ... gourds, olives, a piece of wood, an ape's head, a cheese ... a sea parrot, a toad-fish, an elk's hoof with three claws, a bat as large as a pigeon, a human bone weighing 42 pounds, Indian arrows, an elephant's head, a tiger's head ... a kind of unicorn.[2]

As one might expect, John Evelyn was rather less excited by what he saw, when he took the ferry to Lambeth in September 1657. ('The chiefest rarities', he wrote in his diary, 'were the antient Roman, Indian & other Nations Armour, shilds & weapons'.)[3] And, strange to say, he doesn't mention the Tradescants' trees. Yet these trees were more than mere novelties and oddities. By collecting them, and numerous other plants, from all over the globe, the Tradescants had done more than open a garden to the public. They had opened the eyes of the public to the world of scientific botany. In fact their garden at Lambeth was the prototype of the new style of garden, designed with botany in mind, as well as for pleasure and ornament, a style that would come to dominate gardening for the next three hundred years.

How had this working-class father and son from Suffolk, the John Tradescants, emerged from the shadows? And, to put it bluntly, how did they persuade rich patrons to finance the Tradescants' expensive hobby of collecting plants and other rarities from all over the world? To answer that question we must go back to the first years of the century.

In 1610 John Tradescant the Elder was hired by William Cecil, 1st Earl of Salisbury, to be the new head gardener at Hatfield, his palatial house near London. Politically, Cecil was a giant, courted by the king, James I, himself, and eager to have the best of everything. He must have heard great things about Tradescant. One of the first jobs he gave him was to collect fruit trees, such as medlars, almonds and pears, from plant nurseries in the Low Countries. These were duly planted in the dazzling new garden at Hatfield. Obviously Tradescant was a great deal more than a mere plantsman. After Cecil's death he was hired by another grandee, Lord Wotton, and helped to design and build Wotton's extravagant new garden in the ruins of St Margaret's Abbey in Canterbury. But Tradescant yearned to leave England and hunt for plants abroad.

In 1618 he attached himself to Sir Dudley Digges, who had been chosen to lead a daredevil diplomatic mission to the Tsar of Russia, Michael Federovich. Russia was in chaos, as the country was engaged in a war with Poland, and the tsar was desperate to negotiate a loan of £20,000 from England. To avoid the fighting, an unusual route was chosen for the embassy, involving a long detour by way of Archangel and Arctic Russia. Tradescant joined the expedition, it seems, largely to collect seeds of Russian trees and other plants.

The embassy was a failure as Sir Dudley seems to have lost his nerve. At any rate he turned back before reaching Moscow. But Tradescant came back with a useful haul of seeds of trees.

'I have seene 4 kinds of fir trees', he wrote in his diary of the expedition, spelling the words phonetically: 'and birche trees of a great bignes . . . and littill treese that they make hoops of, whiche the Inglyshe saye they be wilde cheryes, but I cannot believe it is of that kind.'[4] He also collected seeds of various fruits, including some strawberry seeds he later sent to Jean Robin, Louis XIV's celebrated gardener in Paris.

Tradescant's next patron was made of sterner stuff than Sir Dudley Digges. In 1620 James I appointed Sir Robert Mansell to take a fleet and head for Algiers in the hope of persuading the Grand Signior to stop supporting the Barbary pirates. The pirate fleet was based in the harbour at Algiers. Mansell was instructed to demand the release of captured British ships and their crews. Whether diplomacy failed or not, he was to destroy the pirate ships in the harbour. And Tradescant seized his chance to join the expedition. His aim, we can guess, was not to fight with pirates, but to collect rare plants in the western Mediterranean. In due course Mansell's demands were rebuffed by the Grand Signior, and Mansell's fleet pressed home their attack by setting loose a flotilla of fire ships heading for the pirates in the harbour. But success eluded them: the wind dropped at a crucial moment. Mansell had failed. Tradescant, however, returned cock-a-hoop with his new acquisitions. These included a 'sweete and delicate' variety of apricot much admired by contemporary botanists like John Parkinson.[5]

Tradescant's third patron was the dashing Duke of Buckingham, favourite (and reputed lover) of James I. Tradescant's job entailed supervising the duke's sumptuous new gardens: at Burley-on-the-hill in Rutland and New Hall near Chelmsford. He served his master in many other roles. In 1627 Tradescant joined the duke on a reckless expedition to crush the dissident French Protestants besieged at La Rochelle. It proved an unqualified disaster. Two thirds of the duke's force of nine thousand men were cut down or drowned or died of disease. Tradescant was lucky to escape with his life.

The duke himself died the next year, stabbed by a young naval officer called Felton who was outraged by the duke's incompetence. But Tradescant remained in demand. On 20 August 1630 the new king, Charles I, appointed him the Keeper of the Gardens, Vines and Silkworms at the royal palace of Oatlands – in other words the head gardener of Oatlands, Queen Henrietta Maria's country estate in Surrey. It must have been Tradescant's proudest moment. And he must have been happy to be told, before he died eight years later, that he would be succeeded at Oatlands by his only son, John Tradescant the Younger.

It was his thirty-year-old son John who also inherited the twin collections at Lambeth: the garden and the 'Ark'. Already he had proved an accomplished plantsman and plant explorer like his father. In fact he had his father's green fingers without the daredevil streak. Before he was twenty-one he had taken ship for the colony of Virginia to hunt for rare trees, and returned triumphant.

Virginia at that date must have seemed to have a touch of Eden. Trees from the primeval forest grew right down to the shore. As one settler recorded it: 'Nor is the present wildernesse of it without a particular beauty, being all over a naturall Grove of Oakes, Pines, Cedars, Cipresse, Mulberry, Chestnut, Laurell, Sassafras, Cherry...'[6] But there was a darker side to this paradise. The Native Americans naturally resented the newcomers who were parcelling up their lands. In 1622 the local tribes lost patience, and a massacre ensued. Then the settlers took their revenge and an uneasy peace returned.

In 1639 young Tradescant paid a second visit to the colony, and returned with further rarities: seeds wrapped in paper, roots planted in small pots and wooden tubs. For the next few years he was up to his ears working for the queen at Oatlands. Then the storm burst over his head, as Britain was plunged into civil war.

The queen abandoned Oatlands and fled back to France. Oatlands became a prison for Charles I before his beheading in Whitehall. Of course Tradescant was now out of a job, and vulnerable as a former royal servant. But the Puritans running the country had no hang-ups about gardeners. Gardens provided vital food – and vital medicinal plants. Tradescant was allowed to retire to the Ark and cultivate his garden in peace.

In 1656, six years before his death, Tradescant completed a new task he had set himself: to compile and publish a complete catalogue of both his own and his father's collections. This was to be his crowning achievement. His father had attempted part of this task twenty-three years earlier. But his father had merely scribbled notes of his plants on the back of his copy of Parkinson's *Paradisus*. The new lists of both collections proved essential reading for scholars and the public at large. Most of the contents of the Tradescants' museum would eventually be celebrated as the core collection of the Ashmolean at Oxford. (Sad to say, Tradescant's widow, Hester, drowned herself after being cheated out of her inheritance by a rogue scholar called Elias Ashmole, who then took credit for donating the collection. But this is another story.) And the published catalogue of the trees and other plants remained a unique guide to future collectors, following in the footsteps of both the Tradescants.

* * *

Which brings us back to Bishop Compton. We can picture him in the late 1670s, dressed in Carolean gardening clothes, with his copy of Tradescant's catalogue in hand, striding around the 30-acre demesne at Fulham Palace. What did he make of it all?

Out of several hundred botanical rarities in the catalogue, the sixty trees stood out like beacons. Today the list may look a trifle tame. But many of these trees were newcomers only introduced from Europe in recent years, some by the Tradescants themselves. There were half a dozen conifers: ebullient umbrella pines (*Pinus pinea*) from Italy and pinaster pines from France, common silver firs (*Abies alba*) from the Alps, spruce from Norway and other parts of Scandinavia (*Picea abies*), cypresses (*Cupressus semper-virens*) from the Mediterranean. Presumably these had been used in the Tradescants' garden as a backdrop for the deciduous trees. The latter included exotics like both the black and the white mulberries (*Morus nigra and Morus alba*), the Indian bead tree (*Melia azedarach*) the smoke tree or Venetian sumach (*Cotinus coggygria*) as well as better known European trees like the walnut (*Juglans regia*), the sweet chestnut (*Castanea sativa*) and the Cornelian cherry (*Cornus mas*).

Exotics they might be. But these European newcomers were not the star performers on the Tradescants' list. The trees that must have dazzled Compton, judged by later events, were all from America.

In fact there were eleven new introductions from Virginia and the other American colonies, most of which are now well known to British and Irish gardeners. Here's the list, starting with six which were apparently planted by the younger John Tradescant but are *not* thought to have been personally introduced by him: the shagbark hickory (*Carya ovata*), the persimmon (*Diospyros virginiana*), the butternut (*Juglans cinerea*), the red mulberry (*Morus rubra*), the black walnut (*Juglans nigra*) and the locust tree (*Robinia pseudoacacia*).

The last two of these have now become accepted as favourites in Europe – with certain reservations. The black walnut is far more elegant than its European counterpart and its leaves are delightfully fragrant. Unfortunately its nuts are too bitter to eat. The robinia is a tree of choice for English city streets, as it stays where it's put – that is, in the pavement; in summer its feathery green leaves make a painterly contrast with its small white flowers. In France, however, it feels too much at home, and is too happy for its own good. It spreads everywhere; so the French treat it as an invasive weed.

The four American trees actually collected by the hands of John Tradescant are as follows: the Virginian nettle tree (*Celtis occidentalis*), the red maple (*Acer rubrum*), the swamp cypress (*Taxodium distichum*) and the tulip tree (*Liriodendron tulipifera*). It was the last three that were to become celebrated as stars.

Each had something extraordinary to bring to the gardens of Britain and Europe. No other tree could compete with the rainbow of autumn colours displayed by the red maple. The swamp cypress, acid-green in spring, fox-pink in autumn, brought a new glamour to the humble pond. Here was a giant from the Everglades of Florida that would flourish in six feet of muddy English water. And finally there was the tulip tree, that marvel from the forests of Pennsylvania and the Carolinas. If I had to choose one American species for a companion on my desert island it would certainly be this creature, the most heraldic of trees. Its leaf looks like the shield of a medieval knight, with wings at the sides and the end chopped off. In summer it explodes with green-and-pink flowers the shape of tulips. And in autumn it turns the colour of butter fresh from the churn.

* * *

Here was the Tradescants' legacy, and it intoxicated Bishop Compton. Although the Tradescants were dead by the 1670s, and the rows of rare trees in their garden in Lambeth abandoned, their ideas still flourished. Indeed, they swept Bishop Compton off his feet. Virginia was the place for new discoveries, the new botanical Eldorado. So the bishop believed. But who was to act as his agent in that turbulent colony 3,000 miles from Lambeth?

By good fortune the Bishop of London was also responsible for the Anglican Church in the American colonies. Compton acted swiftly. Within a year of moving to Fulham he had chosen a young botanist called John Banister to serve a dual role in Virginia: both as Anglican minister and plant explorer. Although Banister was young and untried he had a high recommendation from the Professor of Botany at Oxford, Dr Robert Morison. (The university was beginning to take botany more seriously since the creation of a small botanical garden there earlier in the century.) Banister reached Virginia in 1678, and made his way through wild country to the Falls, now known as Richmond. At first it was too dangerous for him to botanise. He was befriended by Captain William Byrd, the commander of a fort at the Falls, whose job was to protect the settlers from marauding Indians. Byrd was also a trader who knew the local trails. The raids that year horrified the young botanist. Tribes from the north came to plunder the countryside and even seize the families of some of the settlers. Fortunately at the Falls it was mainly crops and cattle that suffered. As Banister put it, 'blessed God that none of us lost our lives'.[7]

Next year the raids petered out and Banister made his first hesitant sortie into the interior. Mounted on horseback, and with some friendly Indians to guide them, he and a party of settlers spent three days following the course of the James River. Banister was delighted with everything. He wrote home to describe the deafening sound of cicadas, and the heady smell of balsam trampled underfoot. The soil was rich and 'lusty'. All around them were 'Trees, Shrubbes, Herbs etc unknown in Europe.'[8]

In due course Banister compiled a catalogue of two hundred

species of trees and other plants, almost all new to botanists and gardeners. Packets of American seeds began to follow the catalogue. Banister's first loyalty was naturally to the bishop, but the bishop encouraged his young protégé to send packets to a small circle of English botanists and gardeners. These included Robert Morison, his former Professor of Botany at Oxford, and the staff of the Physic Garden at Chelsea. Sometimes Banister would apologise to the bishop for his failure to find the seeds of an important tree. 'My Lord,' he wrote somewhat plaintively,' this comes to beg Your Lordship's pardon that I have not sent the Sassafras berries according to my promise'. He had recently been ill. By the time he recovered, the berries 'had all dropt, or ye birds had eaten them from off ye trees.'[9]

By 1688, despite working so hard to please his backers, Banister was in financial straits. And this was a difficult year for everyone. In London the bishop was swept up in the great conspiracy to depose James II and replace him with William and Mary. Fortunately for the bishop, the coup succeeded. It became the Glorious Revolution, and the crisis passed. By 1691 the bishop's circle of botanists had been much enlarged. In fact it had become a formal club – the Temple Coffee House Botany Club, with about forty members. The new club met once a week and made frequent visits to Fulham Palace to study the bishop's latest acquisitions. And the club's debt to Banister was well recognised. Some of the members corresponded with him, and sent him – somewhat belatedly – the money he needed if he was to continue to explore that distant Eldorado.

Meanwhile Banister's own situation had taken a turn for the better. He had now married and had decided to put down his roots in the colony. The records show that he imported thirty-five new settlers (including, one is shocked to record, two African slaves) to help develop the land allocated him by the Governor of Virginia. Back in London the bishop, and his botany club, could look forward to an even bigger haul of American seeds sent by Banister than Tradescant the Younger had sent half a century before. And then the blow fell, in the summer of 1692, a blow no one could possibly have anticipated.

Captain William Byrd, the man who had befriended Banister when he first came to the colony, had arranged for a small hunting expedition to explore the Occoneechee Islands, a few miles from the coast. The party soon reached the riverbank, and Banister crouched low in the bushes, hunting not for game but for new plants. One of the party approached, and mistook Banister for some kind of game animal. He fired – and killed Banister.

When the news reached London, the bishop lost no time in arranging for Banister's letters and drawings to be sent to Fulham Palace, where they could be studied by himself and his fellow botanists. No one could minimise the extent of the disaster. Banister had been the leading botanist in America, and a fountain of knowledge for European botanists. He had long planned to write a *Natural History of Virginia*, but the work was still unfinished. The bishop and his friends recognised that Banister was irreplaceable. He was 'one of the early martyrs to natural history', wrote Loudon more than a century later, and perhaps it was no exaggeration.[10]

Meanwhile the British public had received the first professional account of the bishop's experiments in botany and horticulture. The account was written by John Ray, the author of *Historia Plantarum* and the leading botanist of the period. In 1691 the bishop had taken him round the garden at Fulham Palace and John Ray was amazed by what he saw. In fact he seems to have been shocked by the bishop's extravagance, but was too polite to say so. (What he did say was that the garden had been created 'at no small outlay'.) The 30-acre garden was 'stuffed full in every place with the stocks of trees he has collected'.[11] The bishop had hired an excellent young gardener called George London, who had been trained by John Rose, Charles II's head gardener. (And George London was already a partner in 'London and Wise', Britain's leading plant nursery.) The bishop proudly showed John Ray his collection: trees newly introduced but once famous in history, like the cedar of Lebanon, and unknown trees from America grown from the seeds sent by Banister. And Ray duly compiled the first list of the Fulham Palace collection.

Ray's list includes a mere twelve species of trees: tantalisingly few compared to those comprehensive catalogues of the Tradescants' garden. In fact it gives us little more than a glimpse of a collection that apparently ran to more than a thousand species of trees and other plants. Twenty years later, shortly before the bishop died, James Petiver, a member of the Coffee House Club, added nine more species of trees identified to be growing at Fulham. Forty years later many of the bishop's collection had been cut down or stolen or sold by his successors. But in 1751 Sir William Watson, vice-president of the Royal Society, made a valiant attempt to describe the survivors at Fulham. He added a further twenty-four species of trees. Modern scholars have built on these lists and the most complete reconstruction of the garden now gives a grand total of about sixty species of trees, and a further twenty-eight species of shrubs.

Nearly half of these trees had been introduced from North America. And it's believed that Banister sent the seeds for eleven of them – many of which are my own favourites, what I would call 'American stunners'. In 1683, in his first consignment to Compton, Banister included the sweet gum (*Liquidambar styraciflua*), a fragrant giant from the swamps of Virginia. At home it can reach 150 feet in height, although it rarely exceeds 100 feet in Europe. Its strongest points are the sweet-smelling resin exuded from its trunk, from which its name is derived, and the astonishing colour of its leaves in autumn. Even the red maple, *Acer rubrum*, introduced by John Tradescant the Younger half a century earlier, cannot compete with these kaleidoscopic, or chameleon-like shifts. A single leaf, shaped like a star, passes from gold to pink and then on to the purple of a bishop's robe – appropriately for Compton.

In 1688 Banister had sent a second consignment. This included the ash-leaf maple (*Acer negundo*) with an elegant trifoliate leaf, and the sweet bay (*Magnolia virginiana*) from the swamps of the east coast of Virginia. Today this small, fragrant, semi-evergreen, glaucous-leaved magnolia gets little attention from collectors or nurserymen, who have hundreds of more spectacular magnolias to choose from. But in the bishop's day this was the only magnolia known to botany and the first of this fascinating genus to cross the Atlantic.

Fifty years later the muscular 'bull bay' (*Magnolia grandiflora*) replaced it as the magnolia of choice. It was much pushier than the sweet bay, with flowers a foot across and yellow-green leaves that were fully evergreen; it was also hardy enough if given a brick wall for shelter. (In Spain and Italy, and the other countries of the Mediterranean, it could grow embarrassingly large, but rarely in Britain.) The bull bay was soon joined by a flood of strange-looking, deciduous magnolias, like the cucumber tree and the umbrella tree (as we shall see in the next chapter).

Meanwhile the bishop was planting out the third of Banister's consignments: seeds and roots which had arrived only a year before Banister's tragic death. The most important of these new trees was the scarlet oak from Virginia, *Quercus coccinea*. Like the sweet bay, it was the precursor of a flood of newcomers: in its case the American red oaks. And, unlike the sweet bay, it was perhaps the most decorative of its genus. Go to any great British or Irish garden in October and the scarlet oak will grab your attention with the flaming colours of the American fall. True, the maples and liquidambars, changing like a kaleidoscope from gold to purple, give a more subtle and more theatrical display. But for homesick Americans I have no doubt that the scarlet oak would win the prize.

Of course, like all collectors of trees, the bishop died too soon. The trees that he had grown from seed were barely adolescent by the time his successor buried him in that modest tomb under the east window of the parish church at Fulham. Some of those trees took more than a hundred years to reach maturity. In 1873 the *Gardener's Chronicle* published a piece on the bishop's garden, illustrated with delightful wood engravings. Two American trees grab the eye, both of which were already near the end of their lives: the black walnut and the black locust. They must have been the bishop's favourites, as he planted them on the lawn where he could see them from the palace, and smell the fragrance of the black walnut. Both had been first introduced to Europe by John Tradescant the younger, but perhaps these trees came from Banister's seeds. Another of his favourites came originally from the Mediterranean: a crumbling, twisted cork oak planted in the shelter of the Tudor courtyard. But none of these three still beckon you to Fulham today.

It's now more than three hundred years after the bishop's death, and only one tree, it seems, has survived to bridge that awesome gap. This is an ancient holm-oak, a mass of huge, competing trunks, planted close to the Thames. Ironically, it's thought to be a relic of an earlier garden and so to *pre-date* the bishop. Still he would have known it and loved it. And if only he could return today, he would be flattered to find that his own garden has come back from the dead, so to speak – as we shall see in the epilogue.

Meanwhile, as the eighteenth century spouted wealth, and

buoyant rents lined the pockets of the great British landowners, a new breed of collectors began to emerge. A brace of dukes took up the hunt for rare trees, and the dukes were followed by members of the royal family. Others in the hunt came from the new rich, including the Quakers. All eyes were focused on America: still the Eldorado for every collector.

In the bishop's day only a trickle of rare trees had crossed the Atlantic. And now the trickle became a flood.

CHAPTER 3

'Forget not Mee & My Garden'

One afternoon in November 1728, fifteen years after Bishop Compton's death, the president of the Royal Society, Sir Hans Sloane, recommended an unusual candidate for a fellowship. He was a thirty-four-year-old Quaker shopkeeper called Peter Collinson. The Royal Society, the leading scientific body in Britain, did not usually elect shopkeepers to its fellowships – nor, for that matter, did they elect Quakers. Many of its Fellows were distinguished scientists; the amateurs included several dukes and peers of the realm; there were also numerous country gentlemen with private means. But Sloane was a popular president and Collinson was duly elected.

Many of the great and the good who voted must have been puzzled. Who was this Peter Collinson? It turned out that the address of his shop was 'at the sign of the Red Lion' in Gracechurch Street in the heart of the City of London: a family business of wholesale drapers and mercers and haberdashers. Collinson, who had rooms above the shop, had worked there since he was seventeen. Recently he had become a friend and protégé of Sloane. The two men had both come from relatively humble origins. Sloane's father was the agent for Lord Clanbrassil, an Irish peer with large estates in County Down. Sloane and his brothers were virtually

Peter Collinson

adopted by the Clanbrassil family, who encouraged Sloane to study botany at a French university.

They now shared a common interest in collecting plants – and in curiosities of every kind. And Sloane had a good nose for talent. He also knew that Collinson, like many British Quakers, had well-oiled trading links with America. But who would have guessed that Sloane's young protégé was going to be the prime mover in a dramatic change to the British landscape in the next half century, by promoting and organising and financing the introduction of American trees?

* * *

By 1728 Sloane was the uncrowned king of Britain's scientific establishment. He was the new president of the Royal Society,

after taking over from Sir Isaac Newton. He was also the president of the Royal College of Physicians and the country's most
fashionable doctor, who had served Queen Anne and was now
physician for George I. He pioneered vaccinations for smallpox;
in fact he had realised they were a godsend a century before Dr
Jenner's discoveries. (Sloane had the courage to make vaccinations mandatory for his young patients.) He was also a property
developer who owned a tasty slice of London, including a large
part of Chelsea. This investment, it is true, was somewhat
tainted – at least by Quaker standards. His wife was a colonial, an
heiress from Jamaica, and her family had owned sugar plantations
worked by unfortunate African slaves. But Sloane was noted for
his philanthropy. He had helped create the Foundling Hospital,
and organised a free surgery in London for those who couldn't
afford his fees.

He had also given a new boost to the Physic Garden at Chelsea
by giving them their site at a peppercorn rent – provided they
supplied fifty new plants every year to the Royal Society. He
arranged for the Physic Garden to have a new curator, Philip
Miller, who would soon become famous, both for making the
Physic Garden one of the best botanic gardens in Europe, and
for publishing, and republishing, a masterly dictionary of plants.
In fact Sloane had his finger in many pies, but botany was his
favourite science.

His scheme for using Collinson to introduce new American
plants seemed simple enough. The commercial market – the
network of nurserymen and their clients – had only supplied a
trickle in the previous century. And it was difficult for professional botanists to examine these new introductions. Bishop
Compton had done wonders by sending out John Banister. But
Banister had died tragically – and proved irreplaceable. Many
of Compton's trees at Fulham had now vanished, either sold

or stolen or simply abandoned. So it was time to bring science to the rescue. Sloane's ingenious scheme was for Collinson to find an amateur botanist in America who would supply him with American seeds *in exchange* for seeds of European trees and other plants. This meant the commercial market could be bypassed; the American amateur would need to be paid little more than his travel expenses. Collinson would be the broker for the transactions in both directions. He would organise the distribution of American seeds to a network of British collectors, and the collection of European seeds for America. And most important of all, he would be able to feed the hunger of international botanists (like the great Carl Linnaeus) with this exciting new material.

Sloane's first step was easy. By pushing – nowadays one says parachuting – Collinson into the Royal Society he had given him the new network of collectors and professional botanists he needed. The society held regular weekly meetings in its elegant classical house in Crane Court, down an alley from Fleet Street. Soon Collinson could write of 'my most Valuable and Intimate friend':[1] that boy wonder, twenty-one-year-old Lord Petre, owner of Thorndon Hall in Essex, and emerging as one of the most successful plant collectors of the day. Other new friends included two great landowners: the Duke of Richmond, owner of Goodwood, and the Duke of Argyll, based on his estate at Whitton, near Twickenham. The most important British botanist was Jacob Dillenius, the Professor of Botany at Oxford. He, too, attended the Society's meetings and rapidly succumbed to Collinson's Quaker charm. But one question remained, one that neither Sloane nor Collinson could answer at present. Where on earth would they find that American amateur who could hunt down American trees in the wilds of the New World and send them as packets of seeds speeding across the Atlantic?

Collinson has left a graphic account of the frustrations he suffered at this period:

My Publick Station in Business brought mee acquainted with Persons that were natives of Carolina, Virginia, Maryland, Pensilvania and New England. My Love for New and Rare plants putt mee often on soliciting their assistance for seeds or plants from those Countries.

I used much importunity for very little purpose – for the turn of the people was entirely the other way. What was common with them (but Rare with us) they did not think worth sending.

Thus I labour'd in vain, or to little purpose, for some years & obtained but very few Seeds or Plants, Neither Money or Friendship would tempt them ... at last some more artful man than the Rest managed to get rid of my importunities by recommending a Person whose Business it should be to gather Seeds and send over plants.[2]

In fact it was not till five years later, in 1733, that Collinson struck lucky. As Sloane had probably assumed all along, it was the American Quaker network that provided the key. Two of Collinson's business associates in Philadelphia, in the heart of Quaker country, suggested he approached a twenty-eight-year-old local farmer called John Bartram.

He had little education, but he was bright. He had picked up some rudimentary Latin, as he had aspirations to be a botanist. He had bought a small farm on the banks of the Schuykill River, a few miles from Philadelphia. He had already begun collecting American trees and other plants in order to create a botanic garden on his farm. So Collinson wrote to Bartram and a deal was struck. Bartram would collect seeds for Collinson and another

British partner – Lord Petre, the owner of Thorndon Hall in Essex. In return Bartram would be sent seeds of European plants and also be paid twenty guineas a year for his travel expenses. The list of partners expanded rapidly. In due course Bartram was packing up boxes of seeds for four more great landowners: the Duke of Richmond, the Duke of Norfolk, the Duke of Argyll and the Duke of Bedford – as well as the man who would later prove to be the mastermind behind the creation of Kew Gardens, the 3rd Earl of Bute.

John Bartram

It sounded simple: posting packets of seeds in either direction. But there were numerous hazards, and many attempts to send seeds across the Atlantic had failed in the past. This was a time of intermittent wars with France. British ships, bound for the colonies, would be seized by French privateers on the high seas, and their cargo confiscated. Any post that they carried would be lost or destroyed. That was only the first hazard. The journey itself – heading for one of the ports on the east coast – took at least six weeks and often much longer. Many ships foundered in storms. And even if the voyage was short and sweet, a cargo of seeds was extremely vulnerable. Damp was the great enemy. Seeds went mouldy in no time, whether exposed to damp in the hold or to salt spray from the deck. Other threats came from an inquisitive member of the crew – and of course from the ship's cat. So constant vigilance was needed. And this is where Collinson showed how well Quaker merchants knew their job.

In one of his first letters to Bartram he explained that he should pick a merchant ship whose captain was fully reliable. He suggested a certain 'Captain Budden' was one of the best. In January 1734 the first two consignments from Bartram duly arrived in London. Collinson went down to the Customs House to do the paperwork – and was delighted.

He wrote back promptly to acknowledge the 'Two Choice Cargos of plants'. They were:

> Curious & Rare & Well worth Acceptance. I am very sensible of the great pains & many Tiresome Trips to collect so many Rare plants Scatter'd at a distance. I shall not forget it but in some measure to Show my Gratitude, tho' not in proportion to thy Trouble, I have sent thee a small token, a Callico gown for thy Wife & some Odd Little things that may be of use among thy Children.[3]

Collinson went on to explain to his new friend that he was sending some waste paper for wrapping up seeds. He was also sending two quires of brown and one quire of 'whited brown paper' for the scientific work, which involved wrapping dried specimens. These herbarium specimens should be 'tied between two broad boards', inscribed with a number and the name of the place where they were collected, and posted off to him in duplicate every year. They would then be identified by 'our most knowing botanists' including Jacob Dillenius, Professor of Botany at Oxford.

In the next decade a steady stream of seeds and herbarium specimens crossed the Atlantic heading for Collinson. The majority of the seeds were from trees that had already been introduced into Britain from America, but were difficult or impossible to obtain from commercial nurseries. These included many of Bishop Compton's favourites – like the liquidambar and the tulip tree and the sweet bay. Bartram's new discoveries, however, were often equally spectacular. He introduced a gigantic new magnolia, whose trunk was so massive that it could be mistaken for a beech. It was to be christened by Linnaeus *Magnolia acuminata*, taking its botanical name from its pointed leaves. But people called it the 'cucumber tree' after the fruit, which were the size and shape of cucumbers. This was to be the first of a new wave of large, deciduous magnolias soon to be discovered along the east coast from southern Canada to northern Florida.

Most of these American magnolias have more impressive flowers than the cucumber tree, whose flowers are small and a rather watery yellow. They have largely replaced it in modern gardens. But the cucumber tree has staged a comeback in recent years, when plant breeders succeeded in giving one of its offspring a flower as yellow as the yoke of an egg. (In fact new versions of the cucumber tree, including 'Elizabeth' – a towering hybrid bred in Brooklyn – are now all the rage on both sides of the Atlantic. John Bartram would have been delighted.)

Bartram also introduced a number of acid-loving shrubs that were to transform British gardens. In fact he started the fashion for highly coloured shrubberies made with rhododendrons and azaleas, whose seeds arrived with one of the first consignments sent to Collinson in 1734. True, the American rhododendron species he sent, *Rhododendron maximum*, is not much planted today in European gardens. The plants can grow 30 feet high, but the flowers are small and unimpressive. There are similar drawbacks to two of the azalea species he sent (now renamed *Rhododendron periclymenoides* and *Rhododendron viscosum*). The flowers can be disappointing by comparison with the flowers of their cousins in China and the Himalayas. But, just like their magnolia counterparts, the American species have made a comeback in the form of popular hybrids.

The famous 'Hardy Hybrid' rhododendrons of Europe are a mixture of Turkish, Chinese and American stock. The same applies to the gorgeous Ghent azaleas. Without those Yankee genes the hybrids would flower too early in the year and might succumb to spring frosts. And some of them would be less beautiful. John Bartram described his amazement when he first saw 'an incredible profusion' of scarlet and orange-coloured azaleas covering a hillside in the Alleghenies. His first thought was that the hill was on fire.

Another important species apparently introduced by John Bartram was the American moosewood, *Acer pensylvanicum*. And this is a tree that has not depended on hybridising to make it fashionable today. The moosewood is perfect just as it is: a small, elegant maple, and the first of the delightful 'snakebarks'. They earned that name from the pale blue or white stripes (technically 'striations') down the length of their barks. The moosewood was introduced in 1755, and for more than a century was the only species of snakebark known to gardeners and botanists. Then half a dozen other species of snakebarks were discovered by plant explorers in China and Japan, including a very vigorous maple discovered by the celebrated missionary, Père David. All these oriental snakebarks are remarkably elegant. But I believe the moosewood is still supreme. Its leaves are strikingly large and green when mature; they open a modest pink, and make their farewells with a sumptuous yellow. In winter their stripes can be dazzling. Enough, you might say, to make a snake jealous.

For thirty years the two self-taught botanists, Collinson and Bartram, exchanged letters and seeds and plants without ever meeting. Usually their letters exuded good humour in the Quaker style. Collinson teased Bartram for flirting with an elderly widow whose 'silk bag', Bartram told him, 'hath past and repast full of seeds several times last fall'. 'I plainly see', Collinson replied, 'thou knowest how to fascinate the Longing Widow'.

Sometimes, it's true, the correspondence became tetchy. Bartram felt he was being exploited. The money he received from Collinson hardly covered expenses, let alone made a decent profit. And Collinson, according to Bartram, had no idea of the difficulties and dangers encountered when hunting trees in the wild. In 1760 Bartram was collecting berries from the top of a holly tree when a branch snapped and he crashed to the ground. He was lucky to survive. As he put it 'my little son Benjamin was not able to help me up my pain was grievous... no house near and A very could sharp wind & above 20 mile to ride home'.[4]

On his part Collinson felt that Bartram owed him a great deal, in fact almost everything. He had put Bartram on the map. When they first corresponded Bartram was a small farmer, self-taught and unknown. Now he was world famous. No other American botanist was in regular correspondence with the great Linnaeus. And if Bartram complained about money, he should realise that Collinson was acting the broker without a 'grain of profit to my self'. He did it 'in hopes to improve, or at least adorn my Country... I had Public Good at Heart'.[5]

Perhaps the tensions between the two men were never fully resolved. But at least the tetchy letters were followed by apologies on both their parts. Collinson wrote: 'I full well know thy many avocations... So I hope for the future thee will never take anything from Mee in a lessening way...' To which Bartram replied: 'Now, my kind and generous friend I shall return thee my hearty thanks for thy care & pains... if thee finds any expressions in my letter A little out of ye way [I hope] thee will not take it in the wrong sense... for I love plain dealing'.[6]

And both men did their best to behave as Quakers should. Bartram's reward came in April 1765 when Collinson wrote to tell him 'that my Repeated Solicitations have not been in Vain for this Day I received certain Intelligence from our Gracious King that Hee had appointed thee His Botanist with a salary of Fifty pounds a year...'[7] To be George III's official botanist in America – that was a reward indeed, even if (as few would have guessed) the king was so soon to lose America.

Meanwhile Collinson's magic circle of collectors, fed by Bartram's seeds and cuttings, had expanded with spectacular results. The young Lord Petre was rich, charming and passionately keen to plant every exotic in the world that could grow on the Thorndon estate. He was at the hub of Collinson's circle for the first decade. In 1741 Collinson described the new Picturesque style of planting at Thorndon:

[He has] Planted out about Tenn Thousand Americans wch being att the Same Time mixed wth about Twenty Thousand Europeans, & some Asians make a very Beautifull appearance great Art and skill being shown... Dark green being a great Foil to Lighter ones & Blewish green to yellow ones & those Trees that have their bark and back of their Leaves of white or Silver make a Beautifull contrast with the others the whole is planted in thickets & Clumps and with these Mixtures are perfectly picturesque...[8]

On another occasion Collinson listed some of the newly introduced American species chosen by Petre:

> A great Variety of pines from North America not found in our Gardens Red Cedars and white Cedars, Great Magnolia (*Magnolia grandiflora*) & the small Magnolia (*M. virginiana*) flower every Year in Great plenty – Sarsifrax (*Sassafras*), Sweet Gum or Liquidambar trees Yew leafed firr (*Tsuga Canadensis*) Balm Gilead (*Abies balsamea*) and spruce firrs from New England and Newfoundland – with a great variety of all other American trees and Shrubbs.[9]

Then in July 1742 Collinson received news that sent him reeling: Petre had been struck down with smallpox and died aged only twenty-nine. He shared his misery with Bartram: 'I have lost my frnd – my Brother the man I loved & was dearer to Mee than all Men...'[10] And what would be the fate of Lord Petre's huge collection of trees and plants (along with a menagerie of cranes, terrapins, tortoises and American cardinal-birds)? All these must now be disposed of, and Collinson realised that it was his responsibility to help the unfortunate Lady Petre. He wrote a touching panegyric: Lord Petre 'was a fine Tall Comely Man Handsome, Had the presence of a prince, But so happily mixt that Love and Aw was begat at the same time... The affability and Sweetness of his Temper is beyond Expression, without the least Tincture of Pride or Haughtyness, with an engageing smile He always Mett his friends... (he had) a great Ardur for every Branch of Botanic Science'.[11]

As for the partnership with Lord Petre, Collinson was inclined to panic. '*All our schemes are broke*', he told Bartram, 'send no seeds for the Duke of Norfolk'.[12] The partnership was doomed. It turned out that the opposite was true. More and more land-owners wished to join the partnership and pay ten guineas for a box of American seeds. And the existing members, like the Duke of Richmond, were encouraged by Collinson to acquire some of Lord Petre's collection of plants that were on the market. The duke wrote to say he would like 'about 40 or 50 of the common Virginia tulip trees... butt upon this condition only, vis, that I may buye them I would not ask them for as a present'. He also wanted a Chinese thuja, 5 feet high, to match his own in the new grove of evergreens at Goodwood. And he planned to extend his grove of American thujas with a further two acres of these trees, as well as planting American hemlocks 'upon the top of a very bleak hill' above the park at Goodwood.[13]

Collinson was a frequent visitor to Goodwood in the 1740s, in the heyday of his friend and partner, the 2nd Duke. But he has left us only these tantalising glimpses of the new planting in the park. We know more about the contents and layout of the estate of the Duke of Argyll at Whitton. He, too, was encour-aged by Collinson to help out Lady Petre by buying part of the collection at Thorndon. Already Argyll had a most impressive collection at Whitton, in the heathland west of London – even more wide-ranging than Collinson's. He had been one of the first landowners to join Collinson's partnership, and buy ten-guinea boxes of Bartram's seeds. He had also struck out on his own, exploiting the new network of nurserymen now emerging in London. The leading nurseryman, with worldwide contacts, was James Gordon, who was based east of the City, in the smoke and grime of the Mile End Road. But Gordon had been trained by the Petre family. He certainly had green fingers, and many of the duke's new introductions at Whitton must have originated there.

Sad to say, no complete catalogue was made – or at any rate, preserved – of this huge collection at Whitton during the duke's lifetime. What we do have is several lists of the remarkable trees and shrubs that remained there half a dozen years after his death.

The most reliable list was composed by a professional botanist, John Hope, Regius Professor of Botany at Edinburgh. In the summer of 1766 Hope embarked on a whirlwind tour of twenty-two of the most important gardens in England. His aim: to track down exotic plants that had yet to reach Edinburgh; he planned to propagate them there from seeds or cuttings. Hope's tour included visits to exciting new private gardens, like Princess Augusta's at Kew and Peter Collinson's at Mill Hill, visits to thriving institutional gardens like Peter Miller's Physic Garden at Chelsea, and to the sad remains of once famous gardens like Bishop Compton's at Fulham Palace.

As one would expect, Hope was particularly impressed by the trees at Whitton. He listed thirty-eight species of trees in Argyll's collection, of which twenty-seven had come from America. Many were already magnificent specimens. The list included a Weymouth pine 60 feet high (*Pinus strobus*), a black locust of nearly 50 feet (*Robinia pseudoacacia*), a Red maple of 40 feet (*Acer rubrum*) as well as an avenue of cedars of Lebanon framing a long canal. There were eight new introductions attributed personally to Argyll. Five of these were shrubs, including a handsome hazel (*Corylus cornuta*), the elegant *Itea virginica* and three important trees: the Canoe birch (*Betula papyrifera*), a thorn called *Crataegus punctata*, and the Kentucky coffee tree (*Gymnocladus dioica*). The latter has been described by a modern authority as 'perhaps the most beautiful of all hardy trees'.[14] It can certainly put up with our winters. But our summers give it the shivers, and it needs to bask in a warmer climate to flower as it would in Kentucky.

Collinson greatly admired the duke – even if he could hardly avoid envying him for the heroic scale of his planting.

There was one other model collection of trees and other plants from which he must have learnt many lessons. This was the Physic Garden in Chelsea, a few miles from the heart of London. Philip Miller, the curator, had created in this four-acre garden beside the Thames a dazzling botanical collection. As a young man he had been hand-picked by Sir Hans Sloane for the task of turning it into a regular botanic garden. By the 1750s he had succeeded. The collection rivalled Collinson's in size – and was conveniently documented in his bestselling *Dictionary of Plants*. Like the Duke of Argyll, Miller had been one of the first to join Collinson's partnership, and had then struck out on his own. His success can be measured by the number of important trees he had introduced.

No fewer than thirty introductions by Miller are listed in Loudon's *Arboretum et Fruticetum Britannicum*. Roughly half the species had been imported from Europe and Asia. The American trees included five important discoveries: two red oaks (*Quercus rubra* and *Q. nigra*) a big-leaved umbrella tree (*Magnolia tripetala*) a pine (*P. virginiana*) and a red spruce (*Picea rubra*).

Miller must have enjoyed convivial visits to Collinson's garden. In fact Collinson had two gardens: one even smaller than Miller's, and the other substantially larger. Let me explain. Collinson moved to the first garden early in his career, inspired by memories of his grandmother, who loved topiary and apparently lived nearby. It was a cottage garden in the pretty village of Peckham, 3 miles south of the City (and his shop). This Peckham garden included all the first batches of Bartram's introductions, as well as numerous other plants given him as presents – or in exchange with partners. One of his friends, a Swedish botanist called Pehr

Kalm, has left us a glimpse of this pioneering Peckham garden in April 1748:

> Mr. Peter Collinson has a beautiful garden, full of all kinds of rarest plants, especially American ones that can bear the English climate... However neat and small this garden... there was, nevertheless, scarcely a garden in England in which there were so many kinds of trees and plants, especially of the rarest, as in this. It was here that Mr. Collinson amused himself in planting and arranging his living collection of plants.[15]

'*Arranging the plants*'. It's hard to imagine how Collinson found room for all Bartram's trees in this small garden: the magnolias, the red and white cedars, the pines, the spruce and the silver firs But it must have been quite a squeeze.

By 1749, however, he had moved to a handsome 'villa' (a small country house) in Mill Hill, 13 miles north of the City. His wife Mary had inherited the villa from her father. Collinson brought with him all the trees and plants that could be dug up and removed. This meant sending them off by the wagon-load, and the delicate job must have seemed interminable; it took two years. But here at last he could stretch his legs – and do justice to his collection. Shrubs and herbaceous plants – rhododendrons, lilies, orchids – rioted in the inner garden (the 'Best Garden'). The place was also perfect for two 'Mountain magnolias' grown at Peckham, like most of the trees, from Bartram's seed. There was room for the pines and spruce and silver firs in two fields behind the house. (There was even a choice of ponds for Collinson's mud turtles.) And no one could miss the prize of the collection: a pair of cedars of Lebanon grown by an enterprising local butcher.

Strange to say, no map of this new and original garden at Mill Hill has survived. Nor did any of Collinson's more celebrated guests – heroes of science like Carl Linnaeus and Benjamin Franklin – leave us with even a sketchy description. What we do know is that Collinson, as a good Quaker, took life as it came. Old age seemed to suit him – as it suited his patron, Sir Hans Sloane, who died in his ninety-fourth year in 1753. But Collinson's wife Mary died the same year, that is, five years after the move to Mill Hill. Mary was a mere forty-nine. Collinson recovered from the shock in due course. Both his children – his son Michael and his daughter Mary – left home to get married. His brother James died in 1762. So he planned to wind up the family business in Gracechurch Street – the drapers and mercers and haberdashers which he had shared with his brother James. He also lost many friends whose friendship he valued most. The 2nd Duke of Richmond died less than a decade after poor Lord Petre. The Duke of Argyll, as we saw, died in 1761.

But Collinson found he could make new friends more easily than most people. The new Duke of Richmond welcomed him to Goodwood, and the new Lord Petre to Thorndon. Collinson was delighted by what he found at Goodwood, although at Thorndon 'All the nurserys (were) overgrown'. He sent the new Duke of Richmond a thousand seedlings of the cedar of Lebanon – some of which bestride the park at Goodwood today. The duke sent him some venison in return, and a jovial message on New Year's eve in 1767: 'You are a lazy old fellow for not coming to see (us) ... Adieu, my Dear Peter, Don't overeat yourself with mince pies ...'[16]

His garden continued to give him the keenest pleasure. This was despite a series of devastating robberies which he suffered in 1762, 1765 and 1768. The robberies cost him many of his favourite plants, including red azaleas from America and agapanthus from South Africa. It was ironic that Collinson, who had done so much to popularise the growing of exotics, should be a victim of his own success.

But he accepted these shattering blows with Quaker humility. He confessed to Bartram that his garden had once 'born the Bell' in any competition. But 'now I very humbly condescend to be on an Equall footing with my neighbours'.[17]

He was now in his early seventies and beginning to put up his feet. 'I am here retir'd', he told Bartram, 'all, alone, from the Bustle and hurry of the Town, meditateing on the Comforts I enjoy; and whilst the old Log is Burning, the fire of friendship is blazeing...'[18] In fact it was his garden outside the windows that was the main source of his comfort, as he made clear to the great Linnaeus early in the spring of 1767. 'I am here retired to a delightful little villa, to contemplate and admire, with my dear Linnaeus, the unalterable laws of vegetation. How ravishing to see the swelling buds disclose the tender leaves!... How delightful to see the order of Nature! oh how obedient the vegetable tribes are to their great Lawgiver!'[19]

And Collinson was not, after all, alone when he walked in his garden. Every tree that he met reminded him of his friends – and the trees they had given him.

'See there my Honble frnd' [he wrote to Cadwallader Colden, Lieutenant Governor of New York]:

how thrifty they look – I see nobody but Two fine Trees, a Spruce & a Larch, that's True, but they are his representatives. But see close by how my Lord Northumberland aspires in that Curious Firr from Mount Ida, but Look Yonder at the Late Benevolent Duke of Richmond, His Everlasting Cedars of Lebanon will Endure when you & I & He is forgot... But pray what are those pines, Novelties rarely seen – that Elegant one with five Leaves is the Cembro Pine from Sibiria, the

other Tall Tree is the very long Leaved Pine of 10 or 12 inches
from So. Carolina. They stand mementos of my Generous Frd
the late Duke of Argyle... But those Balm Gilead Firrs grow
at a surpriseing rate. It is pleasant to See, but they renew a
concern for my Dear Frnd Ld Petre. They came young from
his Nurserys, with all the species of Virginia Pines & Cedars...
Regard but ye Variety of Trees & Shrubs in this plantation
as mountain Magnolia, Sarsifax, Rhododendrons, Calmias &
Azaleas &c &c &c, all are the Bounty of my Curious Botanic
Friend J. Bartram of Philadelphia.[20]

So Collinson's friends welcomed him to his own garden. He died
a year after his last letter to Linnaeus: on 11 August 1768. Modest
to the end, he had chosen to be buried in an unmarked grave
in the Quaker graveyard in Long Lane, Bermondsey. But, as
Linnaeus put it with due solemnity, his legacy was 'the species
of eternity'.

Meanwhile the British landscape was beginning to endure a
dramatic change of style. And nowhere was this more obvious
than at Princess Augusta's revolutionary new garden at Kew.

TRUNKS

CHAPTER 4

Princess Augusta's Collection

'We begin to perceive the tower of Kew from Montpellier Row [in Twickenham]; in a fortnight you will see it in Yorkshire'.[1]

It was 5 July 1761, and Horace Walpole was writing, in his usual mocking style, to his friend the 2nd Earl of Strafford, a rich Yorkshire landowner and amateur architect. The 'tower' was actually the great pagoda at Kew, now rising ten storeys and 160 feet above the fields of Richmond and Twickenham. It was a few miles from Strawberry Hill, where Horace had built his own whimsical Gothic castle – a 'cheesecake castle', as he called it. At Kew the great pagoda, designed by William Chambers, rocketed up past seven Greek temples and other follies. Horace Walpole found the mixture incongruous, and complained that it set an unfortunate precedent. (No doubt he was jealous.) Others reported that Chambers's Chinese pagoda offered a delightful contrast with his Greek temples. Together they made a perfect setting for the collection of exotic trees and other plants that, under the newly coined name of an 'arboretum', would soon make Kew famous.

Chambers, one of the most talented architects employed by the royal family at this time, was a master of the current Palladian style. He was also Europe's leading specialist in Chinese design. As a young man from a Scottish family that had settled in Sweden two generations earlier, he had joined the Swedish East India Company at the age of sixteen. After a couple of years in Bengal, he made two protracted business visits to Canton, in South China. His job was to trade in tea and silk and other Chinese exports. By the time he was twenty-five, he had accumulated enough money to change careers. He had decided to train as an architect. This meant long years studying classical design in Rome and other parts of Europe; in France he sat at the feet of celebrated architects like Nicolas-Henri Jardin.

By 1750 he had established himself as an adviser to Prince Frederick, the boisterous forty-three-year-old son of George II and heir apparent to the throne. Unlike his father and grandfather, Frederick was a dilettante and an enthusiast. No one could deny that at last the Hanoverians had produced a man of taste. He was hungry for Van Dykes, and longed to buy back many of those dispersed after the execution of Charles I. Music was his comfort and his joy. At music parties he played the violoncello, accompanied by his sister Ann at the harpsichord, and his daughter Mary at the mandora. And, most important for the future of Kew, he was a passionate gardener.

One of his visitors, George Vertue, the antiquary, described the happy prince he encountered in the gardens at Kew in October 1750. Frederick was planting 'many curious & forain trees'.

[He] was directing the plantations of trees [and] exotics with the workmen – adviseing & assisting where wee were receivd gratiously . . . for 2 or three hours, seeing his plantations, told his contrivances, designs of his improvemnts in his Gardens, water works, canal, etc great numbers of people labouring there, his new Chinesia Summer hous, painted in their stile & ornaments The story of Confucius and his doctrines, etc

Frederick's garden at Kew had grown by leaps and bounds in the last decade. In fact it was an extension of the family's original estate at Richmond Lodge to the west. This had belonged to the ill-fated Duke of Ormonde – confiscated after he was implicated in the rising of 1715. At first Frederick and his family used Richmond Lodge as their summer retreat. But Kew to the east beckoned. It was nearer London, and handy enough for coaches once a new stone bridge replaced the ferry across the Thames. And there were two fine, contrasting houses on the estate close to the Thames and just behind Kew Green. The first was the 'Dutch House', red-brick and Dutch-gabled; the second a rather dull classical pile called the 'White House'. It was the White House which Frederick commissioned William Kent to double in size. This was to be the new summer retreat for his young wife, Princess Augusta, and their budding family which would eventually total nine children. And it was here, between the Dutch House and the White House, that he was spotted by George Vertue planting his new garden of 'curious and forain trees', and building his 'Chinesia Summer house'.[2]

Poor Frederick! Six months after Vertue had met him in the garden, the prince was dead. But his ideas lived on – especially the craze for 'Chinesia'.

Princess Augusta, widowed at thirty-two, had chosen one of Frederick's closest friends, John Stuart, the 3rd Earl of Bute, to be her mentor and emotional support. Bute was more than unusually accomplished. He was a Scottish polymath – and a mastermind. His mother had died when he was a child, and he had been brought up by her two powerful brothers, successive Dukes of Argyll. The latter, Archibald, 3rd Duke of Argyll, put his own special stamp on Bute's character. It was Argyll, future head of the Campbell clan in Scotland, who had come south in the 1720s and bought the land at Whitton, near Kew. So Bute grew up among his uncle's cedars of Lebanon and Weymouth pines, and the rest of his astonishing collection of rare trees and shrubs at Whitton.

After schooling at Eton, Bute had been sent abroad to study civil law at Leiden university. But he was no conformist. A romantic love affair was followed by a scandalous elopement. (His young wife Mary was the daughter of Lady Mary Wortley Montagu, the pioneer of vaccination against smallpox. Her father, Sir Edward Wortley Montagu, was one of the richest men in the kingdom, and had himself eloped with Lady Mary.) Bute then returned to Scotland where he fathered eleven children. By now he had inherited the family's large and somewhat rundown estate on the island of Bute. For five years he studied agriculture and estate management on this distant island. Science – and especially botany – became his passion. Then he had descended on London, brimming with original ideas of every kind.

He had planned to help Frederick make important constitutional changes. The great Whig families of Britain, the Cavendishes and Cecils and a dozen others, had exercised a monopoly of power ever since they had invited Frederick's grandfather, George I, to come over from Hanover. The king was left humiliated – powerless to impose his own ideas and lead the country. This would all have to be changed, so Bute had once pledged, when Frederick came to the throne. Of course it was now Frederick's son, the new Prince of Wales and future George III, who would have to make these changes. And Bute saw himself as the trusted adviser – what wags like Horace Walpole called 'The Favourite' – of the young prince as well as of his mother, Princess Augusta.

For the young prince the choice of Bute as his tutor was nothing short of miraculous. He was lazy and boorish, according to his first tutor, Lord Waldegrave; even his mother Augusta had found him shy and backward. With Bute he was in his element.

The two men exchanged passionate letters, each beginning 'My dearest friend'.[3] The prince wrote meticulous essays, exploring his old curriculum – in maths and history and politics – with new excitement. And Bute introduced him to a new world of botany and architecture. Bute even arranged for William Chambers, the newly appointed royal architect, to lecture him on architectural design. And it turned out that the prince had himself a talent for the subject; the Temple of Victory, one of the Corinthian temples planned for Kew, is believed to have been designed by the prince himself.

How did his kindly mother regard this astonishing transformation? Of course she was delighted. Augusta was shy, but enjoyed music and the arts. She had always done her best to keep out of politics. By contrast, her mother-in-law, Queen Caroline, had tormented Frederick with denunciations of his political friends. Since Frederick's death, the White House at Kew had proved a very private retreat. By 1757 Augusta at last felt ready to create at Kew the kind of garden that Frederick had planned. It was a way to honour his memory. Prince George was in full approval. And she would have a tower of strength at her side in the shape of Frederick's devoted friend, the Earl of Bute.

There was, it must be said, one problem that neither Bute nor Augusta could resolve. Celebrities attract wagging tongues in any age. And in the eighteenth century there was a pervasive lust for scandal. So the unusually close friendship of Princess Augusta and Lord Bute was assumed by many to be an adulterous affair. The broadsheets spat out the usual accusations. Cartoonists revealed the lovers' secret assignations. Horace Walpole sniggered, and confided that when Frederick wished to be alone with a woman 'he used to bid the Princess walk alone with Lord Bute. As soon as the Prince was dead, they walked more and more in his memory.'[4]

But where was the evidence? Of course there was none. A happily married man enjoying a Platonic friendship with a kindly widow – that was the verdict of sensible people, and it remains the view of modern historians.

Gritting their teeth, no doubt, Bute and Augusta and George now called for their architect, William Chambers, to plan the new garden.

Despite the Seven Years War, which had begun three years earlier, the royal family had no shortage of funds to develop the estate. The first question was to be this: what sort of setting should they give the new trees and shrubs? In other words, would the layout be formal and geometric, or in the so-called 'natural' style?

In fact the new fashion for planting exotic trees, so ably promoted by Sloane and Collinson and Collinson's partners, was now beginning to feed off another new fashion: to create a more natural-looking landscape. The two fashions were made for each other. The designers of British parks in the seventeenth and early eighteenth century had remained loyal to geometry. They had borrowed their ideas, suitably diluted, from the great continental palaces of the Continent: Het Loo in Holland and Versailles in France. This formal style required little variety in the trees planted. A mile-long avenue of lime trees, grown from a single, identical clone; a *patte d'oie* radiating from a carpet-pattern of Italian cypresses; a parterre of yews clipped to give a whiff of the baroque: this had been the fashionable British style for more than a century.

And now its day was over. William Kent (in Horace Walpole's famous phrase) had 'jumped the wall and found all nature a garden'. The new buzzwords were 'natural' and 'Picturesque'; the latter term, as we saw, was already used by Collinson in describing the layout of Lord Petre's park at Thorndon.

By far the most successful landscape architect promoting the new fashion would prove to be 'Capability' Brown. But in 1757 Brown was only a beginner. Chambers was a rival – and no admirer of Brown's work. He deplored Brown's formulas for empty lawns and artificial lakes and lumpish clumps, with monotonous groves of beech and oak. Brown's 'natural' landscapes, he said, were merely bland and insipid. Avenues were cut down and replaced with 'a little grass and American weeds'. Chambers's own instincts were for exotic landscapes created by *improving* on nature.

So the new gardens and landscape at Kew, designed by Chambers, proved richer and more varied than anything Brown would have offered. This would have been obvious from the first moment one of Princess Augusta's visitors left the front door of the White House and stepped out into the garden.

Ahead, on the left, was a gleaming, white-stuccoed Palladian Orangery, loaded with subtropical fruit. Beyond that, covering five acres of undulating grass, was the collection of exotic trees from North America, Europe and the East. At the centre of this astonishing collection (in a place which would be described by the new name of 'arboretum') was the first of seven Greek temples, the Temple of the Sun, a design borrowed from Baalbek in the Lebanon. And beyond a long, bony greenhouse (the 'Great Stove' as it was known) the visitor found a Physic Garden and a flower garden, a menagerie and an aviary.

Away to the west the lawns and gravel paths merged into parkland. Chambers had taught himself to avoid fashionable vistas. So a wall of forest trees – presumably oaks and elms and chestnuts – blocked the way to both Richmond and the River Thames. Instead the visitor followed a mythological walk presenting in turn the six remaining Greek temples: Bellona (the war god, and a topical choice, as Britain was fighting the Seven Years

War), Pan (the god of wild music and misbehaviour), Aeolus (god of the winds, including the winds that decapitated trees), Victory, Arethusa (nymph of the spring) and finally Solitude. There was also a mixed bag of other attractions. Apart from the House of Confucius (Chambers's youthful indiscretion) there was a ruined Roman arch, a theatre dedicated to Augusta, a Gothic cathedral, a Palladian bridge, a Rococo-Moorish Alhambra, and a mosque. And the crowning glory was of course the great pagoda, ten storeys and 160 feet high, mocked by Horace Walpole when it burst into view at Twickenham and Strawberry Hill.

Today, it's generally recognised that Kew's pagoda is a triumph of design. It may not be authentically Chinese. But what's wrong with Anglo-Chinese rococo? The pagoda is also a triumph of construction. More than half the temples and follies at Kew have vanished in the last two centuries – lost to decay or to winter storms or to sheer indifference. But the pagoda, recently restored, has never looked better. Indeed it's two hundred years since its eighty-four blue-and-gold dragons sparkled on every roof-tip. (No one knows why they were ever removed.) Although the woodwork proved short-lived, the brickwork was astonishingly durable. Several bombs landed close to the pagoda in the Second World War. The pagoda didn't make a murmur. The ten storeys proved as indestructible as concrete.

But we must return to Kew in the middle of the eighteenth century (and the middle of the Seven Years War). The core of the gardens was obviously the new arboretum of five acres, guarded by the Temple of the Sun. What species of trees should they plant? That was the question. Chambers himself would not have been responsible for the choice. It rested with the princess and her mentor, Lord Bute. Of course they were not short of advisers. In 1759 they took on an energetic young gardener called William Aiton who had been trained by the redoubtable Philip Miller at

Chelsea. Like Miller, and so many other successful gardeners, Aiton was a Scot who had come south to make his fortune. And he certainly succeeded in transforming Kew in the next thirty years. Meanwhile the princess and Bute leant heavily on the advice of an odd sort of botanist, Dr John Hill.

Hill was an oddity even in age of professional eccentrics. Sometimes he seemed no more than a mountebank. He had flirted with more than half a dozen careers. Actor, apothecary, novelist, gossip columnist, zoologist, geologist, astronomer: he had tried and discarded them all. His heart was in botany and horticulture. By 1757 he had published a bestselling *British Herbal* and a gardener's guide called *Eden*, both dedicated to Lord Bute. It's not clear if he now gave his advice to Bute free of charge. (Later he was paid a large salary as director of Kensington Gardens.) What is certain is that he helped assemble the large number of young trees and shrubs needed for Kew's new arboretum.

One tiresome problem had finally been resolved: the problem of naming trees and other plants. For years the world of garden-ers and botanists had been lumbered with impossibly awkward names. New plants would be choked with a bramble-bush of Latin. But now the confusion had been ended at a stroke. In 1753 the Swedish master-botanist, Carl Linnaeus, had published his revolutionary volume, *Species Plantarum*, explaining his long-discussed binomial system. All names of plants (and animals, too) could be reduced to two simple Latin words. For example, *Acer rubrum* was the new name for the American Red Maple, instead of that baffling and tongue-twisting string of Latin words: *Acer foliis quinquelobis subdentatis subtus glaucis pedunculis simplicis-simis aggregatis*. A genus was followed by a species – just like a surname and a Christian name. It was a simple as that. And of course it had transformed the task of anyone trying to assemble a collection of exotic trees.

What species of exotic trees were now available and hardy enough to be planted outside at Kew, guarded by the Temple of the Sun in the five-acre arboretum? By the middle of the eighteenth century the list was still surprisingly small – if we accept the estimates of John Loudon, prepared in the next century.

First to be introduced were about twenty trees from Europe and the Near East, like the walnut and the sweet chestnut, the Mediterranean cypress and the horse chestnut, and the mighty cedars of Lebanon. The younger Tradescant had added half a dozen new species in the inaugural wave from North America, including the false acacia, the red maple and the black walnut. Bishop Compton had followed. With John Banister's help he had collected about fifteen important new species from across the Atlantic, including the first magnolia (*M. virginiana*) the liquidambar, the scarlet oak and the tulip tree. By 1700 the total number of new species – of *trees* as distinct from shrubs – barely reached forty. About ninety more introductions, according to Loudon, followed in the next sixty years.

Some, like the 'cucumber tree' (*Magnolia acuminata*) and the silver maple (*Acer saccharinum*) had come by way of Bartram and the Quaker network, commissioned by Peter Collinson. Many others had been given to the world by Philip Miller, who had turned the Physic Garden at Chelsea into a clearing-house for rare plants. Miller's introductions included the water oak (*Quercus nigra*), the red oak (*Q. rubra*), the American thuja (*T. occidentalis*) and the American lime (*T. americana*). A dozen other rich British collectors, using a newly created network of dealers, had imported exotic trees, or their seeds, from America or elsewhere. Many of them owned great estates – like the Dukes of Bedford, Norfolk and Argyll. Others were humbler folk: doctors or country parsons. But the grand total of all their efforts in two centuries of exploration was only 130 new trees – if we accept Loudon's estimates.

So in 1759 this was the challenge for Lord Bute and the princess, and for young William Aiton, the new gardener at Kew: to hunt down as many as possible of these new introductions, and to ransack the world for hundreds more.

They had three striking advantages. First, Aiton had been Philip Miller's protégé at the Physic Garden in Chelsea. So he could rely on Miller to give him every assistance – not only advice but seeds and young plants – to build up Kew's arboretum. Second, in October 1760, a year after the building of the first of Chambers's new temples, the twenty-two-year-old Prince of Wales had succeeded his grandfather, George II, as king of Britain and Ireland. He was now George III, and, despite the Seven Years War, far better equipped to splash out large sums on the new gardens at Kew. Third, in 1761 Lord Bute's uncle and former guardian, the Duke of Argyll, had died aged seventy-eight. Argyll had no children, and had left the Whitton estate to his mistress, Mrs Williams. So Bute was able to strike a dazzling bargain with the executors. Before the Whitton estate was sold, Bute could remove the smaller trees and replant them at Kew. Whitton was only a few miles upriver. So a treasure trove of rare trees were duly dug up, and dispatched on the short journey by boat.

It's unfortunate that no one made a scholarly list of this Whitton bonanza. All we know is that the Duke of Argyll's young trees became the core of the new collection at Kew.

Of course the majority of the Whitton trees were now too big to be moved. Two lists of these large trees have survived. There's one from the notes of Professor Hope, the Scottish academic who made a whirlwind tour in 1766 to inspect seventeen important English collections. The most impressive of all his discoveries were the forty fine trees at Whitton, many of them planted in the 1720s and 1730s, and now dominating the landscape. One of the cedars of Lebanon was 60 feet high with a girth of 8 feet;

a Weymouth pine was nearly the same height, and of the same girth as the cedar; there was also an American tupelo, 25 feet high and 'the best in England', a Sassafras with 'a fine round head' and an American plane with a 'beautifully tapered stem'.

The second list of the Whitton specimens was compiled by the gardener Daniel Crofts, in 1765, a year before Hope's visit. It was printed with the catalogue when Whitton was put up for sale, and gave no indication of size or condition. Many of the names are difficult to interpret, and obviously Crofts was not a man of learning. What is clear is that, even after Lord Bute had taken the smaller trees to Kew, the remaining collection at Whitton was still enormous – perhaps the largest in Britain. Crofts listed 340 varieties of trees and shrubs. Fortunately the estate passed into good hands. After some vicissitudes, the lease was bought by none other than Kew's celebrated architect, Sir William Chambers. (By then the king of Sweden had made him a Knight of the Polar Star.) No doubt Chambers found it handy to live near his Greek temples and his beloved pagoda.

* * *

The question remains: which trees from Whitton did Bute remove to Kew? And it seems that little is known for certain. Two trees, it is true, are cited by Professor Hope, in his notes on his visit to Kew, as having come from Whitton a few years earlier. One was a Kentucky coffee tree (*Gymnocladus dioica*) that was then 12 feet high. The other was a Kermes oak (*Quercus coccifera*) that Hope was informed had been brought from Spain by the Duke of Argyll himself. He tells us nothing of the origin of the other thirteen trees he describes at Kew. Perhaps they were *all* trees from Whitton; after all, they were small enough. The majority, as one would expect, were Americans: a snowbell tree (*Halesia monticola*), a red juniper, a swamp pine (*Pinus palustris*) and a foxtail pine (*Pinus serotina*), a chionanthus (*C. virginicus*) and a bull bay magnolia (*M. grandiflora*). But Hope only mentions one tree which was later to prove one of the stars of Kew's arboretum. This was the mighty persimmon (*Diospyros virginiana*) planted close to the Temple of the Sun. According to W. J. Bean's invaluable five-volume work, *Trees and Shrubs Hardy in the British Isles*, this tree was brought from Whitton and became the champion persimmon in the British Isles. It grew to the remarkable height of 65 feet, with a girth of 5 feet 6 inches, and was celebrated for the shagginess of its bark, which was cut into rectangles. It died full of years, preceded by the Temple of the Sun, which was smashed in the 1930s by a falling tree.

Today it appears that three other trees brought from Whitton in 1762 are still alive and well and living at Kew. They are known as the 'Old Lions'. Two of them, it must be said, have seen better days: a false acacia with its stomach held together by iron bands, and a sophora (now called *Styphnolobium*) half encased in a bed of bricks and concrete. But their delicate flowers still open summer after summer, and smell sweet enough. The third tree is a prodigy, one of the more remarkable trees of Europe – an age-defying ginkgo from China. Every spring its pale green leaves emerge, shaped like a butterfly's wing, every autumn they paint the sky yellow. It's hard to believe that this many-headed creature is 260 years old. But temple ginkgos in China and Japan are believed to live for more than a thousand years. No doubt Kew's prodigy, soon to be the last survivor of the duke's garden at Whitton, brought downriver to Kew by Lord Bute, will serve as a worthy memorial to both men.

Poor Bute! His masterly work at Kew was never acknowledged by the public. (How could it be, when it was a private royal garden?) Instead he was vilified by the press and threatened with assassination. What happened was this.

In October 1760 his devoted friend and protégé, the Prince of Wales, became George III. Together the two men, as we saw, had a vision for the future. It was idealistic – and perhaps impractical. They wanted to end corruption and corrupt patronage. They wanted to give the monarch more than a nominal role in deciding national policy. This would mean breaking the power of the great Whig families which controlled both Houses of Parliament. Foreign policy, if the two men had their way, would be less dependent on European alliances, and tilted more in favour of the colonies. Of course they would need the cooperation – or at least the acquiescence – of the men now ruling the country, the leaders of the great Whig families whose power they threatened. The Whig prime minister was the sixty-seven-year-old Duke of Newcastle, and the man who managed the Commons – and the war policy – was William Pitt the Elder. Would *they* cooperate with Bute? It was not impossible if they were offered enough pickings. Or at least they might be outmanoeuvred.

In March 1761 the young king promoted Bute to the rank of secretary of state with a seat in the cabinet. That same summer the long-awaited peace negotiations with France began. All sides were now exhausted in this global battle of giants: Britain and Prussia against France and Austria and Russia. Bute led the peace negotiations, and they looked like succeeding. Then Pitt suddenly resigned. He had insisted they launched a pre-emptive attack on Spain, a plan to which the rest of the cabinet (including Bute) strongly objected. And the Duke of Newcastle soon followed Pitt's lead. He resigned in May 1762, unhappy with Bute's handling of the subsidies paid to Prussia. The king could not pretend to be displeased: the new prime minister was Lord Bute.

One might have thought that Bute now had the world at his feet. The Seven Years War was over at last, leaving most of the combatants exhausted and nearly bankrupt. (Maria Teresa, the ruler of Austria, had to pawn her jewellery.) But for Britain the spectacular gains in the war had more than offset the costs and losses. The French had been expelled from both India and Canada. The British colonies in the Caribbean flourished as the sugar trade boomed. Best of all, from Bute's point of view, he had flushed out the leading Whigs – Pitt and Newcastle – who found compromise impossible. Now for the programme of modest reform agreed with the king, a programme that would set the seal on the reputation of both Bute and George III.

But Bute had not bargained for the ferocious response of the Whigs. A deluge of abuse broke over his head: in Parliament, in the press, in every town and village. He was hustled on the streets, and threatened with assassination. No one had a good word for him. Bute was the man who had sold out to the French in the recent agreement to end the war. He had betrayed Britain's allies, the Prussians, by reducing their subsidies. His aim, no doubt, was to restore the absolute monarchy of the Stuarts. (After all he was a Stuart himself – even if his ancestors had been born on the wrong side of the blanket.) And Bute was a Scot, a rebel at heart, if not actually involved in the '45 rebellion.

Of course Bute did his best, in the House of Lords, to defend himself from these slanders. But he was not fitted for the rough and tumble of eighteenth-century politics – too honourable, perhaps, for that tawdry world of dealers and fixers. He hated the mean compromises that come naturally to politicians. And, what was worse, his own shyness made him seem cold and arrogant.

After a year as prime minister he could stand it no more. On 9 April 1763 he handed in his resignation to the king. Within six months he had left politics for good.

What of the great garden at Kew that, with the king and his mother, he had worked so hard to create? Did it prove an antidote to humiliation in politics, as Bishop Compton had found with his great garden at Fulham Palace? Sad to say, Bute soon became estranged from the king. By 1766 they had ceased to correspond. Bute had denounced the king for accepting Pitt as his latest prime minister. And Bute had already found a new garden of his own to lavish with money and ideas.

By now Bute had become one of the richest men in the kingdom; his wife, Mary, had inherited more than a million pounds in cash, as well as the vast Wortley estates. Bute spent much of the cash buying the estate at Luton Hoo, pulling down the house and rebuilding it to the designs of Robert Adam. He spent three years travelling in Italy. And he chose a new career as patron of literature, science and the arts. His beneficiaries included Samuel Johnson, Tobias Smolllett and Thomas Sheridan. He poured money into botany – creating a chair at Edinburgh for Dr John Hope, and paying £12,000 for a 26-volume work, *The Vegetable System*, commissioned from Dr John Hill, the Kew eccentric.

Tiring with Luton Hoo, he built a villa, Highcliffe, at Christchurch in Hampshire, overlooking the Isle of Wight. It was there he lived in melancholy grandeur for the last twenty years of his life, conducting his botanical studies, and collecting books, prints and scientific instruments.

Meanwhile poor Princess Augusta had succumbed to a painful cancer, and George III had suffered the first of his mental breakdowns. But William Aiton, in charge of the garden and arboretum at Kew, was proving one of Britain's most talented gardeners. And his success owed a lot to the help of a young explorer who had recently returned from circumnavigating the globe.

CHAPTER 5

Sir Joseph Takes Charge

Everyone was eager to meet the dashing young explorer, Joseph Banks. He had just returned from circumnavigating the globe in Captain Cook's *Endeavour*. Not least of his admirers was the king, George III. He received Banks 'graciously' (according to the newspapers) at St James's Palace. The date was 2 August 1771, and Banks must have hit it off with the king. They met again several times that month at Richmond Lodge, the king's summer retreat next to Kew Gardens. Banks showed him some of the drawings of plants he had collected on the voyage. And Banks brought along Dr Solander, the distinguished Swedish botanist and favourite pupil of the great Linnaeus. Solander had served as Banks's adviser (and friend) on the daredevil three-year voyage.

Like many of his subjects, the king must have anxiously followed the course of Cook's expedition during those three years. In fact the king had a personal interest in its success. Early in 1768 he had been approached by the president of the Royal Society to ask him to subsidise a scientific expedition to some island in mid-Pacific from where an astronomer could observe the transit of Venus. The transit of Venus across the path of the sun was a key to new astronomical discoveries, but if this chance was missed it would not occur again for another century. The king agreed to pay £4,000 out of his own pocket. In due course the navy was persuaded to supply a ship and a hundred sailors. The ship was the *Endeavour* with Cook as the captain; the island where the astronomer would erect his observatory was Tahiti. And what better place to consort with Venus than this newly discovered island where love came free?

Now Banks himself was a friend of Lord Sandwich, the First Lord of the Admiralty, and Eton and Oxford, plus a private income of £6,000 a year, had made him an insider in society. Although he had inherited a large family estate in Lincolnshire, he was not one of the fox-hunting squires. Plant-hunting was more his style. He had already made a trip to Labrador on a ship commanded by Lieutenant Constantine Phipps, an old friend from Eton. He brought back a good haul of birds, fishes, insects and plants. His talents were recognised, and he had been elected a fellow of the Royal Society when he was only twenty-three. He had duly got wind of this new scientific expedition to observe Venus. He applied to join the expedition. But why restrict its objects to astronomy? Why not explore the *botany* of these vast unexplored regions of the world?

Lord Sandwich had been most helpful. If Banks could organise – and pay for – a team of botanists, that was fine by the navy. So when the *Endeavour* set sail, in the autumn of 1768, it had nine extra men in the great cabin: Banks and Dr Solander, with two artists, a secretary and four personal servants, including two Black men.

In due course the voyage of the *Endeavour* proved a triumph. Cook was the first man to chart the west coast of New Zealand, and the east coast of Australia. He redrew the map, filling the void with accurate soundings and meticulous surveys. He exposed the mistakes of his predecessors. There was talk of a ghostly continent, *Terra Australis Incognita*, somewhere south of New Zealand. Cook showed it was indeed a ghost.

For their own parts Banks and Solander made numerous botanical discoveries. Despite the dangers and difficulties (including near-shipwreck on the Great Barrier Reef) they brought back the seeds of many hundreds of plants and thousands of dried specimens ready for the herbarium. They shot and preserved hundreds of rare birds and animals. They were the first Europeans to describe an Australian kangaroo. They found the perfect place for a convict settlement – at Botany Bay, next to modern Sydney. But one wonders how much Banks chose to tell the king when they met at Richmond Lodge after his return.

The ship had reached Tahiti in good time to record the transit of Venus on 4 June 1769 – and to enjoy the favours of its beautiful women. Banks spent as much time exploring Tahitian behaviour, what he called 'enjoying free liberty in love', as he did in exploring Tahitian plants. And Banks's inexperience led to the unfortunate deaths of two of his party. On the first leg of the trip he had taken his men on a botanical ramble near Cape Horn. Although it was high summer the weather changed with alarming speed. The party spent the night snowbound, and two of the servants (Black men called Thomas Richmond and George Dorlton) were left behind and died of exposure.

In fact the death rate on the voyage – largely due to a mistake of Cook's – was terrifying. Of Banks's original party of nine, only three survived the trip. Both the artists, Sydney Parkinson and Alexander Buchan, died of some tropical disease. So did Banks's secretary, Herman Sporing, and one more of the servants. Disease played havoc with the ship. Charles Green, the astronomer, succumbed. So did the ship's surgeon, William Monkhouse, and Zachary Hicks the second in command, and about thirty sailors. Cook's disastrous error was to leave the ship's company in the Dutch East Indies Company's port of Batavia (modern Jakarta) while the *Endeavour* was being repaired; its hull had a temporary patch of sailcloth after being punctured by the coral of the Great Barrier Reef. Batavia was famous for the skills of its shipwrights, and famous, too, for its diseases. Banks and Solander were lucky to survive – no doubt because they had spent the weeks botanising outside the port.

A year after his return, Banks was excited to hear that the Royal Society was planning another scientific expedition to the Pacific. The navy had agreed to provide two ships and their crews, and once again Cook had been chosen as leader. The scientific aim was geographical and, it must be said, somewhat negative: finally to confirm that *Terra Australis Incognita* – the Great Unknown Continent – was simply a myth. But Banks gathered the trip would mean a return to Tahiti, and the discovery of other exotic islands and their delectable peoples. Banks hurried to his friend Lord Sandwich. Could he join the expedition? And could he adapt the *Resolution*, Cook's new ship, to the requirements of his own party? He had to admit that they had found conditions rather cramped on board the *Endeavour*. Once again Lord Sandwich agreed. If Banks was prepared to pay, that was fine by the navy, although refitting the ship would delay the expedition.

At this point events took a farcical turn. Banks's refinements proved not merely unsuitable but grotesque. At colossal expense – over £10,000, more than double the original cost of the ship – Banks had arranged for a luxurious new upper deck and poop deck to be superimposed on the existing ones. It was too much to bear (quite literally) for the good ship *Resolution*. On its sea trials it rolled like the devil; in a decent wind it would certainly capsize. Cook took care to avoid the row that followed. But he must have been relieved when he heard Banks was not joining the expedition after all. Banks had finally lost the support of Lord Sandwich, and went off licking his wounds. He had paid a colossal bill, and merely made a fool of himself.

His first reaction was to hire a ship for himself and Solander, and cool off, in every sense, on a botanical trip to Iceland. A lesser man might then have thrown in his hand and reverted to the usual hobbies of country gentlemen: hunting and shooting animals, chasing women, pursuing local politics. Banks was made of sterner stuff. From his humiliation he drew a useful lesson. He must listen to people. His passion was botany, and science in general. His strong suit, apart from his wealth, was his energy and enthusiasm. He enjoyed lobbying. He had great gifts for organising people. He loved to arrange every detail of a plant-hunting expedition, down to the design of the shipboard containers for plants and the beads and metalwork for the natives who would barter for them. (Today he would be called a control freak.) But among eighteenth-century botanists he was merely a talented amateur. He must listen to the experts, like Solander and his successors. They were pupils of Linnaeus and their advice was unrivalled.

A calmer phase of his life now began. In 1777 he gave up his bachelor chambers in Piccadilly, and bought a grand house in Soho Square. He needed plenty of space for his collection of dried plants and other specimens, now accumulating fast. He also needed space for his family. He paid off his mistress, Sarah Wells, and married an heiress called Dorothea Hugessen. In 1781 he was created a baronet. His reputation restored, he was elected president of the Royal Society. This was much more than an honour. Now he had the authority to lobby the government on anything from convict settlements to whale-hunting. But nothing was so close to his heart as his aim to make the king's estate at Kew the finest garden in Europe.

The two men must have met at Kew some time after Banks's return from Iceland. Banks had decided to rent a country retreat near the river at Isleworth. It was an unpretentious suburban villa only a couple of miles from Kew and the great pagoda. After Princess Augusta's death in 1772, the king had inherited the Kew estate, which ran immediately to the east of his own estate at Richmond. The two could be combined in due course. But the king had an embarrassing problem. Neither he nor his wife, Queen Charlotte, knew much about gardening. Architecture, not horticulture or botany, was the king's passion. So this is where Banks saw an opening for himself. He would become the unofficial director of the garden, supervising William Aiton and his staff. He had the skill and the know-how, and the instinct when to get expert advice. (As for self-confidence, he had it in spades.) Here was an informal arrangement which suited both men. It flattered Banks to be advising a king. And it wouldn't cost the royal family a penny.

Banks's plan for the arboretum at Kew might appear simple. It was to be a fully comprehensive collection. This meant that *one day* the collection should include every single species of tree and shrub hardy enough to grow in the open at Kew. But would that day ever come? A start had been made in the decade and a half since Chambers had laid out the five-acre arboretum, centred on the Temple of the Sun, and spread out between the Dutch House and the Great Stove. Aiton, who had learnt his trade at Chelsea's Physic Garden, was proving a success. He had added hundreds of new trees and other plants to the core collection transferred from the duke's garden at Whitton. Some of the newcomers had been propagated from seed or cuttings grown in the greenhouses at Kew. Others were donated by fellow collectors in Britain.

The most determined of these fellow collectors – and rivals – was the 6th Earl of Coventry. As a young man, in 1751, he had inherited the family's estate at Croome Court in Herefordshire and soon changed it out of all recognition. Lord Coventry, unlike Joseph Banks, was a dedicated aesthete. He was the dashing young peer who had married the famous beauty, Maria, elder of the Gunning sisters; he also kept a mistress, Kitty Fisher, London's best-known courtesan, painted by numerous artists including Reynolds. At Croome Court he had hired 'Capability' Brown to redesign the landscape with clumps and romantic vistas and a serpentine lake. And not only the landscape. Brown was also commissioned to knock down the family's house – a red-brick Jacobean manor – and replace it with the dressed stone corner towers and portico of a stylish Palladian mansion. After Maria's early death from lead poisoning (apparently the result of the toxic face cream then in fashion), Lord Coventry had begun to collect trees and other plants on a heroic scale. His sources, it seems, were some of the excellent plant nurseries now blossoming in the south of England: those of James Gordon at Mile End, Lee and Kennedy at Hammersmith, and Conrad Loddiges at Hackney. Before he died Lord Coventry was reckoned to have collected the astonishing total of 242 species and varieties of trees, hardy enough for a Herefordshire winter. These trees were scattered over 45 different genera. Only Kew could boast a larger number.

Of course Banks, too, ransacked the English plant nurseries for exciting rarities. But Banks had noticed that so much seemed left to chance. Since the death of Peter Collinson there had been no organised syndicate to share plants from America. (The firm of Lee and Kennedy, however, had found their own substitute for John Bartram on the east coast of north America, and had a collector in South America, too.) There was no shortage of be-your-own-gardener books. But the eighth and final edition of Philip Miller's indispensable *Dictionary of Gardening* had been published in 1768, and now Miller was dead.

And which 'tree-munger' (to use Horace Walpole's mocking term) had published a catalogue of their own collection of trees and shrubs? Only one had bothered, and that one was the late

Princess Augusta. She had commissioned the eccentric botanist Dr John Hill to compile a catalogue of Kew trees and shrubs which was duly published in 1768 with the sonorous title of *Hortus Kewensis*. But this was incomplete at the time, and soon out of date.

What was needed seemed obvious to Banks. Kew's energetic gardener, William Aiton, must be set to work compiling a *complete* list of the trees and shrubs at Kew. The king must have agreed with Banks although the list took more than a decade to compile. (It was finally published in 1789, and shared, confusingly, the same sonorous title as Hill's.) Meanwhile Banks had taken a bold step in organising the flow of new plants to the arboretum. If the British nursery trade couldn't organise the import of rarities, then it was up to the royal gardens at Kew. And this meant that Kew had to hire its own collectors who would have to risk their lives in some of the wildest parts of the globe.

A start had been made in 1771 when it was decided to send out a collector to South Africa. The man chosen was one of Kew's own gardeners, Francis Masson, recommended by his boss, William Aiton. And it was Banks, it appears, who had suggested where he was to be sent. Banks himself had yet to assume the role of unofficial director of Kew. But he and Solander had been impressed by the opportunities for plant-hunting at the Cape, when they paid a visit on the way home in the *Endeavour*. The Dutch East India Company had founded a colony at the Cape a hundred years earlier. Now, in the 1770s, it was one of the hubs of the world: an international staging post for ships on the long voyage to and from India and the East. Cape Town had bred an energetic population of five thousand, mainly white settlers and their black and brown slaves, and a mixture of all three, and was blessed with a magnificent natural harbour under the shadow of Table Mountain.

Masson duly arrived that autumn, after being given a lift in the *Resolution*. (The navy gave him a passage on the first leg of Cook's second voyage.) And when he returned to Kew in 1775 he brought many treasures. As Solander put it: Masson has arrived back 'with a great cargo of new plants... a glorious collection'.[1]

They certainly included some exciting new house plants – like the many coloured ice-plants (Mesembryanthemums) and the scarlet geraniums (Pelargoniums). Two of Masson's other discoveries were particularly astonishing. He found a flower which had a beak like a pelican's, and out of this beak sprang a cockade of orange and blue flowers. It was christened *Strelitzia reginae* in honour of George's wife, Queen Charlotte. (Her father was Duke Charles of Mecklenburg-Strelitz.) The popular name was 'bird of paradise plant'. Masson also discovered a treasure trove of proteas hidden between two coastal ranges in the western Cape. There was nothing in Europe quite like this gorgeous flower, its jewelled disc pollinated by sunbirds and sugarbirds.

But there was a problem with all Masson's discoveries in South Africa. Most of them were house plants and herbaceous. But even those which were shrubs were of no use for the arboretum. To earn a place there a new exotic tree or shrub must be able to survive the winter at Kew *in the open*. That meant that it couldn't depend on the shelter of a greenhouse, let alone the Great Stove. Hence Banks and Solander's botanical discoveries on their trip round the world had added virtually nothing to Kew's arboretum. True, they had filled volumes with dried specimens, and enriched the world of science. But Cook's route to Tahiti and beyond had condemned Banks to hunt plants in the tropical lowlands of the South Pacific, and the subtropics of Australia. Masson's plant-hunting was in the Cape: that is, in the warm temperate zone of South Africa. It was in the *cool* temperate regions of the world where Banks must search for his Eldorado ready-made for the arboretum.

And Banks was well aware that there was no shortage of these regions – even in the tropics – if the plant hunter was prepared to climb mountains. Of course mountains in the tropics had a totally different climate from the lowlands: a cool temperate climate similar, in some ways, to Europe's. (In fact a plant's *altitude* neatly offset its *latitude*: a tree in China at an altitude of 10,000 feet, and 25 degrees of latitude, faced much the same climate as one at sea level, and 50 degrees of latitude – like the trees at Kew.)

So Banks's eyes turned to China. Was this where he would find his Eldorado?

Already his grand house in Soho Square was stuffed with books and pictures which gave tantalising glimpses of China and its plants. For more than a century the Chinese emperors had allowed European Jesuits to live and work near the so-called Forbidden City – a series of imperial palaces and gardens at the heart of Peking (now Beijing). One of the most beguiling missionaries was Fr Pierre d'Incarville, who was sent to China by his order in 1740. His mission was no fewer than to convert the Quinlong emperor; unsurprisingly, he failed. But the two men became friends. Fr d'Incarville was an amateur botanist and presented the emperor with a number of European plants which he had grown himself from seeds sent from France. The emperor reciprocated by encouraging Fr d'Incarville to send seeds of Chinese plants to the royal gardens in Paris. It was a fair exchange. The Chinese seeds grew into fruitful specimens: a pagoda tree (*Styphnolobium japonica*), a tree of heaven (*Ailanthus altissima*), a golden rain tree (*Koelreuteria paniculata*), and a Chinese mahogany tree (*Toona sinensis*) Examples of all four species soon reached England – including the pagoda tree which, as we saw earlier, Lord Bute had sent from Whitton to Kew after the death of his uncle, the Duke of Argyll. And this was why Banks, in the shadow of the great pagoda at Kew, longed to send out collectors to sample more of the botanical booty of China.

But China was not like South Africa: open and accessible to wandering plant hunters. The Jesuits had been exceptionally privileged. No ordinary travellers were permitted to visit, let alone live in, Peking. Indeed, since 1757 the only other Europeans licensed to work in China were the staff of the British East India Company, based at their trading post at Canton, in the far south. Even that licence was limited to a monkish, six-month trading season for the 'supercargoes', as the European staff were called. No women were allowed to accompany them to Canton. So as soon as the six months were over the supercargoes would retreat to the Portuguese island of Macao, where they could live a more normal life with their wives and families and mistresses.

For nearly a decade, Banks waited his chance – and then it came. Late in the winter of 1782, Banks received a letter from two influential members of the British team at Canton: the resident surgeon, John Duncan, and the company's 'chief of the council of supercargoes', William Pigou. Together they offered to serve Banks as plant collectors, although they confessed they knew little or nothing about botany. Banks reassured them. He would send them a hit list ('my desiderata', he called them) of Chinese plants that he knew had not yet reached Europe. After the first consignments began to arrive, Banks got to work; he successfully lobbied the directors of the East India Company to raise Duncan's salary by £200 a year.

The very first consignment had included a magnolia new to science. It was called by the Chinese the 'yulan', meaning the 'lily tree', and no doubt Banks was told that potted yulans were common in the gardens of Canton and the local plant nurseries.

But their lives were short. The species couldn't stand the heat of the tropics, as it was native to the mountains far to the north. So the Cantonese would throw away the plant as soon as it had flowered – and buy a young replacement.

What Banks must have gradually realised was that this yulan, with the pure white flowers of a lily, was the very icon of imperial China. It had been collected in the wilds of eastern China during the Tang dynasty (AD 617–908) – China's first golden age. Buddhist monks planted the tree in the precincts of their temples, and carried it proudly with them to their temples in Japan. In due course it decorated the gardens of later dynasties, including the current Manchu dynasty at Peking. By the late eighteenth century, the French Jesuits had already described its exotic fascination. In his *Memoires*, published in 1778, Fr Cibot wrote: 'It is said to resemble a naked walnut tree with a lily at the end of each branch'.[2] No wonder Banks longed to possess it.

But it turned out that this prodigy still remained tantalisingly out of reach. The first consignment sent by John Duncan in January 1784 by a ship called the *Morse* docked six months later in London. The yulan had died on the voyage. Three years later John Duncan tried again, sending two yulans in a ship called the *Worcester*. Both plants were dead on arrival. The six-month passage across the world simply proved too much for them. It was not only the violent swings from one climate to another – from the searing heat of the Pacific to the rigours of Cape Horn. A potted plant on an eighteenth-century ship was under constant attack from salt spray on deck and from sea water in the hold, from hungry pigs and hens and caterpillars; and there were times when thirsty plants came last in the queue for a water ration. Of course seeds generally survived better than living plants. (How else could one explain Fr d'Incarville's success in sending those dazzling new species of trees to the royal gardens in France?) But magnolia seeds seemed particularly vulnerable.

To compensate Banks for these disappointments, John Duncan sent him other plants from his hit list, mostly flowers, including several mountain peonies, called in China the moutan, and recognised since the time of the Tang Dynasty of the ninth century as the 'king of flowers'. Somehow one of these delectable plants (now famous as *Paeonia suffruticosa var. banksii*) survived the perils of the journey.

John Duncan then retired from Canton, but his brother Alexander took over his job, after Banks lobbied hard to get it for him. In December 1788 Alexander dispatched four yulans by the *Talbot*.

And, somehow, one survived. No one knows how Alexander finally succeeded in coaxing a yulan to stay alive during the six-month passage to London. Or perhaps he struck lucky with seeds. By 1789, at any rate, Banks had introduced this astonishing new species to Europe. The tree grew rapidly and flowered for the first time about 1800. And then its Chinese magic was at last revealed.

Hitherto the only magnolias known to Europe were those from North America. Bishop Compton had acquired the first: *Magnolia virginiana*, the elegant little tree with glaucous leaves. This was followed by half a dozen new species of American magnolias brought to Europe, including the giant cucumber tree and that aptly named evergreen, *Magnolia grandiflora*. But all these American trees shared a conventional pattern of flowering: the flowers emerged *with* the leaves. What was new and magical in the yulan – and this was a gift of almost all Asiatic magnolias – was the timing of the flowers. The flowers emerged on the ends of bare branches *before* the leaves. Hence that romantic description by Fr Cibot, the French Jesuit at Peking, of the 'naked walnut tree with a lily at the end of each branch'.

Meanwhile Banks was waiting on tenterhooks to hear the result of a far more ambitious botanical scheme than anything he had previously attempted. This was his plan to dig up and remove more than a thousand breadfruit plants from Tahiti in the South Pacific and transport them to Jamaica 12,000 miles away in the Caribbean. It sounds a hare-brained venture. But Banks was confident in the scheme, if it was left to him to arrange things. The aim was to find a cheap food for the slaves in the sugar plantations of the British West Indies – cheaper, at any rate, than their current diet of plantain fruit, a crop vulnerable to hurricanes. In 1787 Banks had persuaded Pitt to put a 215-ton sloop at his disposal, ingeniously adapted to carry the breadfruit. He chose the crew of forty-six men, including an experienced gardener from Kew, called David Nelson. The small ship attracted no particular attention when it sailed from Spithead in late December 1787. The ship was called *Bounty*, and its captain William Bligh.

Back at Kew, Banks continued to manage the royal gardens with his usual tact and efficiency. He would meet the king most Saturdays. 'What-what-what' was the usual way the king would begin the conversation. Then they would talk farming and gardening – Merino sheep and Highland cows and Chinese plants – like any two middle-aged country gentlemen. And perhaps the king would tell Banks of how he planned to knock down the rather unimpressive White House, the Palladian pile facing the arboretum at Kew built for his father by William Kent. He would replace it with a sprawling Gothic castle designed by James Wyatt. It wouldn't be cheap. (The bill eventually came to more than half a million – before it was demolished.) But the king was sure the public would expect it of him. They admired magnificent architecture.

And then came a twist of fate that no one could possibly have predicted.

In mid-October 1788 the king began to show signs of a terrifying affliction. By early November several of the king's doctors believed he was dying. Others thought the king would remain a cripple for life, and the Prince of Wales would take over as regent. This would have spelt disaster for Pitt's government, as it was assumed that the prince would replace Pitt and the Tories with his own cronies. For Banks, too, it spelled disaster: an end, at any rate, to his well-laid plans for Kew, and his ambition to give it the finest collection of trees in the world. He must abandon his plans for sending expeditions to find new plants in China and America. Without the king's support he would be helpless.

December came and the king's doctors remained baffled by the king's disease. They had no name to give it. Only one thing was clear. The king had gone mad.

CHAPTER 6

Dr Menzies' Discoveries

Today George III's mysterious disease is recognised by most historians as a case of manic depression. Porphyria, a disorder of the nervous system, is no longer believed to have been the king's problem.

The symptoms, described by the queen, were certainly alarming: his eyes were 'nothing but blackcurrant jelly, the veins in his face were swelled, the sound in his voice was dreadful; he often spoke till he was exhausted, and the moment he could recover his breath began again, while the foam ran out of his mouth'.[1] No fewer than seven doctors attended him, all charging handsome fees. Their treatment gave him great pain and was unfortunately futile. As well as dosing him with emetics and purgatives, they repeatedly blistered his scalp and legs, and 'cupped' him with a heated glass vessel applied to the skin.

By late November it was decided to send him to the White House at Kew, which now became his prison, with the king and his jailers on the ground floor and his family on the floor above. Despite his jailers' efforts, he tried to escape to his family, but was caught and restrained. No one listened to the queen. Her hair turned grey; she was clearly on the verge of a breakdown.

It's possible the seven doctors would have killed him with their purgatives and blistering and cupping. Fortunately Pitt's cabinet saw sense in December and decided to call in a new doctor who specialised in mental illness. Dr Willis was a clergyman and managed an asylum for the insane. He treated the king humanely as far as he could; when the king became violent he was confined in a straitjacket. By January the king was slowly recovering, although still prey to sudden attacks of delirium. He was now allowed to walk in the garden at Kew, and one day he seized the keys of the Great Pagoda. A struggle ensued between him and his attendants. He lay on the grass, like an angry child, and refused to get up. Eventually he had to be carried home on the shoulders of his attendants. He was often abusive to Dr Willis and resented his company. But by early February his sense of humour was returning. One day, when he and his attendants were walking in the garden, he met William Aiton, the head gardener, who offered Dr Willis a basket of exotic fruit. 'Get another basket, Aiton,' said the king, 'and pack up the Doctor in it and send him off at the same time.'[2]

As the king had now reached convalescence, Willis encouraged him to meet his personal friends. One of the first to see him was Joseph Banks. No doubt Banks congratulated the king on his recovery. But did they discuss the Regency Crisis precipitated by the king's breakdown? In November, as we saw, the seven doctors had warned Pitt and the cabinet that the king's illness might leave him a hopeless wreck. The Prince of Wales, and the Foxite Whigs in Parliament, had then seized their chance. If the prince could be appointed regent, he in turn could replace Pitt with Charles James Fox. Pitt did his best to drag his feet. But by February Pitt had been forced to present a Regency Bill to the Commons. In a matter of days this could have passed the Lords. So the king had only kept his throne by the narrowest of margins.

By April the prince and the Foxites could only grind their teeth as the nation celebrated the king's recovery with a crashing

Te Deum in St Paul's, followed by a magnificent ball at Windsor attended by 228 guests. And with the king's support Banks was beginning to plan a new expedition to America.

For two hundred years – ever since the days of the Tradescants – the British colonies on the *eastern* side of North America had proved a treasure chest for Europe to plunder. Banks's new plan was to explore the *north-west* coast for botanical treasure. The area in which he was most interested lay to the north of the ill-defined frontier where British and Russian fur-trappers met Spanish immigrants from what was then northern Mexico and would eventually become the state of California. In fact that jagged coastline had never been properly surveyed, and there was even wild talk of a great rift in the north of the continent which might enable ships to sail directly from the Pacific to the Atlantic, and vice versa, without wasting months rounding Cape Horn. (Another version of this rumour suggested that a great river in the west would provide a link to the Atlantic by way of the North-West Passage.) What was clear was that fur-trapping was proving lucrative, and three different nations – Britain, Spain and Russia – might soon be competing to create settlements in the area.

Of course Banks, as a life-long supporter of imperial expansion, was keen that Britain should strike first. But plans for a British settlement ground to a halt when the Spanish government seized a number of British ships at Nootka Sound in the summer of 1789. Nootka was an obscure outpost on the western side of what was later to be christened Vancouver Island. When the news reached Britain, Pitt's government ordered a general mobilisation of the fleet, and war with Spain seemed imminent. After their escape from the Regency Crisis the cabinet was confronted with the Nootka Crisis. But if there was to be war, what exactly was it for? A war for a handful of fur-trappers? Both countries came to their senses. By the autumn of 1790 the Nootka Sound Convention was signed by Britain and Spain. The next step by Britain was to send out a ship to survey the area (which Cook had somewhat sketchily surveyed ten years earlier) and tidy up the details of the convention. And this was Banks's chance. The survey would serve many purposes, political, diplomatic, and, crucially from Banks' perspective, botanical.

The ship chosen was a newly launched warship, HMS *Discovery*, honoured with the same name as Cook's own ship on his second and third voyages. The new ship's captain, George Vancouver, had served on both those voyages, first as a midshipman, then as a fourth lieutenant. He shared one of Cook's most remarkable gifts – his skill in navigation and surveying – but was otherwise a much less attractive character. He was liable to sudden, inexplicable outbursts of rage. He bullied the midshipmen, and even flogged one of the Pitts, called Lord Camelford, for stealing some of the ship's stores and using them to buy the favours of the girls in Tahiti. (This was a particularly rash undertaking by Vancouver, as the young peer was a cousin of William Pitt, the prime minister, and there was no precedent for flogging midshipmen.)

Before the expedition sailed, Banks found Vancouver rude and uncooperative. When Banks proposed that his young protégé, Archibald Menzies, should be the surgeon-cum-naturalist for the expedition, Vancouver bluntly rejected the proposal, and appointed a surgeon who knew nothing of botany. The news came as a slap in the face for Banks. But Banks was used to rebuffs. He won the next round, by lobbying Pitt and the government. Menzies was appointed as the official naturalist for the expedition, and would take his instructions directly from Banks.

The *Discovery* finally sailed from Falmouth in April 1791, and reached the west coast of North America a year later, after short

Dr Archibald Menzies

stops for food and other comforts at the Cape, Australia, New Zealand, Tahiti and Hawaii. Already relations between Vancouver and Menzies were tense. One problem was the experimental plant cabin erected on the quarterdeck. This was a large, glazed wooden structure, personally designed by Banks, with sliding glass panels to protect the plants. Vancouver made no secret that he found it a tiresome obstruction. But Banks and Menzies believed it was the key to success. Without this strange new device they saw no chance of bringing home living plants for the king's garden at Kew.

Surveying the coast proved both tedious and dangerous. The jagged coast was dotted with islands, including the 300-mile-long giant soon to be known as Vancouver Island. Every bay and cove, every twist and turn of the forested coastline had to be inspected by the team in small, open boats. But Menzies, despite the hardships, was in his element. In January 1793 he wrote a full report to Banks, detailing his work up to that date.

In the straits to the east of Nootka Sound they found 'fine level Country... abounding with extended lawns & rich pastures, not inferior in beauty of prospect to the most admired parks in England'. As for trees and other plants, Menzies confessed that he could not pass this beautiful country without 'often regretting my not being able to land & examine it more particularly'. It would appear that Vancouver did little to accommodate Menzies. Still Menzies was able to report to Banks what he had found on his botanical forays on the eastern side of the great island: 'there is a greater variety of Hardwood scattered along the Shores here than I have observed on any other part of the coast, tho' not in great abundance.'[3]

By the end of August 1792 they had rounded the end of the island and turned south to Nootka Sound. Here they met the Spanish grandee, Bodega y Quadra, who was both governor of the region and commander-in-chief of the Royal Navy of Mexico and California. It was Quadra's responsibility to arrange with Vancouver the details of the handover of the Nootka settlement. This had been agreed by Spain and Britain when they signed the Nootka Convention. But, although Quadra proved friendly and hospitable at first, there were unexpected difficulties. As Menzies reported to Banks:

> On our arrival, he told Captain Vancouver that he would put him in possession of those territories agreeable to his orders & the wish of his Catholic Majesty, giving up all the Houses, Gardens &c. as they stood, and that he would haul down the Spanish colours before he went away, & on our hoisting the English Colours that he would then salute the British flag. But on the arrival afterwards in the port of an American trader,

Captain Ingraham, he wonderfully prevaricated from these intentions, as was thought by the advice of that man and he would not then give up the port, but only a small corner of it, about a hundred yards square...[4]

To resolve this impasse, Quadra and Vancouver agreed there was nothing for it but to pass the buck back to the two governments in Europe. So a young officer, Lieut. Zachary Mudge, was dispatched in a fur-trading vessel on a year-long voyage to take the news back to London by way of China. Meanwhile Vancouver was free to pursue his surveying, and Menzies could continue his search for rare plants. Many of the species were already familiar to him. To Banks he sent a preliminary list: oaks, ash, birch, alders, maples and poplars. There were also 'other new and rare plants' which included a new species of arbutus, berberis and lonicera. Menzies promised to give Banks a full account of his discoveries after his return – when he would have the opportunity of consulting other professional botanists.

Menzies' brief, and rather threadbare, list might seem strangely disappointing to us today. Here he was in a botanical paradise – a coast which later generations of plant explorers would reveal to be teeming with new species of trees and other plants. A modern list of the trees on Vancouver Island would include the gigantic Oregon maple (*Acer macrophyllum*), the incense cedar (*Calocedrus decurrens*), the golden oak (*Quercus chrysolepis*, and numerous other trees and shrubs now common in British and Irish gardens. Still Menzies had spotted a new arbutus, as he told Banks in his letter. This was the giant of the genus, the madrone; it was duly named *Arbutus menziesii*. Menzies had also spotted three gigantic conifers. Two of these – the Douglas fir (*Pseudotsuga menziesii*) and the Sitka spruce (*Picea sitchensis*) – are today the dominant species in British and American forestry. And the third is the tree we now recognise as the tallest tree in the world, the coastal redwood (*Sequoia sempervirens*).

Menzies failed to spot so many other vegetable wonders. But who can blame the ship's surgeon-naturalist? Better to blame the captain.

A new, ironic twist now occurred in Menzies' tense relations with Vancouver. Dr Cranston – the ship's surgeon whom Vancouver had appointed in preference to Menzies – had proved quite inadequate. He had been ill half the voyage, and was now to return home from Nootka in a store ship. So Vancouver went to Menzies with 'earnest solicitations' to see if he could be persuaded to take the job. Menzies agreed – 'with this proviso that he will be careful it will interfere as little as possible with my other pursuits'. Fortunately there were two assistants to help him in his new duties and the ship was 'in general healthy'. These new arrangements, Menzies believed, offered a useful bonus. As he reported cheerfully to Banks: 'I have by this means got an additional Cabin, which will be very serviceable in preserving my collections'.[5]

Poor Menzies! He could hardly have guessed then how these new arrangements could lead to disaster. But I am anticipating.

The winters in the far north-west were too cold and stormy for surveying the coast in small boats. In October 1793 Vancouver took *Discovery* south to Monterey, the headquarters of the Spanish settlement in California in October. Here they were received with unexpected hospitality by the governor, Don Quadra. Menzies collected many new plants in this area; some were dried as specimens for the herbarium, others were kept alive in the plant cabin on the foredeck. (It is possible the living plants included the Monterey pine and the Monterey cypress – both now world-famous garden plants.) Then the *Discovery* set sail for the Sandwich Islands (now the islands of Hawaii) where Cook had been killed in that tragic fracas with the islanders fourteen years earlier. Relations with the British were now reasonably good. Menzies collected more plants and seeds, and showed his spirit by making the first ascent of Mona Roa. (Menzies estimated the height of this awe-inspiring volcano, now known as Maunaloa, as 13,634 feet above sea level, only 40 feet less than a modern survey records.)

By the spring *Discovery* was back in the north-west and nearing the end of their three-year survey of the coast. Vancouver was now able to answer the all-important question: *was* there any chance of a northern route by water across the American continent? His answer: a resounding no. There was no truth in the stories that 'Cook's River' would lead to that route. It was not even a river – only an inlet that extended a mere 4 or 5 leagues beyond the point where Cook's boats had left off their researches in 1779.

Vancouver was delighted, no doubt, by these discoveries, negative as they were. For Menzies, however, the result of this northern foray was most frustrating. As he explained apologetically to Banks:

At the head of this great Inlet, we were much entangled & perplexed with drift Ice, and about the latter end of April, encountered heavy falls of Snow, and intense frost... and I am sorry to acquaint you that this severe & quick transition of climate, killed the greatest part of the live plants I had in the Frame on the Quarter deck, and this is more to be regreted [*sic*], as I am afraid it will not be in my power to replace many of them, particularly those from California...[6]

With their survey of the northern coast complete as far north as latitude 61/12, the crew of *Discovery* returned in September to Nootka Sound 'in perfect health, & in high spirits', as Menzies put it. They were heading for home at last, they believed. It turned out that the two governments – of Spain and Great Britain – had still not settled the contested issues of the Nootka Convention. Vancouver gave it a month, and then, by agreement with Quadra, decided to head south for Monterey, en route for Cape Horn. His instructions from home had been to avoid Chile for fear of diplomatic complications. But, soon after passing one of the Galapagos Islands ('a large dreary barren island... whose shores were inhabited with vast numbers of seals, Penguins, Guana Lizards & Snakes'[7]) they realised they had sprung the main mast.

It was clear *Discovery* needed urgent repairs, and there was nothing for it but to break the journey at Valparaiso, the main port of the Spanish colony of Chile. In the event a new mast proved impossible to obtain. All they could do was patch up the old one and hope for the best. But they had no need to fear political complications. The president and governor of Chile was a colourful Irish expatriate, born plain Higgins, but now known as Don Ambrosio O'Higgins. As soon as he heard of their arrival, he invited them to be his guest at the capital, Santiago, three days journey to the east on horseback, in the shadow of the Andes.

Menzies reported to Banks that he and the other officers spent nine days in the capital where 'the President and the Principal Inhabitants vied with each other in showing us every civility and kindness'.[8] What Menzies *didn't* say was what happened at a ceremonial banquet that the president gave in their honour. The story goes that Menzies secretly pocketed a handful of 'pine' nuts put on the table for dessert. He could not identify the species. But when he returned to *Discovery* the following week he sowed the nuts on board, and five small trees resulted.

Perhaps the story has improved in the telling. What is certain is that Menzies sowed the nuts and brought the mysterious small trees back to England. And it was a time when Menzies must have felt he deserved a bit of success. His precious plants in the frame on the foredeck had once again fallen victim to the weather. The previous year's batch had died of cold in the far north. Now most of the current batch died of heat in the tropics. As he put it, sadly, 'Our tidious [*sic*] & Sultry passage from Monterey, proved fatal to many, of my little favourites, the live-plants, from the North-west coast & California, notwithstanding my utmost attention & endeavours to save them...'[9] Still, despite these disappointments, Menzies was able to fill up the plant cabin once again with healthy plants, and he looked forward to adding even further to his collection when they sailed from Valparaiso in April 1795.

But he had not reckoned with Vancouver. The tensions between the two men, half hidden for so long, had finally broken surface. In mid-September Banks received a desperate SOS from Menzies. *Discovery* had arrived in the Shannon estuary in the south-west of Ireland, waiting for an escort to bring it safely home. 'I now beg leave to inform you that I am under an Arrest since the 28th July last for insolence and contempt...'[10] He was threatened by a court martial. Vancouver had flown into a rage, it appeared, after Menzies had reproached him for interfering with the management of the plant cabin. The result of this interference had been disastrous. A sudden downpour caught the plant cabin with the lid removed, and almost all the precious plants there had been destroyed once again.

Back in Soho Square, Banks dealt with the crisis with his usual tact and efficiency. Perhaps Menzies had used strong language in dealing with Vancouver. But to court-martial the poor man would be hardly appropriate. Banks persuaded Vancouver to accept an apology from Menzies and cancel the court martial.

Despite the loss of successive batches of living plants put in the plant cabin, Menzies had made some important discoveries.

His seeds were already germinating in the gardens at Kew. His dried specimens were now being examined by other professional botanists. In due course four of his discoveries would honour his name, although three of them were not to be introduced until a later generation of plant explorers brought back the seeds. The first was a new genus of giant conifer which Menzies had found while Vancouver was surveying Vancouver Island and the north-west coast in 1792. Today it's commonly known as the Douglas fir, as David Douglas introduced it in 1825. But its botanical name is *Pseudotsuga menziesii*. The second was a new species of giant spruce, the Sitka spruce, *Picea sitchensis*. Together these two new giants now dominate commercial forestry in many parts of the world. Menzies' third discovery, was the madrona (*Arbutus menziesii*), a larger and more elegant tree than either of the European arbutus.

His fourth discovery was the most remarkable, and this was a tree which he both discovered and introduced. Somehow five living specimens had escaped the disastrous fate suffered by most of the inhabitants of the plant cabin. They had originated as the 'pine' nuts which Menzies was said to have had slipped into his pocket at the banquet in Santiago given by President O'Higgins. Several trees resulted, including one planted at Kew: strange, spiky creatures that might have shared their world with dinosaurs. Some people thought them repulsive and others competed to be the first to grow them. The new species was christened *Araucaria araucana* – after the Araucano Indians of the Andes, whose diet included these nuts. But it soon acquired a more expressive name. It was called the monkey puzzle.

CHAPTER 7

Kneeling to Greet the Emperor

Despite all the setbacks, and the painful relations with Vancouver, Menzies had done wonders. But his achievements were over-shadowed at the time by a crisis of a very different sort that no one could possibly have anticipated.

In December 1787, nearly a year before the onset of the king's illness, Banks had launched by far the most ambitious of all his schemes to move plants about the world. Banks's plan, adopted by the king and Pitt's government, was to move more than a thousand breadfruit plants from Tahiti in the South Pacific to Jamaica, 20,000 miles away in the Caribbean. The idea had originated as a brainwave of some of the white plantation owners. The newly discovered breadfruit would provide them with a cheaper food for their black slaves than the current rations of plantains or mealies.

The expedition would also serve a second purpose: the men would include an experienced gardener from the royal gardens at Kew. As well as looking after the breadfruit he would be instructed to collect tropical plants from both Tahiti and the West Indies.

The *Bounty* had sailed in December 1787 with a crew of forty-six and a thirty-three-year-old lieutenant, William Bligh, in command of the ship. Bligh seemed ideal for the job. He had served as master on the *Resolution*, for Cook's third voyage, and shared Cook's unusual skill in navigation. He also had a practical experience of growing breadfruit, as he had spent some weeks on Tahiti during that voyage and even picked up a smattering of the language. Still, Bligh was not a popular commander. He had little sympathy for his crew and a biting tongue. Fortunately, as it appeared, he had chosen as master's mate (and acting lieutenant) a man who was generally liked: Fletcher Christian, a twenty-three-year-old sailor from Cumberland who had already served with Bligh on several voyages.

Then, in March 1790, the news hit Banks like a kick in the stomach. Ten months earlier, *Bounty* had been taken over by mutineers, led by Fletcher Christian. Bligh himself, and those loyal to him, eighteen in all, had been cast adrift in an open boat with only a small sail and six oars. They had no map, little water and hardly any food, but miraculously survived the forty-eight-day, 4,000-mile journey to the nearest Dutch settlement on the island of Timor. Sad to say, two of the survivors, including David Nelson, the gardener from Kew, died of fever contracted on Timor.

It was to be another year before anyone could piece together the bizarre details of the mutiny and its aftermath. Did the lure of life on Tahiti – even life as an outlaw – encourage the mutineers? Or had Banks, and the naval experts, failed to provide a ship big enough to carry an armed guard to protect the officers from mutiny? One thing that is clear is that the crew of the *Bounty* had deeply resented Banks's arrangements for the breadfruit. The thousand pots and tubs had taken over the main cabin and the quarterdeck, displacing the sailors. It only needed Bligh's abusive treatment of Fletcher Christian to turn half the crew to mutiny.

As it was, the navy dispatched a ship, ominously named the *Pandora*, to bring Fletcher Christian and the other mutineers to justice. More than half of them were tracked down in Tahiti where the *Bounty* had left them after the takeover. Some had gone native, and taken Tahitian 'wives'. Others had done their best to hide. They were all put in irons, and packed off in a cage on the deck of the *Pandora*. But that ship then struck an uncharted reef somewhere east of Australia. Four of the mutineers drowned, still in irons, together with thirty of *Pandora*'s crew. Ten men survived to be tried by court martial in England, and six were found guilty of mutiny. Three of those found guilty were blessed with a royal pardon, and three were hanged from the yardarm.

But where were Fletcher Christian and the remaining mutineers? They seemed to have vanished from the face of the earth. Then, in 1808, a whaling boat spotted a campfire on Pitcairn island, far to the west of Tahiti. It turned out that the mutineers had set fire to the *Bounty* on their arrival at Pitcairn, and then split into factions. There was fighting with some Tahitian men they had treated as slaves. One of the Tahitians had killed Fletcher Christian, and all but one of the mutineers was dead.

Meanwhile Banks had received some heart-warming news. Despite the fate of the *Bounty*, Pitt's government was prepared to finance a second expedition to take breadfruit from Tahiti to the West Indies and Jamaica. Bligh would once again be the commander. And Banks was invited once again to make all the arrangements for dealing with the breadfruit. The *Bounty*'s successor, the *Providence*, was twice its size, and had fifteen armed marines ready to prevent trouble. It came with a tender, the *Assistant*, also equipped with armed marines. Preparations went smoothly. Banks chose a new gardener to replace the unfortunate David Nelson. The great cabin was redesigned as a plant nursery. The two ships sailed from Portsmouth in August 1791. Banks must have breathed a sigh of relief. This time, please God, nothing would go wrong. And nothing did.

Two years later the two ships returned to England with their mission accomplished. Over a thousand breadfruit plants had been delivered to the botanic gardens of St Vincent and Jamaica. And there was a bonus for Banks and the royal gardens. These West Indian gardens, in turn, had sent a rich collection of tropical plants for the greenhouses at Kew. It was a time for Banks to congratulate himself. The great experiment in moving plants across the world had ended in triumph.

In triumph? It soon turned out that one crucial question had been forgotten or ignored. Would the slaves in these West Indian plantations actually *eat* the breadfruit? The answer, to everyone's surprise, was no. The plants flourished, but the slaves stuck to their traditional diet of plantains or mealies. They dug in their toes and refused to eat breadfruit. At enormous cost – in money and ships and human lives – Banks's great experiment had ended as a magnificent, and tragic, failure.

As for the world to which Bligh and the *Providence* had returned – that world had changed out of all recognition. In January 1793 the tumbrils rattled through Paris and the revolutionary mob cheered as King Louis XVI was devoured by the guillotine. The queen, Marie Antoinette, shared his fate nine months later. The executions precipitated a war between Britain and France that lasted, with only a year's intermission, for the next twenty-two years. At sea, Britain soon got the upper hand. Lord Howe's fleet won a striking victory in 1794 that came to be known as the 'Glorious First of June'. On land, the revolutionary armies swept all before them. It was to be more than fifteen years before a British army won their first substantial victory; this was Wellington's defeat of the French at Vimeiro, which ended their invasion of Portugal.

Despite the war, whose tentacles soon extended their grip to British and French colonies throughout the world, Banks still dreamt of sending men to collect plants in temperate China.

It was fortunate, he realised, that the British navy was in the ascendant; the French navy would not be much of a problem. But how to persuade the Chinese authorities to allow British plant hunters to pursue their quarry in temperate China – that is, in the central and northern regions of that vast country? The Duncan brothers, Charles and Alexander, had had little success in collecting plants for two different reasons. First, they were stuck in tropical Canton with no authority to hunt for plants further north. Second, they had to rely on the captains of British merchant ships, sailing from Canton, to carry their precious cargo of small plants safely to Britain. The problem seemed insoluble while the eighty-two-year-old Qianlong emperor ruled China.

The Qianlong emperor

Then Banks heard the wonderful news. Pitt's government had decided to send an embassy to Peking, financed by the East India Company. It would be led by two persuasive Irishmen: Lord

Macartney, a former governor-general in India, and his friend and assistant, Sir George Staunton. The aim was for nothing less than a commercial and diplomatic breakthrough. Britain wanted its ships to be given access to Chinese ports, in addition to Canton, with much-reduced tariffs. At present Britain enjoyed a brisk trade with China – importing thousands of tons of tea, silk and chinaware – but the trade was all in one direction. A trade deficit with China was accumulating at an alarming speed. To arrange things would mean installing a permanent diplomatic mission at Peking. This would safeguard the interests of the ever-expanding British Empire. It would also steal a march on the French, whose Jesuit missionaries had (until their recent expulsion) been suspected of systematic intrigues against the British.

Sedan chair for a mandarin

Banks's plan, predictably, was to exploit Macartney's mission for his own good purposes. Here was a heaven-sent opportunity for importing trees and other plants from China. George Staunton was an old friend, and before he became a diplomat and administrator had practised as a doctor. He would be just the man to take charge of the arrangements for collecting plants for Kew Gardens. Banks sent him a long list of the plants he was hoping to acquire. Some, like the yulan and the peony, were already growing at Kew, after living plants were sent by Alexander Duncan. But Banks' hit list included many that were only known from Chinese and Japanese pictures, like *Magnolia kobus* and *Clerodendron trichotomum* – an exotic, summer-flowering tree with bright blue fruit and crimson lobes. Banks also suggested to Staunton that he should try to find Chinese counterparts of European forest trees like the oak and the sweet chestnut. These new introductions 'Either as Luxuries or for the Food and refreshment of the Middling Ranks' would be preferable to 'those that are merely Curiosities to the science of Botany.'[1]

No expense was spared in making Macartney's embassy splendid enough to impress the Qianlong emperor. It was a hundred strong, and included two Chinese interpreters (students from a Catholic seminary in Naples), two artists, a doctor, the eleven-year-old son of Sir George Staunton, who had been learning Chinese since he was ten, and two gardeners. Although Banks had been able to arrange for these gardeners to join the expedition, it was unfortunate that he had failed to find a professional botanist to accompany them. Another surprising omission was in the list of presents destined for the emperor. For some reason no British manufactures were included – although this was, after all, a mission to boost British exports. There was talk of bringing one of Matthew Boulton's steam engines, but Macartney decided it would be too cumbersome. (It was also hoped to bring a hot-air balloon, but no professional balloonist was prepared to join the party.) In the event the presents consisted mainly of scientific instruments: telescopes, globes and the famous Planetarium.

The travel arrangements, however, proved excellent. To ensure the party's safety from French warships and privateers they were installed on a 64-gun warship, HMS *Lion*, supported by the East India Company's *Hindostan* and a half-battalion of marines. The ships left port in September 1792, with war impending, and followed a laborious route to China via Tenerife, Rio de Janeiro, Batavia and Macao. By August 1793 they had reached the Gulf of Bohai, east of Peking. A month later Macartney and his party were kneeling to greet the emperor at his summer palace, Jehol, about 75 miles north-east of the Great Wall.

Bronze lion at the palace

The state reception in a circular tent had been carefully timed to coincide with the celebration of the emperor's eighty-second birthday. Macartney certainly rose to the occasion. He wore a sheaf of ostrich plumes in his hat, with the mantle of the Order of the Bath, and the collar, a diamond badge and a diamond star. (Sir

George could only manage the scarlet silk of an Oxford Doctor of Laws.) The emperor, dressed in a blue silk gown like his mandarins, faced the British delegation from a gilded throne four steps up on a raised platform. Macartney climbed the steps and, bending on one knee, presented the emperor with a large square box. The box was made of gold and adorned with jewels. Inside was a letter from George III formally explaining the purpose of the embassy. Both the George Stauntons (that is, father and son) then climbed the steps in turn, and the twelve-year-old George was apparently able to charm the old emperor with his fluent Chinese. Presents were then given to all the British delegation. The reception was followed by a sumptuous banquet, served with tea, and conducted in a dignified silence, according to the Chinese custom.

Next day Macartney and young George were taken in a yacht to see the imperial gardens at Jehol, the 'Garden of Ten Thousand Trees'. For Macartney this was a revelation. Here was a Chinese painter's landscape brought to life on a vast scale. As he put it: 'The shores of the lake have all the varieties of shape which the fancy of a painter can delineate, and are so indented with bays or broken with projections, that almost every stroke of the oar brought a new and unexpected object to our view'. There were islands in plenty, each with its own character, 'One marked by a pagoda, or other building, one quite destitute of ornament, some smooth and level, some steep and uneven, and others frowning with wood, or smiling with culture'.[2]

Macartney left the yacht to look at some of these buildings, and was astounded. They were furnished with 'stupendous vases of jasper and agate; with the finest porcelain and japan'. Then he saw something that filled him with dismay. He saw 'spheres, orreries, clocks and musical automatons of such exquisite workmanship, and in such profusion' that he realised that their own presents to the emperor 'must shrink from the comparison'.[3]

Within a few days Macartney's worst fears were confirmed. Far from discussing new arrangements for trade, and for a permanent British diplomatic presence in Peking, the mandarins seemed only

The governor's boat

concerned with getting rid of their guests. The penny dropped – with an unmusical clang. Belatedly Macartney and Staunton realised that the two countries had, from the first, been at cross purposes. The Chinese thought the British simply wanted to send a tribute to the emperor on his eighty-second birthday. The British were eager for a complete change (what we would now call a reset) in their relations with China. Not only would British exports reap the harvest; Britain would have a powerful ally to counter French aggression in India and the East. But smooth talk from mandarins in Canton had fooled the British. Nothing was to change. Nothing.

Before Macartney and his hundred men were hustled out of

China, taking the overland route direct to Canton, they were given the emperor's formal reply to George III's letter – the one in the golden box. The reply, contained in a large roll covered in yellow silk, was first exhibited in a gilded hall of the emperor's palace, and then brought to Macartney's quarters. To sweeten the pill, the emperor had showered presents on his visitors, including the humblest servants. But the reply was an unqualified negative. No, there would be no permanent diplomatic presence in Peking for Britain, or indeed any other country. No, there would no access to other ports than Canton. As for those presents Macartney had brought – the orreries, the telescopes and so on – they were no use at all.

This was the disappointing message which Macartney, Staunton and their advisers had at least half expected. But they were quite unprepared, it appears, for the bluntness of the emperor's language. In fact bluntness is hardly the right word. Making no pretence of the politeness due to equals, the emperor's letter to George III was downright rude.

> You, O King, from afar have yearned after the blessings of our civilization, and in your eagerness to come into touch with our . . . influence have sent an Embassy across the sea bearing a memorandum. I have already taken note of your respectful spirit of submission, have treated your mission with extreme favour and loaded it with gifts, besides issuing a mandate to you, O King, and honouring you at the bestowal of valuable presents. Thus has my indulgence been manifested.[4]

But he gave a curt dismissal to the ambassador's petition to open up trade with China. It was 'inconsistent with our dynastic usage'. He also turned down flat the ambassador's request for 'barbarians' to be given 'full liberty to disseminate their religion'. The request was 'utterly unreasonable'. He told George III he did not forget 'the lonely remoteness of your island, cut off from the world by intervening wastes of sea'. But he had ordered the departure of the mission.

The emperor ended with a final slap in the face for George III.

Peradventure you yourself are ignorant of our dynastic regulations and had no intention of transgressing them when you expressed these wild ideas and hopes ... Tremblingly obey and show no negligence.[5]

Macartney knew better than to reply, and he made sure that the text of the insulting letter from the emperor was kept hidden from the British public. A year later, sailing in a large convoy to protect them from the French, Macartney's embassy returned somewhat sheepishly to Portsmouth.

Banks now took charge of the plants and seeds and dried specimens collected in China and destined for Kew. By contrast with Macartney, Banks had at least something to show for his efforts. It was true that the Chinese had made sure that their British guests had very little opportunity for collecting plants. Staunton confessed to Banks that 'my voyage in point of Curiosity' (that is, of collecting rare plants) 'has been almost totally frustrated'.[6] Even when the two gardeners could snatch a chance to collect specimens they had little support from their hosts. As one of them wrote in his journal: 'I was surrounded by a crowd of People who ... began hooting and Running after me & as the soldier who protected me rather encouraged them they began to pelt me till I Returned to the boats.'[7] Worst of all, Banks had failed to provide the expedition with a professional botanist. The result was that the new specimens for Banks's herbarium were hopelessly muddled. Often there was no description of the live plant attached to the dried specimen. This made it impossible for Banks's professional botanist in London, Dr Dryander, to identify and classify the new plant, if new it was.

When Staunton came to write up the botanical discoveries in his sumptuous two volumes, *An Authentic Account of An Embassy From The King of Great Britain To The Emperor of China* (1797), he claimed that members of the mission had collected about four hundred plants as seeds or as dried specimens for the herbarium. But few of them proved new to science or worth planting in the royal gardens. Nearly twenty years later, William Townsend Aiton, the head gardener at Kew, listed the plants collected by the mission, introduced by Sir George Staunton and at that time growing at Kew. Alas, there were only four. None were trees, and the only shrub of significance was a handsome evergreen rose, *Rosa bracteata.* It had large white flowers and a delicate fruity perfume. Known as the Macartney rose, it was a striking addition to Kew's arboretum. Unfortunately it was short-lived – like Macartney's hopes of a deal with the Chinese emperor.

* * *

These recurrent setbacks would have crushed a man less resilient than Joseph Banks. But Banks proved irrepressible. In 1804 he decided to send out to China a young Scottish gardener he had spotted at Kew: his name was William Kerr.

If northern and central China were still firmly barred to plant hunters, the door had stayed open at Canton and Macao. And Kerr could succeed where the Duncan brothers had failed. He was young and knowledgeable and ambitious. Above all he had no other duties than to comb tropical markets and gardens in a hunt for temperate plants.

In his first year at Canton, Kerr sent back a series of hardy living plants: *Cunninghamia lanceolata,* a strange, spiky tree related to the monkey puzzle, and *Juniperus chinensis*, a much more decorative form of juniper than those common in Europe. In his second year he sent a yellow-flowering shrub that is now one of the best-loved symbols of spring in European gardens: *Kerria japonica* (honouring his name after his early death). By 1811 he had racked up a huge score of novelties – over two hundred new plants, according to one account. They included a variety of the elegant white *Camellia sasanqua* that had long been one of the most popular of all camellias in China and Japan. It had been spotted by Macartney's mission and illustrated in Staunton's *Authentic Account*. It remained for Kerr to claim the honour of introducing it to the wider world.

And, what must have given particular pleasure to Banks, Kerr sent home a new rambling rose named *Rosa banksiae* after Banks' long-suffering wife, Dorothea. In this original form the rose was fragrant and double white. Most plants today are double yellow and rather less fragrant. But you can choose any form of 'Lady Banks's Rose' and you will find it a stunner.

By 1814 poor William Kerr was dead – a victim, it would seem, of addiction to opium in Ceylon, where he had been appointed to look after the botanic garden. Banks himself was now sixty-nine, and for years he had been a martyr to gout. He was still president of the Royal Society but he conducted business from a wheelchair. Most of his friends – and most of the people he had inspired – had died many years before. The king, once at the centre of his life, was now out of reach and effectively dead. His madness had finally taken control in 1810, leaving the country at the mercy of the prince regent and his whims.

Banks himself had many astonishing achievements to celebrate. For forty years he had been the dynamo that made the plant world hum. Despite the endless setbacks and frustrations, he had helped elevate botany from a hobby to a serious science. He was himself a distinguished amateur who employed distinguished professionals. By default his library at 32 Soho Square had served as an international centre for botanical research. It was here that the herbarium sheets were critically examined by botanists like Dr Solander and Dr Dryander, and the fate of a new plant decided for at least the next generation. A new genus – or *only* a new species ? Not even that – merely a new variety? An old plant with a new name? An old name for a new plant? The answers were more likely to come from Soho Square than from any British university – or even from the royal gardens at Kew.

It was Kew's arboretum that served as a showcase for Banks's work. It made a pair with Soho Square by providing a place for a living collection of trees and shrubs. Collaboration was no problem because Banks had appointed himself unofficial director of the royal gardens; he gave instructions to both the Aitons, father and son, who were head gardeners in turn. When the younger Aiton, with Banks' help, brought out the second edition of *Hortus Kewensis* in 1812, it included over six thousand species and varieties of plants cultivated at Kew. Of these less than two thousand were trees or shrubs hardy enough to grow in the open in west London. But it was thanks to Joseph Banks that Kew's arboretum, where the trees and larger shrubs had put down their roots, was now one of the most complete in the world.

Banks died in 1820, a few months before his friend, the king. Perhaps both men had lived too long. New ideas, including the itch for democracy, were slowly eroding the power of the old aristocracy. Arboretums, once the symbol of old wealth, were becoming the fashion for a pushy new middle class, and even for the public at large.

CHAPTER 8

Dr Wade Leads the Way

One day in the spring of 1796 a large public notice was posted up in the streets of Dublin, printed across four columns.

Headed 'The Dublin Society', the notice proudly announced that the society had taken 16 acres of 'Ground at GLASNEVIN, for the purpose of forming a BOTANIC GARDEN ... [and] has made some progress in laying them out ...'

This was followed by a detailed prospectus for the proposed layout, beginning with 'HORTUS LINNAEENSIS [in] three parts HERBACEOUS [Herbarium] The SHRUBS [Fruticetum] and The Trees [ARBORETUM].'[1]

What did the Dublin Society mean by this exotic new word 'arboretum'? In fact the original Latin word, used since the time of the Romans, meant nothing more than a 'grove of trees'. But by 1796 it had begun to acquire a romantic new meaning. It now meant, as defined by a modern botanist, a 'collection of trees, duly documented, and arranged either for education or for ornament'. And it was in Dublin, somewhat surprisingly, that the term first came to be given publicity. (The arboretum at Kew was still part of a private garden belonging to the royal family.) In fact this new arboretum at Glasnevin, in the suburbs north-west of Dublin, was to be a jewel in the Irish parliament's crown: the first *public* arboretum in Europe to be laid out for the promotion of scientific knowledge. It was encouraged and financed by the Irish parliament. And the scale was princely: the new 27-acre botanic garden, of which the arboretum was part, would be much larger than any of its predecessors, like those at Pisa, Padua, Leiden or Oxford.

Other parts of the proposed botanic garden were designed to promote modern agriculture. There was to be a cattle garden ('for the instruction of common farmers'), a hay garden, an esculent garden ('for every Plant that furnishes Food to Man') a bog garden – and of course a nursery for propagating plants.

The notice ended with an appeal to patriotic Irishmen to send 'such Plants and Seeds, as their several Collections, or their Neighbourhood can furnish'[2] to a certain Dr Wade, who was undertaking to arrange the arboretum, and would serve as the professor and lecturer in botany. Walter Wade was a well-known doctor and botanist in Dublin, who had successfully petitioned the Irish parliament, back in 1790, for the creation of a public botanic garden. But the man behind the project was a masterful Irish politician, John Foster, Speaker – and chief manipulator – of the Irish House of Commons.

Foster did not belong to one of the great Anglo-Irish families, like the FitzGeralds or Butlers or Hills, who controlled more than half the seats in the Irish Commons. His own family had risen from humble beginnings. His grandfather was a mere country attorney who had scraped together enough money from his profession to buy 500 acres of impoverished moorland near Slane, County Meath. But for ten years Foster had led the 'junto' of intransigent Protestant nationalists who were defending the Protestant ascendancy and blocking Catholic emancipation. In fact Foster was the man who had humiliated Lord Fitzwilliam and sent him packing. Fitzwilliam was the liberal-minded viceroy appointed by Pitt to lead the British executive in Ireland. Blocked

John Foster

by Foster in 1795, he was forced to resign, leaving Ireland to its fate; his departure was followed by the disastrous rebellion of 1798 and the Union of 1800.

It was fortunate that Foster loved planting trees as much as he loved manipulating people, and here, at least, he had few opponents. His personal collection of trees – a private arboretum created at the family's estate at Collon – was the most complete in Ireland. He had a 'rage for planting', as he told John Ellis, a well-known English botanist. His ambition was 'to Plant every tree & shrub in plenty that will stand our climate'.[3] In due course he had amassed a collection of 1,700 different trees and shrubs that were hardy enough to stand the Irish winter.

To collect trees and shrubs on this scale was quite an achievement. Back in the 1780s plant nurseries in Ireland had little to offer, as few Irish country gentlemen collected trees at this date. Foster relied on the plant nurseries in London, like the Hammersmith nursery of Lee and Kennedy, and the firm of James Gordon in the Mile End Road. They could supply collectors with the latest introductions. For basic information he could rely on Philip Miller's famous *Dictionary of Gardening* (which had appeared in an Irish edition in 1768). He had also the benefit of *Hortus Kewensis*, William Aiton's recent catalogue of the 3,000-odd trees and shrubs in the royal collection at Kew. And he was kept in touch with the latest twists in botany by associates (and admirers) of the celebrated Linnaeus, like the English botanist John Ellis.

Yet, despite all these advantages, Foster was only an amateur – and tree-collecting was only one of his numerous interests. In fact he had his finger in a dozen pies. He was vice-president of the Dublin Society, founded earlier in the eighteenth century, mainly to promote the improvements in agriculture on which the Irish economy depended. The society also awarded premiums to landowners who afforested their estates. Irish-grown trees, especially oaks, were vital for building the ships of the British navy which defended Ireland – a topical issue in 1796.

For it was the defence of Ireland, and Irish politics, that dominated Foster's life in those years of crisis leading to the 1798 rebellion and the Union. Already, in 1796, Ireland had found itself in the front line of the war with revolutionary France. The French Directory had sent an armada of forty-five French ships with fifteen thousand French soldiers and instructed them to land in Bantry Bay, in south-west Ireland, in January of that year. Their commander was Bonaparte's main rival, General Lazare Hoche. There was no Irish or British force strong enough to stop Hoche's rapid advance on Dublin – once his armada had landed. But the hurricane blew, scattering Hoche's fleet like confetti. Not a ship landed its soldiers. Ireland, and the Protestant ascendancy championed by Foster, had escaped by the skin of their teeth.

Four months later that large public notice to celebrate the new botanic garden at Glasnevin was posted up in the streets of Dublin. And, as we saw, it reported that a certain Dr Wade had agreed to be responsible for choosing and arranging the trees in the arboretum and other plants in the garden. In fact Walter Wade was a protégé of Foster's who had been angling for this job since the beginning of the decade.

To his rivals, Wade was a somewhat ludicrous figure. In an anonymous article he was described as an old-fashioned prig, and a coxcomb, who delivered his lectures in a sky-blue waistcoat. 'Tricked out in apparel as tawdry as the pie-bald vestiture of the high priest of Flora herself, and thoroughly imbued with that dancing-master style...'[4] Of course Foster rallied to his protégé's defence. Wade, he said, was 'a man of great worth, zeal and knowledge in that part of the science which is strictly termed Botany... I believe no man could excel him in... the clearness and accuracy with which he explained the simplicity and beauty thereof...'[5]

What was clear was that, even if Wade played the fool in his botanical lectures, Glasnevin owed Wade a great deal for his choice and arrangement of trees and other plants. The 27-acre site was picturesque but demanding. Half a century earlier it had adjoined the romantic retreat of Dr Patrick Delany, scholar of Trinity and bosom friend of Jonathan Swift. Delville was then the name of the house, and today Delville has vanished under bricks and mortar. But Glasnevin still has the River Tolka and its mill stream at its feet, and what Swift mocked as a ridiculously small estate:

And hills and vales, and woods and fields
And hay, and grass, and corn it yields...[6]

It was here in Ireland that Dr Delany pioneered the new informal style of landscape gardening, based on the writings of Joseph Addison and the practical work in England of William Kent. Here, too, that Delany's second wife, Mary, sketched the view of temples and grottoes, and perhaps learnt how to create her astonishing plant mosaics, cut from coloured tissue paper: the works of art that would later make her famous.

Did Dr Wade pay due respect to all these ghosts from the past? Judged by the first published plan of his layout for the new garden, the answer is probably not, although the Dublin Society may well have been attracted to acquire Glasnevin because of its romantic associations with Swift and the Delanys and their pioneering garden. But Wade, too, was a pioneer. As one would expect, the arboretum provided the most striking feature of Wade's layout. Together with the fruticetum (the place for shrubs) it occupied a large slice of land on the western side of the site, with a gravel path running up the centre. Herbaceous plants, a 'rock mound', a Hibernian garden, and specialised areas for cattle, sheep and goats, dominated the centre. And, away to the east, where the ground sloped sharply down to the Tolka, there was still more land reserved for meadows and rough pasture.

This layout might seem uncontroversial enough. But in one respect Wade had invited sharp criticism – indeed he had stepped on a hornet's nest.

According to which scientific system were the trees and shrubs to be arranged? This was the question which would bedevil many arboretums in the future, and there were no easy answers. But, broadly speaking, there were two alternatives. The designers of an arboretums could stick faithfully to the system of the great Linnaeus, that is, following his rigid principles of classifying trees and other plants. Or its designers could show their independence by adopting one of the so-called 'natural' styles of classification now favoured by many continental botanists.

Wade, it turned out, had opted for Linnaeus. His enemies labelled this absurdly old-fashioned. The fact was that in 1753 Linnaeus had inaugurated a system of dazzling simplicity for naming trees and other plants. Known as the 'binomial' system, it abolished long-winded descriptions by reducing them to a mere pair of names: the genus and the species. Within a few decades the binomial system had conquered the scientific world. Linnaeus had then followed this up with an equally dazzling attempt to define *groups* of genera. He named the groups 'classes', subdivided into 'orders,' and called it a 'sexual' system. At first this was welcomed with open arms. There were only twenty-three classes, and you needed no special skill to name the class where a given plant belonged. All you needed was a pair of eyes sharp enough to count how many stamens one of its flowers contained, (these stamens were 'male' reproductive parts) or, failing that, to count its pistils ('female' parts). But had Linnaeus been *too* ingenious – that is, oversimplified the grouping of plants? By 1796 there were serious doubts, and a system of grouping genera by 'families' was coming into vogue.

The squabble might have seemed unimportant to most people. But it had dramatic effects in the design of an arboretum. Wade's layout, following Linnaeus, was highly artificial. It meant lumping together trees and shrubs which had nothing in common except that they shared the same number of stamens or pistils. The incongruity became obvious as soon as the first trees were selected for the new arboretum. If Wade had followed the new system proposed by the French botanist Antoine Laurent de Jussieu, the classification would have seemed more natural and more reasonable. Jussieu had published his radical work *Genera Plantarum* seven years before Wade began his layout for Glasnevin. It was

1789, Year One of the French Revolution. Fortunately for Jussieu, he was on the side of the revolutionaries, and was appointed to take control of the prestigious Jardin du Roi in Paris, duly renamed and reinvented as the Jardin des Plantes. Jussieu named a hundred families for trees and shrubs and herbaceous plants. He used carefully graded criteria when he chose a botanical family for a particular genus – 'weighing not counting', as he put it. His proposals were simple but had a touch of genius. Many of his families are still in use today.

Perhaps Wade believed that these radical ideas would soon be forgotten and die with the French Revolution. He certainly had many other pressing concerns. His patron John Foster was famous for his skill in manipulating the Irish House of Commons, but he had only succeeded in squeezing the minimum subsidy for the new botanic garden and its arboretum. Wade himself generously gave the Dublin Society his fee for a course of lectures. But a head gardener had to be lured from England – John Underwood, recommended by William Curtis, the editor of one of the first gardening magazines. John White, like Dr Wade a protégé of Foster's, was appointed under-gardener. Labourers had to be hired. Cartloads of gravel were needed for the paths, and cartloads of peaty soil for the lime-hating plants. To build the range of architect-designed greenhouses cost nearly £3,000. No wonder there was little cash for buying exotic trees and shrubs – although Dr Wade had to spend £370 buying plants from the celebrated London firm of Lee and Kennedy.

Fortunately the Irish nursery trade responded generously to the appeal for plants. In the last two decades the Irish nursery trade had begun to find its feet. Plants were sent free of charge from Charles and Luke Toole's nursery at Cullenswood; in 1797 they said they had 'a great number of curious plants'[7] which they believed were not yet at Glasnevin. Other Irish nurseries donated plants or seeds. They were thanked for their patriotism.

John Foster, however, was not easily satisfied. Never one to doubt his own powers of persuasion, he sent a personal appeal to the new viceroy, Lord Camden (the one who had succeeded the unfortunate Lord Fitzwilliam). Foster hoped his request would not appear presumptuous, but would Camden kindly arrange for rare trees and shrubs to be sent from the royal gardens at Windsor. If 'His Majesty would be pleased to order us such plants from his garden at Kew, as can be spared from thence, we should not only be saved a large expence, but be supplied with many, which money could not procure . . .'[8] But John Foster had met his match in Joseph Banks. As the king's unofficial director at Kew, Banks had issued instructions to the head gardener, William Aiton, not in *any* circumstances to give away surplus plants. And it would appear that no exception was made in this case – at any rate no record exists of a donation of plants from Kew to Glasnevin.

Fortunately Foster had a treasure trove of surplus specimens on his own estate at Collon. Tulip trees, red maples, yellow-flowering chestnuts, pagoda trees, pin oaks, arbutus – the collection was the most complete in Ireland. He could also rely on the generosity of a growing number of professional men addicted to collecting exotic trees and shrubs. David La Touche, heir of the banking family, had a fine estate at Marlay in County Dublin. He offered to donate several very rare and valuable plants. There were already several grandees in Ireland well known for their passion for trees. One of the most enterprising was the 2nd Earl of Clanbrassil. His father had discovered a miniature version of the Norway spruce on his estate at Tollymore, County Down. The little freak had been given the name *Abies excelsa* 'Clanbrassiliana' (now *Picea abies* 'Clanbrassiliana') and was perfect for small gardens. Another

Irish landowner whose trees had made him famous was the Earl of Enniskillen. One of his tenants had discovered a strange, upright form of the common yew, and a specimen was now growing at Florence Court, Lord Enniskillen's house in County Fermanagh. Soon that mother tree (which, miraculously, still exists today) was used to make cuttings for the nursery trade, and became the ultimate mother of millions of incongruously upright Irish yews from California to Australia.

Of course it was slow work, making an arboretum from scratch. But by 1800 the Dublin Society was welcoming the public to the new garden. Following the rules prescribed by Linnaeus, each of his twenty-three botanical classes was represented in a separate plot in the linear arboretum. Many were from familiar genera: elms, oaks, willows, poplars and so on. But Wade had the courage to take one step away from the path prescribed by his hero, Linnaeus. Specimens were supposed to represent a basic species, not a variety of a species. Wade's arboretum included trees and shrubs with intriguing variations: silver and gold blotches on the leaves of forest trees like oaks, cut-leaved and copper-leaved varieties of beech, and all kinds of oddities among the fruit trees like plums and apricots. No doubt some of his fellow botanists were shocked. But Wade knew when it was time to play to the gallery.

For the next two decades that oddly assorted trio – Walter Wade, John Underwood and John White – continued to expand the collection at Glasnevin, under the wary eyes of John Foster. Of course there were tensions. Wade complained that his lectures – a course of sixteen, including two in praise of Linnaeus – were not taken seriously enough. Underwood's detractors claimed he was rather too keen on the bottle. Money was always short. Relations with the committee of the Dublin Society were cool. Part of the trouble was that John Foster no longer had the clout provided by his role as Speaker of the Irish House of Commons. The Irish parliament, the hub of the Protestant ascendancy, had ceased to exist – swept away, despite all Foster's efforts, by the Act of Union of 1800. Foster himself was a mere Irish MP in Westminster, although Pitt gave him a role as Irish Chancellor of the Exchequer for two years, and he continued as a commissioner. (Eventually he was fobbed off with an English peerage – as Lord Oriel.)

Meanwhile expansion of the collection meant exciting improvements to the layout. A map of the botanical garden printed in 1818 shows that the arboretum, formerly squeezed into a narrow strip along the western frontier, had now been combined with the fruticetum (for shrubby specimens) and extended to the middle of the garden. A new Linnean garden had been created to replace the original Cattle Garden, now moved to the large meadow on the extreme west of the site. Most dramatic, a long, snake-like pond, fed from the River Tolka, now uncoiled itself along the eastern corners of the garden. It was here that the most ornamental trees would be installed, dominated by a triple-trunked black pine planted in 1798, and a brutish Cephalonian silver fir. But most theatrical of all the rarities was the Norfolk Island pine (*Araucaria heterophylla*).

Originally 15 inches tall, it had been bought in 1798 from the London nursery of Lee and Kennedy for the sum of seven shillings and sixpence. By 1819 it was 16 feet tall and the pride and joy of Glasnevin. But there was a problem. No one knew how well it could survive out in the open. This strange, triangular species of monkey puzzle had been discovered by Captain Cook in 1774 on his second voyage around the world. It was endemic, meaning only found on Norfolk Island, marooned in the Pacific 1,000 miles north-east of Sydney, Australia. Collectors had snapped up the first plants brought to Europe – preceding the species of monkey puzzle introduced by Archibald Menzies from the Andes. That Chilean species, *Araucaria araucana*, certainly proved hardy. But its Australian cousin seemed happier in the subtropics. At any rate, to play safe, the Glasnevin tree had been installed in a conservatory next to the professor's house. And now the tree was the centre of a furious row that threatened to tear the garden apart and lead to the sacking of the unfortunate John Underwood.

Predictably the tree had already outgrown the conservatory by 1814. Arrangements for a replacement were slow in coming. As usual, when money was needed, the Dublin Society dragged its feet. Nobody was blameless, although no one knew how urgent was the problem. By the autumn of 1819 the old conservatory had at last been removed, and builders started on its replacement which was to be 40 feet high. Then, on the night of 24 November, ten days before the new building was ready, the thermometer at Glasnevin fell to 20 °F (-7 °C). It didn't seem much, but in the next few months it was clear that the tree had been mortally injured, and there was hell to pay.

Wade tried to see the humorous side of the disaster: 'I am sorry to inform your Lordship', he told Foster, 'that Lady Norfolk [meaning the tree] is Pine-ing away very fast and all our hopes of recovery at an end – even Doctor Underwood has given her over.'[9] Foster and the Committee of the Dublin Society were not amused. It was decided to sack Underwood for failing to protect the tree. Underwood responded with a passionate plea for forgiveness. But he claimed he was innocent of the charges. He had not been guilty of incompetence or neglect. The exceptional frost could not have been predicted. He was ill that night and could not leave his bed. No one had told him that the replacement was supposed to be finished by September. Finally, if he was sacked, 'his helpless children would be instantly involved in all the miseries of want and starvation'.[10]

Fortunately the Committee relented. It was agreed that Underwood should only be 'severely censured'. But the affair left a permanent wound. It seems he was unjustly blamed: the Norfolk Island pine is not hardy in Ireland. From this period Underwood's work began to deteriorate – and no doubt whiskey played a part in his sad decline.

Meanwhile, in the world outside Ireland new generations of landowners were beginning to take pride in their collections of trees. Some would have taken their cue from the royal gardens at Kew, others from Glasnevin. Many were responding to the new bonanza of plants on offer from plant nurseries, now that the long war with France had finally ended on the field of Waterloo.

CHAPTER 9

The Stonemason's Son

David Douglas landed in New York on 6 August 1823, glad to leave the packet, *Ann Maria*, after a frustrating two-month voyage from Liverpool. He was well provided with letters of introduction to the great and the good of eastern America. But who would have guessed that this shy young gardener from Scotland would prove himself, within a decade, to be one of the most celebrated plant explorers of the century?

He was twenty-three years old, the second of an underpaid, working-class family of six children; his father was one of the eight stonemasons employed at Scone, the palatial estate of the Earl of Mansfield. He had left school when he was twelve, and served a seven-year apprenticeship as a gardener at Scone, then picked up a job as under-gardener at Valleyfield near Edinburgh, before moving to the newly created botanic garden in Glasgow. It was here that he had the good fortune to meet one of Britain's most enterprising and original scientists, William Hooker, Professor of Botany at Glasgow University. Hooker spotted Douglas's unusual gifts: his fascination with nature in all its forms coupled with relentless energy. Soon Hooker became the friend and mentor of the young man. Douglas was encouraged to attend his crowd-pulling lectures at the university. At weekends the two men would comb the countryside for unusual plants, tramping over the moors and hunkering down in some abandoned croft when caught by a sudden storm.

Before he was twenty-three Hooker got him a job as foreman of the botanic garden, and then offered him a far more alluring prospect. This was to scour the east coast of America for rare trees and other plants, working as a collector for the newly founded Horticultural Society of London, and its masterful secretary, Joseph Sabine.

The Horticultural Society had begun modestly enough in 1804. At first it seemed more like a gentleman's club. It was the brainchild of John Wedgwood, son of the famous potter, and held its inaugural meeting in Hatchard's bookshop in Piccadilly. The founder members included two 'Right Honourables': the connoisseur and statesman, Charles Greville, father of the diarist, and Sir Joseph Banks, the ageing unofficial director of George III's garden at Kew. Most of the newly elected Fellows were amateur gardeners, anxious to tell their friends of their important discoveries at home in their potting sheds. (Sir Joseph Banks wrote a learned article about growing potatoes.) These horticultural discoveries were duly published in the *Transactions of the Horticultural Society* launched in 1807. But business was not the strong point of the Fellows. By 1810 the accounts were in hopeless confusion, and the society seemed close to collapse. It was rescued about 1815 by a young lawyer, Joseph Sabine, who had agreed to serve as the unpaid secretary, and it was Sabine who ruled the society for the next fifteen years in a style that his friends called masterful and his enemies called 'despotic'.

Sabine had many advantages compared to his bumbling predecessors. He was young and energetic and had a house conveniently close to Hanover Square in central London. Somehow he had managed to secure a well-paid sinecure as inspector-general of taxes; this left his hands free to transform the society. His aims, though ambitious, seemed practicable. The royal gardens at Kew were now in a state of slow decline. The last plant collectors sent out to China from Kew had been withdrawn. Sir Joseph Banks was too old and gout-ridden to play much part in its affairs. The king himself had sunk into the final, most tragic phase of his madness. But Kew, influential as it had been, had never been a public garden. By contrast it was Sabine's ambition to make the Horticultural Society serve a large swathe of the public. And high time, too, now that the war with France was finally over, the nursery trade was booming, and the import of exotic plants never easier.

The first step was a membership drive to exploit the new taste for gardening – and boost the society's income. Sabine realised that they needed to woo the celebrities of the day, including royal grandees like the Duke of York. (The duke took the bait and agreed to accept honorary membership.) Distinguished foreigners were shamelessly pursued. By 1823 the society had enrolled as foreign correspondents many crowned heads in Europe, including the kings of Denmark, Bavaria and the Netherlands, as well as the Tsar of Russia. Membership soared: from 1,500 to over 2,000 in a couple of years. No wonder the Fellows gave Sabine a gold medal for his pains, and agreed to splash out thousands of pounds on a new garden designed to demonstrate both the science and the art of gardening.

In turn the society rented land in the suburbs of west London: first a 1.5-acre plot at Hammersmith and then a 30-acre site at Chiswick whose landlord (and neighbour at Chiswick) was the benevolent bachelor duke, the 4th Duke of Devonshire. Sabine's main aim was to create a new arboretum at Chiswick stocked with all the trees and other plants reckoned hardy in Britain. This arboretum would be much bigger, as well as more up to date, than the one Banks had supervised at Kew. British nurserymen, like the firms of Loddiges and Lee and Kennedy, would provide many of the young trees and plants. Donations of plants from enthusiastic gardeners at home and abroad would be gratefully received. But the society needed to recruit and send out its own trusty band of collectors. And this is where Sabine might fairly have been accused of hubris. At any rate he met his first serious setback.

In 1822, a year before young David Douglas landed in New York, Sabine had dispatched three separate collectors to search out new plants in the wilds. All three expeditions had the backing of both the East India Company and the British government. John Potts, a young gardener employed by the society, was sent to Bengal and then to China. He brought back a collection of tropical plants, but he was crippled with disease and only survived his return to Britain by a few weeks. Another young gardener, John Forbes, was sent out to accompany a naval expedition to East Africa, and made an interesting collection of tropical plants on the lower Zambezi. He died at Senna less than a year later from the effects of the climate. The third expedition, led by George Don, had better luck. He found some new plants – and at least he survived.

But the lesson for Sabine and the society seemed clear. The tropics were too hazardous for plant explorers. And after all, no tropical plants could survive the British winter out of doors. Their role for the society was strictly limited. Doomed to spend their life in a greenhouse, they would be of no use for the society's new arboretum. It was in *temperate* zones that the future lay. Hence the dispatch in 1823 of young David Douglas to seek his own – and the society's – fortune in eastern America.

Sabine and Hooker had given Douglas only a rough idea of what was expected of him. Initially he was to concentrate on the most civilised parts of the east, including New York State and Pennsylvania, for which he was well provided with letters of introduction. His brief was to report on American horticulture and its exponents. This would mean visiting local markets where he could collect living trees – especially fruit trees – and send them back carefully packed for the two-month voyage to London. He was also to collect seeds of all kinds: herbaceous as well as those from shrubs and trees. Both commodities could be sold to raise funds for the society. Later he was to explore the Iroquois country beside Detroit and Lake Erie where botanists had already identified a treasure trove of native American oaks. Many of these venerable oaks would be new to Europe – or at any rate only known from a few young specimens in European botanic gardens. By sending back acorns from the trees, Douglas would help to put these exotic giants on the map.

From his first day in America Douglas was struck by the opulence of the landscape.

'This morning can never be effaced', he wrote in his journal that day, 6 August, 'it had rained a little during the night, which cooled the atmosphere and added a hue to Nature's work, which was truly grand – the fine orchards of Long Island on the one side, and the variety of soil and vegetation of Staten on the other. I once more thought myself happy.'[1]

For the next four weeks, armed with flattering introductions from Sabine, he was busy collecting seeds and cuttings in the gardens of the rich and powerful. Everywhere he was hospitably received: the young Scottish gardener, son of a stonemason, welcomed by the merchant aristocracy of New York. Their hospitality was all the more striking because it was only eight years since the recent war with Britain, which had led to the burning of the White House in 1814, and ended a year later with the Battle of New Orleans. (Fortunately for Douglas, the Americans had won.) In late August he took the coach and paddle steamer down to

Philadelphia. He found the peaches and apples in the market there much superior to those of New York. He was taken to see a rich merchant called Landreth who had 'a great many fine plants', including three species of American magnolia (*M. cordata, M. fraseri* and *M. macrophylla*) and a large plant of *Maclura pomifera* (the bizarre Osange orange) 'about twenty feet high, very rustic, leaves large, ovate, at the stalk of which is a large thorn'. He was offered two stout plants propagated by cuttings taken from this tree – plants which 'I feel glad to have the pleasure of carrying to England'.[2]

Even more bizarre than this American freak was the English-style estate of Joseph Bonaparte which Douglas passed on the way back to New York. Joseph was Napoleon's elder brother and former king of Italy and king of Spain in turn. In 1814, when Napoleon was packed off to Elba, Joseph had escaped to America in disguise, carrying the Spanish crown jewels. Their subsequent sale enabled him to create a magnificent estate at Bordenstown – 'a most splendid mansion... pleasure-grounds in the English style; there are many fine views.'[3] Joseph entertained his guests as lavishly as if he was still a reigning monarch. But, for once, young Douglas was not hospitably received, nor invited to inspect Joseph's collection of trees.

Back in New York at any rate he was paid a rare honour: an invitation to a committee meeting of the New York Horticultural Society. This had been called specifically to give him advice and assistance. Douglas found their welcome somewhat overwhelming. The president, a wealthy merchant called Hoffman, 'uses me with all possible attention imaginable; he invited me to stay at his house all night, which I did.'[4]

By early September he was ready to set off for Iroquois country. He caught the paddle steamer *James Kent*, heading north up the River Hudson, bound for Albany. The scenery along the

Hudson proved captivating. Apart from the picturesque villas, 'perpendicular rocks covered with woods gave it an appearance seldom to be met with'.[5] In Albany he went straight to the state's governor, De Witt Clinton, and Clinton fell for him immediately. Clinton was keen for Douglas to explore the oak forests beside Lake Erie. In fact Lake Erie was very close to Clinton's heart. He was a naturalist of some distinction. He was also one of the leaders of the campaign to open up eastern America using canals and paddle steamers. In 1817 he had defied sceptics by raising $7 million of the state's money to build a canal linking the Hudson River with Lake Erie. (This new canal would in turn link Albany with Buffalo, and was to be a great commercial success as soon as it opened in 1825.) Loaded with new letters of introduction from Clinton, Douglas headed off by stagecoach and paddle steamer, finally reaching Amherstburg on Lake Erie in mid-September.

'This is what I might term my first day in America',[6] he confided to his journal on 16 September. What he meant was that he had left civilisation behind and reached the wilds at last. At heart he was still the young boy who had tramped the Scottish moors with Hooker and hunkered down in some abandoned croft. He now felt reborn.

He was dazzled by the size of many of the trees: several species of oaks, 'some of immense magnitude', two kinds of walnut, a hickory and an American ash. Fortunately for Douglas he had been given an introduction by Joseph Sabine to a man called Briscoe, a friend of Sabine's brother who had met him during the recent war; the man took Douglas to see trees in the forests on the Canadian side of Lake Erie. Despite torrential rain, all went well when the two men explored the lakeside. But later Douglas was left alone and made the mistake of hiring as a guide a runaway slave from Virginia. No sooner had Douglas climbed an oak tree to collect acorns and dried specimens than the former slave ran off with Douglas's coat which he had left below. Douglas 'descended almost headlong',[7] as he put it, but the man escaped into a wood. Douglas was shocked by this experience. Apart from losing the coat and its contents – his botanical notes, 19 dollars in paper and a small vasculum for collecting plants – he was forced to admit that he had fallen into a beginner's trap.

The weather continued wet as winter approached. To add to his troubles he now learnt that Briscoe was being sent off to Kingston by the first steamboat. So he decided to abandon his original plan to head north to Detroit and then go to Canada. He had already made a good haul of acorns and other seeds. He would return with Briscoe by the way he had come. And on the way to Albany they would hire a canoe and visit Niagara Falls.

In the event Douglas, despite his passion for the natural world, found the Falls surprisingly unimpressive. It's true that he mentioned their 'grandeur' – but only in passing. Perhaps he was still unnerved by the loss of his coat and the blow to his self-esteem. Or perhaps he had no eyes for waterfalls when surrounded by so many wonderful species of trees. 'Out of the cliffs of the rock', he wrote in his journal on 30 September, 'grow Red Cedar [*Carya amara*, a species of hickory] and *Quercus*'[8] (one of the innumerable species of oaks). Next day they took a canoe 4 miles down from the Falls. 'Opposite what is called the Whirlpool grew three species of *Quercus* on barren rocks, with narrow serrated leaves, acorns small and olive-shaped; they are certainly different from any in my possession'.[9] Douglas duly added these to his large collection of dried specimens destined for the Horticultural Society's herbarium.

He was back in Albany in early October and what he found there finally restored his good humour. The town was 'all in an uproar – firing of guns, music etc'. It was all to celebrate the opening of the western branch of the new canal. Governor

Clinton was in his element, and welcomed Douglas on his return. He recommended a day's ramble close to the city. That afternoon Douglas added an unidentified new oak to his list of specimens – 'a stately tree almost everywhere, foliage large and entire, fruit small and yellow. The trees were covered with pigeons pecking the fruit.'[10] Clinton also recommended that he should pay a call on Stephen van Rensselaer, a tycoon of Dutch origin and supposed to be the richest man in America. He invited Douglas to breakfast but the visit surprised him – and perhaps disappointed him. He was told that this flower garden, tastefully directed by the tycoon's daughters, was a novelty in America 'as little attention is paid to anything but what brings in money or luxury for the table.' And most of the best plants in the garden had been imported from Europe: roses from France, herbaceous plants from Germany, annuals from London.

Back in New York, Douglas continued the search for seeds and specimens that Sabine had commissioned him to collect. He attended a second meeting of the New York Horticultural Society, and was given a sheaf of new contacts. Soon his tally of oak specimens totalled sixteen, including three recent acquisitions (*Quercus muehlenbergii*, *Q. stellata*, and *Q. cuneata*). But he was still determined to return to Philadelphia to try once again to pay his respects to the garden of America's earliest botanist, John Bartram. He finally made the pilgrimage there in early November. Bartram had supplied Bishop Compton with a treasure trove of American trees (including the famous Scarlet oak) more than a century earlier. So Bartram was one of Douglas's heroes. He had died in 1777, and his son William had preserved the collection of trees as best he could for the next fifty years; fortunately the Bartram family's farm was only a few miles from Philadelphia. Sad to say, William Bartram had died a few months before Douglas's visit and the garden was now in a 'deplorable state'.

Still William's niece showed Douglas an impressively large cypress in front of the house. It was 90 feet high and 23 feet in girth. The tree had been planted eighty-five years earlier, and Douglas was told that William Bartram had 'held the tree while his father put the earth round'.[11] Douglas spotted two more oaks – *Quercus lyrata* and *Q. macrocarpa* – that flourished in the area. He also collected specimens from some other oaks growing on rocky soil in a wood nearby. And he collected seeds from one of Bartram's trees that turned a brilliant scarlet in the fall. It was a 40-foot-high sorrel tree (*Oxydendron arboreum*) beside the pond. He was also pleased to find that there were still five species of American magnolias in the garden. But he was astonished to see how small they were. 'In miniature' he called them. They were nothing compared to the pampered specimens of magnolia back in England at Kew and the Physic Garden in Chelsea.

Douglas spent December packing up the large number of trophies he had collected: boxes and boxes filled with trees from Philadelphia, Burlington, Baltimore and Flushing, presumably numbering more than a thousand plants. Most of these species, he knew, were rarities in England, and would delight Joseph Sabine, as they would fetch high prices in England. Douglas wrote to Sabine every week to keep him abreast with his discoveries. One of the most exciting was a new species of *Berberis*, known as the Oregon grape, which had been brought from the western side of the Rockies twenty years earlier by the famous explorers Lewis and Clark. (It was later to be renamed *Mahonia aquifolium* and become commonplace in Europe, but when Douglas's plants reached London they sold for £10 apiece.)

Douglas also assembled a small menagerie to take back to England, including pigeons, ducks and a quail. In mid-December he had paid his last social calls and was finally all set to depart. The *Nimrod* sailed on 12 December, and after a short tussle with a north-easter soon caught a following wind. The voyage home was uneventful enough apart from a little trouble with his menagerie. 'My ducks were very sick for two days and ate nothing; the pigeons and the quail continued well'.[12] A month after leaving New York the *Nimrod* was back in the quayside in London.

* * *

Of course Joseph Sabine was delighted with the achievements of his protégé. Sabine had taken a gamble with the shy young Scotsman and the gamble had proved a triumph. He celebrated the success of Douglas's mission with a fulsome tribute in the *Transactions*, the official records of the Horticultural Society: 'This mission was executed by Mr DOUGLAS with a success beyond expectation: he obtained many plants which were much wanted, and greatly increased our collection of fruit trees by the acquisition of several sorts only known to us by name'.[13] And Douglas had also distinguished himself with a display of unsuspected diplomatic gifts. Many tributes followed from his new friends in America including one from Governor Clinton himself. 'He unites enthusiasm, intelligence and persevering activity',[14] he wrote of Douglas. An invitation followed, proposing Douglas as a corresponding member of the New York Horticultural Society.

Sabine's next move was perhaps predictable enough. It was thirty years since Captain Vancouver and Dr Archibald Menzies had explored the north-west coast of America and Canada in the good ship *Discovery*. They had found that distant coast teeming with new, unrecorded trees and other plants. But for various reasons, including his stormy relations with Vancouver, Menzies had been unable to bring back living plants, or even viable seeds. (The only exceptions were the nuts of those astonishing monkey puzzles he had collected in Chile on the slopes of the Andes.) Why shouldn't the Horticultural Society now succeed where

Menzies and Vancouver had failed? Sabine was convinced that it could – and the cost would be minimal. A new kind of expedition was needed. It was no good for the society to try to share a British naval survey, like Vancouver's. They must choose one *independent* man to be their collector: someone of extraordinary gifts, including relentless energy. Sabine believed he had found the man. It was David Douglas.

Six months after returning to London in the *Nimrod*, Douglas embarked on the Hudson Bay Company's ship, the *William and Ann*, bound for the estuary of the River Columbia 6,000 miles away on the Pacific coast of North America. He was not yet twenty-five, but he had learnt a lot in the last year. He was now an accomplished amateur botanist as well as a resourceful traveller in the wilds. But ahead lay a challenge few men had faced. Paid a mere £100 a year, he was to risk his life hunting for trees and other plants among unpacified tribal natives thousands of miles beyond the frontier with civilisation.

Despite the low salary, Douglas had barely hesitated when he received Sabine's latest offer. He had always longed to be an explorer.

CHAPTER 10

Hunting Giants

The square-rigged, two-masted brig *William and Ann* finally came to anchor in Baker's Bay, in the mouth of the Columbia River, on 7 April 1825. 'With truth', David Douglas recorded in his journal, 'I may count this one of the happy moments of my life'.[1]

The voyage from London had taken eight months and fourteen days, with little to relieve the grinding monotony. True, they had two days on Madeira, where Douglas confessed himself 'amazingly gratified'.[2] He had climbed the highest peak, with his friend John Scouler, the ship's surgeon and a keen botanist. He had a glimpse of the famous dragon tree (*Dracaena draco*) and added a number of new plants to his herbarium. He also bought seven pounds' worth of wine from the local vineyards, to be shared with Scouler.

By the end of September 1824 the ship had cast anchor in the celebrated harbour at Rio, dominated by the Sugarloaf, and crowned by enormous palm trees. Brazil was ruled by Pedro I, the newly proclaimed, Portuguese-born emperor of Brazil. Douglas spent an enjoyable fortnight there, although relentless rain prevented him collecting good specimens for his herbarium. Joseph Sabine had given him several useful contacts in Rio. They included the governess of the emperor's daughter, a keen botanist called Maria Graham, and an enthusiastic gardener from

Liverpool, William Harrison, who showed him his collection of about seventy species of the orchid family. Douglas also attended midnight mass in the emperor's private chapel. Although a Presbyterian himself, the Catholic ritual appealed to the romantic side of Douglas's nature. He confessed that 'the gorgeous tapestry hung round the saints, the brilliance of the candles... gave me pleasing sensations', although he found the palace disappointingly ordinary. The walls were 'plain rubble-work and would only do for a potentate' in South America.[3]

By mid-November they were heading for Cape Horn, and its forbidding climate. Despite the pitching and rolling of the ship, Douglas occupied himself with catching numerous kinds of seabird. He found stormy petrels easy to take with a hook and a line baited with pork fat. Other birds were harder to ensnare, although he had no conscience (unlike Coleridge's Ancient Mariner of a generation earlier) about killing the iconic albatross. In fact he recorded, bluntly enough, that rough seas made the job easier. 'It is only when the wind blows furiously and the ocean is covered with foam like a washing tub that I could take the Albatross.'[4] In the event he took and killed forty-nine of these huge brown birds. (Two were later sent back to England as specimens.) Off Cape Horn itself he found another variety of albatross with a pale blue neck. He took and killed another pair, including an understandably aggressive bird that attacked one of the sailors helping Douglas, and cut out a piece of his thigh 'as if with a knife'.[5]

After ten days rounding the Cape, hammered by continuous storms, with waves breaking over the ship and sleep only barely possible, the *William and Ann* sailed north up the west coast of Chile. Soon they were in a kinder climate. Douglas caught new kinds of seabirds (including a snow-white Wandering Albatross) and saw a strange porpoise with a pure white stripe, which evaded capture. Otherwise the voyage was almost featureless, his journal an uncharacteristic blank. And then, in mid-December, Douglas made an unexpected discovery, leading to a strange encounter, that delighted him.

Three hundred miles off the coast of Chile, in search of fresh water, the ship anchored beside a wooded and mountainous island. Known as *Mas-a Tierra* ('Nearer-the-Land'), this was the second largest of the Juan Fernandez group, and was considered the original of Robinson Crusoe's island in the novel by Defoe. At any rate it was here that the flesh-and-blood Alexander Selkirk had been marooned from 1704 to 1709. And now, in 1824, a new Robinson Crusoe had established himself on the island. His name was William Clark and he was an eccentric English sailor, born in Whitechapel, London.

Clark had arrived in Chile five years earlier, and later came to this island with a party of Spaniards who made their living killing seals and wild bullocks, both of which were numerous. He now lived alone in a hut made of turf and stones, and thatched with straw from wild oats. A log of wood to sit on was his only furniture, and his meals were cooked in a cast-iron pot with a *wooden* bottom. (This struck Douglas as taking eccentricity too far, and he advised Clark 'under the circumstances' to try roasting beef instead of boiling it.) He seemed intelligent and well-informed, but dressed for the part of a castaway. 'His clothing was one pair of blue woollen trousers, a flannel and a cotton shirt, and a hat, but he chose to go bare-headed; he had no coat'. Douglas and his friend John Scouler, the ship's surgeon, gave him some extra clothing from their own small stock. And what delighted him even more was their present of a single dram of rum, which 'made him forget his exile'. Soon he was rolling drunk, and like a Trojan hero 'slew the slain three times'. But while still sober he impressed Douglas with his library of seventeen volumes. They included the Bible, the Book of Common Prayer, Scott's *Old Mortality* and – inevitably – a fine bound copy of *Robinson Crusoe*, of which he was 'himself the latest and most complete edition'.[6]

Apart from this encounter with Clark, there was little to do on the island except botanise – which suited Douglas perfectly. He spent two days collecting plants, many of which (as it later proved) were only to be found on Juan Fernandez. He listed seventy-eight species or varieties, mostly annuals and perennials, like cardamine and lobelia. But the list included large shrubs like a species of *Vaccinium*, which grew right up to the summit of the principal mountain. There were also a few substantial trees, including what he took to be a species of *Eugenia*, a tree of the myrtle family; this was 40 to 60 feet high and the main forest tree on the island. Would any of these subtropical plants be hardy enough to grace the Horticultural Society's new arboretum? Douglas could hardly guess. The first step, on his return to England, would be to get the dried specimens identified by the society's professional botanists. But Douglas took understandable pride in his new discoveries. He found a filmy fern in a shady ravine below the mountains, and flung himself down on a carpet of them, beside a crystal stream. 'Although a plant of humble growth, its delicately veined and crisped foliage contrasts beautifully with the more princely of the tribe'.[7] Of course he, too, was a plant of humble growth, the son of a stonemason, who had been welcomed by the great and the good in London.

Next day the *William and Ann*, its water barrels refilled, weighed anchor. They left Clark standing on a large stone on the shore. He had presented them with a fine female goat ('but not one of Robinson Crusoe's, for it was young') and he hoped they might return next day. But a strong south-easterly set in, and the ship was forced to make for the open sea. By Christmas Day they had reached latitude 27 south, and were riding on the back of the south-east trade wind. 'We dined on the goat given to us by Clark; were comfortable and happy; in the evening we drank the health of our friends in England'.[8]

On 10 January they anchored at James Island, one of the smaller Chatham Islands. It was to be the final stop before they reached the Columbia River – and a sad disappointment. Douglas was only allowed to go on shore for six hours. The ceaseless rain made collecting plants unusually frustrating. He collected 175 species, many of which were new to him. He was only able to save 40. 'Never in my life was I so mortified, touching at a place where everything, indeed the most trifling particle, becomes of interest in England, and to have such a miserable collection to show I have been there.'

If the rain had let up, he would have at least made a fine collection of birds and animals. 'The birds are very numerous, and some of them pretty... Many of the smaller ones perched on my hat, and when I carried my gun on my shoulder would sit on the muzzle.' He killed forty-five of nineteen genera. There was no need to shoot them. They were easily killed with a stick. He skinned them all carefully but 'had the mortification to lose them all except one species of *Sula*' (probably the blue-footed booby). He had no better luck with animals. There were large tortoises and lizards, 3 feet long. Both made 'good eating'. But he only managed to skin the lizard and soon lost it, before he had even time to write a proper description.

The rain finally stopped for an hour, and the sun broke through and 'raised a steam from the ground almost suffocating'.[9] His thermometer stood at 96 °F and there was not a breath of wind. Next day they sailed, and the rain hammered on the deck for the next fortnight almost without a pause. So Douglas had little chance of drying any of the specimens that still survived.

For the next three months the winds played cat and mouse

with the *William and Ann*. Sometimes the ship seemed tantalisingly close to their objective, the Columbia River. Then the wind turned 'boisterous and frightful', and it was useless to think of approaching land. 'We were tossed and driven about in this condition for six weeks', Douglas recorded. 'Here we experienced the furious hurricanes of North-West America in the fullest extent, a thousand times worse than Cape Horn.'[10] Sleep was almost impossible, and it was dangerous to go on deck; the second mate lay in excruciating pain after falling on deck and fracturing his right thigh. But on 7 April their luck finally turned, and a kindly north-easter brought them close to the coast. 'All sail was set, joy and expectation was on every countenance, all glad to make themselves useful. The Doctor and I kept the soundings.' They slipped past the sand bar, where many ships had been injured or wrecked, and at four in the afternoon cast anchor in Baker's Bay, the gateway to the Columbia River. This was the day when Douglas wrote in his journal 'with truth I may count this one of the happy moments of my life.'[11]

Yet the task he had set himself – and agreed with Joseph Sabine – would have left many men crippled by shock. He was to search several thousand miles of wilderness for unknown trees and plants. But there were no roads, not even many tracks. Away from the great river, the place was almost unexplored and unmapped by Europeans. It was Indian country, and tribal wars were alarmingly common. Who was in charge? Certainly not the governments of Spain or British Canada or the United States east of the Mississippi. No firm frontiers had yet to be agreed between these three rival powers; and in 1825 none of the three seemed to have an appetite to colonise the wilderness. If anyone could exercise authority this side of the Rocky Mountains it was a commercial organisation, the 150-year-old Hudson Bay Company, whose business empire stretched from north-east Canada more than 3,000 miles to the mouth of the River Columbia. The main purpose of the company was to feed the voracious European market for Canadian and American furs. These were pelts of beaver and otter sold to the company by local trappers, mainly the so-called 'Indians', the indigenous peoples of the area. In return the company sold them European goods of various kinds, cheerfully including barrels of rum (despite its disastrous effects on indigenous society) in ever increasing quantities. To manage this business, the Hudson Bay Company had its head office in London; in 1821 it had merged with another similar company, the North West Company based in Montreal, after a vicious trade war. Now the two companies combined had imposed a trading monopoly on half North America, and their power was confirmed by a network of more than twenty forts and outposts straddling both sides of the Rocky Mountains.

From the first Douglas recognised his overwhelming debt to the company – and to Joseph Sabine who had persuaded their executives in London to pay for this expedition. Douglas had travelled out as a guest on board their ship, the *William and Ann*. Now he found himself at Baker's Bay on the north side of the river, a few miles upriver from the company's nearest fort. He would rely on the company for his own most vital needs: passage upriver in the company's boats and canoes, food and shelter at their various forts along the river and its tributaries; above all, information and advice about the dangers of travel, including the ever-present threat from tribal natives.

What a gigantic task he had set himself, compared to that of Archibald Menzies in the 1790s. Menzies had never strayed far from the sea, as his base was Vancouver's survey ship, *Discovery*. Menzies had made a number of important discoveries of both trees and other plants. But in one respect Menzies had failed. He had not managed to bring back any of the seeds, or living plants, to introduce his discoveries to Europe (apart from the famous monkey-puzzle nuts smuggled out of Chile). By comparison Douglas had two great advantages. First, he could exploit the company's new network of forts to help him hunt for plants as far inland as the Rockies – or even beyond. Second, he could rely on the company's ships, like the *William and Ann*, to carry his seeds, and living plants, safely back to England. How different from the fate of poor Archibald Menzies, arrested by Vancouver for protesting at the ill-treatment of those precious collections!

And what a cornucopia of new plants awaited Douglas from the first moment he left the ship. 'On stepping on the shore *Gaultheria shallon* was the first plant I took in my hands. So pleased was I that I could scarcely see anything but it. Mr Menzies correctly observes that it grows under thick pine-forests in great luxuriance and would make a valuable addition to our gardens.'[12] As well as this new evergreen shrub, Douglas collected the seeds of a salmonberry (*Rubus spectabilis*) a decorative currant bush (*Ribes sanguineum*), several lupins and the soon to be celebrated camassia quamash. This was the bulb with the startling blue flower which coloured whole prairies in the north-west. The bulb, boiled or roasted, was also a staple source of food for indigenous tribes (and for European explorers like Lewis and Clark, whom the bulb saved from starvation during their epic journey across the continent).

And even more spectacular discoveries beckoned. The hills either side of Baker's Bay were dominated by what Douglas took to be pines. In due course he collected seeds from what proved to be three new *genera*, later identified as the western hemlock (*Tsuga heterophylla*), the balsam fir (*Abies balsamifera*) and the tree that would above all make him famous: the Douglas fir. (Appropriately enough, its botanical name, *Pseudotsuga menziesii*, honoured the man who had collected the first dried specimen of the tree, Archibald Menzies.)

As well as making these exciting botanical discoveries, Douglas had his first encounter with the indigenous people whose ancestors had made their homes for thousands of years in the vast forests and sprawling plains of the north-west. In the months ahead, when he had left the Columbia River and the shelter of the Hudson Bay Company, Native Americans were to play a crucial part in his search for trees and other plants. They were to guide him and feed him and defend him from dangers of many kinds. But at first he seemed only mildly interested in them. A canoe with a 'Canadian' (a 'voyageur', or professional canoeist, often of mixed race) and several indigenous people called at the ship, offering various kinds of food for sale: dry salmon, fresh sturgeon, game and roots prepared with dry berries. Douglas noted that 'the natives viewed us with curiosity and put to us many questions. Some of them have a few words of English and by the assistance of signing make themselves very well understood.' He found they had the 'singular habit' of perforating the septum of the nose and ears with 'shells, beads, bits of copper, or in fact any hardware.' But they soon showed they were smart enough at bargaining, and got a good price for their salmon.[13]

By 19 April Douglas was all set to go upriver to Fort Vancouver, the company's new headquarters 70 miles from the sea. Fortunately John McLoughlin, the chief factor and one of the grandees of the company, was down at Baker's Bay. McLoughlin was an impressive figure: tall, with a shock of white hair. (Later he would fall out with the company over the help he gave prospective American settlers; he himself then took American citizenship. But at this period he was one of the most articulate leaders of the company, and his word was law.) On his return to his new headquarters he gave Douglas a lift in his canoe. As the current was against them the journey took two days of hard paddling by the crew of the canoe: a Canadian and six Indians. The Europeans slept in the canoe, pulled up on the beach, after a supper consisting of bread and tea and sturgeon. The Indians spent all night roasting and eating their share of the sturgeon. They paddled off as soon as it was light. Douglas lay back and admired the scenery.

The country had become mountainous, 'and on the banks of the river the rocks rise perpendicularly several hundred feet in some parts, over which are some fine waterfalls'.[14] Soon they saw a distant range of snow-capped mountains, including Mount Hood, Mount Jefferson and Mount St Helens. And everywhere along the riverbanks there were new trees and other plants ripe for collection.

Fort Vancouver itself, on the north bank, was unimpressive, though the scenery was inspiring; opposite the fort was an island named in honour of Archibald Menzies No houses had yet been constructed, so Douglas was at first given a tent to sleep in, followed by a hut made of red cedar bark. For the next year this small bark hut was to be the base where he could write up his notes and dry his precious seeds and herbarium specimens. But most of the time he was away hunting for plants, with nights spent sleeping under an upturned canoe or in the shade of a giant pine tree.

In fact Douglas pushed himself to the limits – and beyond. Sometimes he collapsed with exhaustion. In the first few weeks he covered hundreds of miles and listed nearly three hundred plants that he had collected. Many had been discovered by Menzies but none had yet been introduced into Europe. There were many kinds of lupins, a phlox that he named after Joseph Sabine, more examples of the 'Oregon grape' (*Mahonia aquifolium*), more kinds of currant and bramble, penstemons galore and hundreds more shrubs and herbaceous plants.

The stars of the collection were of course the trees. Douglas was dazzled by a 90-foot giant maple that he found beside the Columbia River: 'its large foliage and elegant racemes of yellow fragrant flowers contrast delightfully with the dark feathery branches of the lordly pine'. In due course it would be christened by botanists the 'big-leaf maple' (*Acer macrophyllum*) which sounds ordinary enough, although the leaves are indeed much the biggest in the maple family. Douglas also discovered a red-flowered maple in the forest, the vine maple of botanists (*Acer circinatum*). The trees had many crooked trunks and these were arched in every direction. The Canadian voyageurs called them *Bois de diable* ('trees of the devil') as their twisted and interlocking trunks made the forests almost impenetrable. But the Indians were grateful for the trees. The wood was white, and so hard that it was used to make hooks for catching salmon.

After a few weeks Douglas was anxious to explore the country north of the river, and hoped to join the company's ship that was heading for the famous Nootka Sound (where Vancouver had confronted a northern outpost of the Spanish empire thirty years before). But Douglas was warned by his kindly patron and host, the chief factor, John McLoughlin, that the natives were 'turbulent' in that area. There would be little chance of collecting plants. Europeans could only travel in large, well-armed parties. So Douglas decided he would explore the upper reaches of the Columbia and the burning plains beyond. In mid-June he joined an official party of canoeists sent out to various posts in the interior. About 200 miles from the ocean they came to the Grand Rapids of the Columbia.

Here the river, squeezed by rocks to a channel a quarter of a mile wide, plunged over a series of limestone and granite terraces. Above, there were three islands, including one that served as a graveyard for the Indians of the south bank. Below, lying between layers of rock, were many huge petrified trees. Douglas spotted two kinds of tree – soft wood and hard wood – which he took to be the balsam fir and the big-leaf maple respectively.

Both banks were crowded with native people. The river was now ripe for fishing, and many people had travelled for miles to come here to fish for salmon. Douglas was told that salmon in 'almost incredible numbers' were caught here with nets made of Indian hemp. He bought a 35-pound salmon for a mere half-ounce of tobacco, worth no more than a penny, and ate it under the shade of a great tree. 'It is very wonderful the comfort, at least the pleasant idea of being comfortable, in such a place surrounded by multitudes of individuals who, perhaps, had never seen a white person before, and were we to judge them by appearance are very hostile'. In fact he was warned by his guides not to be too trusting. Most of the coastal tribes – Chenooks, Cladsaps, Clikitats and Killimucks – were 'not unfriendly'. But here in the interior, 200 miles from the ocean, the natives were reported to be 'inquisitive in the extreme, treacherous . . . [and] will pillage and murder when they can do it with impunity'.[15]

Despite the warning, Douglas made several expeditions in the neighbouring forest, groping his way through thickets, and crossing gullies choked with stones and dead wood. He returned so hungry and exhausted that he could no longer stand. Twice he had to crawl to a small abandoned hut. Fortunately he was a good shot and brought down two partridges, then fell asleep, too tired to eat them.

Fifty miles further upriver were the Falls, first described by Lewis and Clark on their pioneering journey across the continent. Douglas found they were nothing to compare with the Rapids. Although the Falls stretched across the whole river, the actual decline was a mere 10 or 12 feet. And to search for plants was futile. The riverbanks were almost bare – apart from a few shrubs like *Mahonia aquifolium*. In fact the river was now a slice through a burning wilderness. Douglas had to cross a 19-mile stretch of white sand, which left his feet badly blistered. With relief he turned back towards Fort Vancouver and the comfort, if comfort it was, of the great forest.

By mid-July he was back on the coast, hunting for the cyperus – a vegetable claimed to be as edible as the potato. A twelve-day search north of Cape Disappointment proved abortive; and he was warned not to travel any further north, as several of the tribes were at war in that quarter. Douglas then paid a visit to Cockqua, the chief of the local Chenooks, who was known to be exceedingly fond of 'all the chiefs who come from King George', meaning European explorers like Vancouver and other captains of English ships. Cockqua greeted Douglas in great style. 'He imitates all European manners; immediately after saluting me with a "clachouie", their word for "friend", or "How are you?" and a shake of his hand, water was brought for me to wash and a fire was kindled.' Supper was served from an enormous sturgeon, 10 feet long, and Douglas was invited to choose which part he would like to have cooked; his choice of flesh from the spine earned him a fine compliment from his host.

But it turned out that the Chenooks were at war with the Cladsaps, the tribe on the opposite bank of the river, and an attack from the Cladsaps was expected that very night. Douglas watched as three hundred of Cockqua's men, naked except for their warpaint, danced the war dance and sang several death songs. Cockqua then pressed Douglas to spend the night in the safety of a cabin he had built for him within the stockade of the tribal lodge. Douglas politely declined. He knew that the lodge would have its floor well stocked with fleas. He was also keen to prove he was no coward. Cockqua's offer 'I would have most gladly accepted, but as fear should never be shown I slept in my tent 50 yards from the village.' Fortunately there was nothing to disturb his sleep. But in the morning Cockqua told him 'he was a great chief, for I was not afraid of the Cladsaps'.[16]

To add to his reputation Douglas then gave a demonstration of his skill with a gun. The locals had never seen a bird shot on the wing. Douglas spotted a large white eagle perched on a dead tree stump close to the village. 'I charged my gun with swan shot, walked up to within forty-five yards of the bird, threw a stone to raise him, and when flying brought him down'. His hosts were amazed. Many covered their mouths with their right hands – a token of astonishment or terror. Douglas then added another party trick from his repertoire. Someone threw up his hat high in the air. To everyone's astonishment, Douglas shot the crown to pieces, leaving only the brim. 'My fame' as he put it, understandably enjoying his moment of triumph, 'was sounded through the camp'. And Cockqua paid him a final compliment: 'Cladsap can't shoot like you'.[17]

* * *

A year passed, and Douglas continued to push himself to the limits. There seemed no end to the botanical treasures he could discover in places too distant from the coast for Menzies to have visited. But to reach them meant following the lesser tributaries of the Columbia River, and then cutting a path through thousands of miles of wilderness. He explored the Blue Mountains, north of the Columbia, wading through deep snow to reach one of the peaks, and arriving back at the camp so exhausted that it took him days to recover. Sometimes he had little to eat, except a handful of hazel nuts or camassia roots. Once or twice they had to shoot one of their own horses to give themselves a meal. His respect for his indigenous companions continued to increase. He had made friends with important chiefs like Cockqua, and perhaps that was easy enough. But he needed guides and trackers and porters, which meant learning at least a smattering of their languages – which were frustratingly numerous. Now he could pick their brains for news of new trees and other plants. Two of his most exciting discoveries were made in the autumn of 1825, high up in the Blue Mountains.

The first was the noble fir (*Abies procera*), which he thought 'in point of elegance justly claims pre-eminence'. It grew to a height of 170 feet with a 'white, smooth, polished bark.' Often the concentric whorls of leaves were bright blue, and so were the outsize fir cones. (Today, nearly two hundred years after Douglas sent its seeds to England, the noble fir is acknowledged to be one of the most elegant exotics in Scottish forests, and also serves as a favourite choice for a Christmas tree.) The other newly discovered species he described as having 'a singular beauty' was appropriately named the lovable fir (*Abies amabilis*). It grew as tall as the noble fir, but its charm lay in its glossy green leaves and purple cones and the delicious smell of oranges that arose from a crushed leaf.

By the summer of 1826 it might have seemed that Douglas's appetite for new discoveries had at last been satisfied. But he was haunted by the thought of a tree he had missed. He had failed to track down a specimen of the gigantic pine tree reported to grow somewhere south of the Columbia River. He had first heard of this prodigy the previous year, when looking at the tobacco pouches of some friendly Indians. In the pouches were some very large, and very edible seeds. He understood these seeds came from one of these pine trees in the Umqua mountains which lay far to the south – beyond the boundaries of northern California.

He finally set off for this little-known territory on 20 September 1826, after joining a party of thirty Europeans and Indians who were searching for beaver pelts. The weather was perfect: clear and dry with dewy or foggy evenings. The party averaged about 16 miles a day, which gave time enough for hunting. And Douglas found what he thought was an evergreen species of sweet chestnut – now called the golden chestnut (*Castanopsis chrysophylla*). This gave him great pleasure. 'Nothing can exceed the magnificence of this tree, or the strikingly beautiful contrast with the sable glory of the shadowy pine'.[18] The party had now divided, and on 19 October Douglas had an alarming accident.

He was alone, and was pursuing a large buck which he had wounded in the shoulder, when he fell into a deep gully stuffed with dead wood, and was knocked unconscious. He awoke at 5 p.m. 'I was on my belly and my face covered with mud . . . [and] a severe pain in the chest'.[19] Fortunately six members of the Calapooie tribe found him, and helped him to limp back to his camp, leaning on a stick and his gun. He was pleased to be able to reward his rescuers with food. Next day the pain had left him; he bathed in the river. He rejoined his comrades and they continued the march to the south.

By mid-November they had crossed the border with California and were still making good progress through forests and thickets. The party then divided again, and Douglas was alone, apart from a single guide. On 24 November his camp was struck by a tremendous thunderstorm –'one of the most dreadful I ever witnessed'. His fire was extinguished, his tent flattened, and he lay in the grass soaked and shivering. 'Sleep of course was not to be had, every ten or fifteen minutes immense trees falling (and) producing a crash as if the earth was cleaving asunder . . .' His terrified horses ran to him for protection, 'hanging their heads over me and neighing'.[20] But next day dawned cold and clear. Douglas headed for some open country where there were three tribal lodges. They gave him salmon for which he was grateful.

He left after a short stay, aiming for a ridge of hills where he hoped to find the pine.

At daybreak on 26 November he set off alone from his camp, leaving his guide to take care of the horses, and dry the sheets of paper used for wrapping seeds. An hour later he met a Native American who strung his bow and threatened him. Douglas calmly put his gun on the ground, and indicated that the man should do the same with his bow and quiver. Then he waved the man forward. Douglas struck a light and 'gave him to smoke and a few beads'. Before long Douglas was showing him a rough sketch of the long-lost pine and pine cone. The man immediately pointed at some hills about 15 or 20 miles to the south, and proceeded to show him the way. 'At midday I reached my long-wished *Pinus* (called by the Umpqua tribe *Natele*) and lost no time in examining and endeavouring to collect specimens and seeds'.

The great tree was no disappointment. (If Douglas lost no time looking for seeds, he was certainly lost for words.) All he could say was that it was 'beautiful and immensely large'. The tallest he could measure was a giant blown down by the wind: it had been 215 feet tall and had the enormous girth of 57 feet at three feet from the ground. The largest trees had clean trunks for two thirds of their height, and the pine cones hung down from the upper branches 'like small sugar-loaves in a grocer's shop'.[21] Later it would be christened the sugar pine.

But how could he collect the seeds when the cones were impossible to reach? Douglas got three cones, each more than a foot long, and packed with seed – but they nearly cost him his life. Let him tell the story in his own words.

Being unable to climb or hew down any (cones), I took my gun and was busy clipping them from the branches with ball when eight Indians came at the report of my gun. They were all painted with red earth, armed with bows, arrows, spears of bone, and flint knives, and seemed anything but friendly. I endeavoured to explain to them what I wanted and they seemed satisfied and sat down to smoke, but had no sooner done so than I perceived one string his bow and another sharpen his flint knife with a pair of wooden pincers and hang it on the wrist of his right hand, which gave me ample testimony of their inclination. To save myself I could not do so by flight, and without any hesitation I went back six paces and cocked my gun, and then pulled from my belt one of my pistols, which I held in my left hand. I was determined to fight for life. As I as much as possible endeavoured to preserve my coolness and perhaps did so, I stood eight or ten minutes looking at them and they at me without a word passing, till one at last, who seemed to be the leader, made a sign for tobacco, which I said they should get on condition of going and fetching me some cones. They went, and as soon as out of sight I picked up my three cones and a few twigs, and made a quick retreat to my camp, which I gained at dusk.[22]

Even then his troubles were not over. Two hours before dawn his guide gave a loud scream. 'I sprang to my feet, thinking the Indians I saw yesterday had found me out.' But it was a grizzly bear that had attacked the guide. Douglas waited till it was light, then shot the bear, and its two cubs. He promptly paid off the guide with the carcass of the bear cub ('he seemed to lay great store by it') and set off to rejoin the main party.[23]

* * *

A further year of danger and discovery passed before Douglas finally returned to meet his employers in England. Characteristically he had chosen the hardest route: travelling overland across the continent, riding the so-called 'Hudson Bay Express'. Of course this was not a vehicle, but an infinitely laborious expedition by canoe and on horseback and on foot, bringing members of the company 3,000 miles back to the harbour in Hudson Bay.

Back in London Joseph Sabine and William Hooker waited excitedly for the return of their protégé. They had much to celebrate. Douglas had achieved more on this second trip than they could have dared to hope. In fact his boxes of seeds, sent ahead of him in the company's ships, were a revelation. Thirty years before, Archibald Menzies had brought back dried specimens for the herbarium, the ghosts of great trees and other plants. Now Douglas had breathed life into them. And he had added hundreds of new plants that Menzies had missed. As Douglas's seedlings began to germinate in the greenhouses of the Horticultural Society in Chiswick, it was clear that this modest young son of a stonemason had made a major contribution to botanical science. And, what was even closer to Joseph Sabine's heart, the sale of Douglas's surplus plants would in due course earn hundreds of pounds for the Horticultural Society.

Meanwhile Sabine hoped to complete the society's new arboretum at Chiswick, the first of a second generation of arboretums which would soon sweep across Britain and Ireland. But Sabine had a problem which he had kept secret from all but his closest friends. As secretary of the society, he had been spending thousands of pounds more than the society earned. And now in the late 1820s it was quietly going bankrupt.

CHAPTER 11

The Downfall of Joseph Sabine

David Douglas finally reached London on 11 October 1827 and became an instant celebrity. He had risked his life in the wilds of north-west Canada and America – and survived to tell the tale.

He was showered with honours: fellowships (and free membership) from the Linnean, Geological and Zoological Societies. Everyone wanted to meet this new British hero, and to hear from his own lips the tales of his escape from grizzly bears and savage Indian tribes.

At first Douglas was too exhausted and ill to appear in person. As secretary of the Horticultural Society, it was Joseph Sabine who read Douglas's paper prepared for the society, describing Douglas's daredevil hunt for the sugar pine.

In the following months Sabine must have been delighted to find that Douglas's new collections of seeds were germinating in enormous quantities. Earlier, when Douglas was still in North America, Sabine had reported in the society's *Transactions* that Douglas's expedition had 'hitherto succeeded beyond the most sanguine expectations of his employers'. Members were told that 'it was hoped that, from this expedition, our gardens will become as well filled with the beautiful vegetation of the borders of the Columbia, and of the Rocky Mountains, as it is already with that of the Ohio and Mississippi'.[1] Now, with Douglas back in London, the extraordinary nature of his achievements was becoming clear.

Sabine, writing in the society's *Transactions*, duly reported that Douglas had introduced 210 new species, which were now growing in the society's garden in Chiswick. Of these, 80 'presented no other interest than as Botanical curiosities'. But the other 130 were being used to propagate seedlings in huge numbers, and the resulting treasure trove of small trees and other plants had been distributed to the Fellows, and to public gardens all over Europe. The 'peculiar value attached to these plants', according to Sabine, was that they could stand the British winter without protection, and many were 'also distinguished by their great beauty'.[2]

What Sabine *didn't* choose to say was equally significant. The whole cost of Douglas's three-year expedition had only amounted to £400, including his wages and all expenses. In fact Douglas was only paid the wages of a junior gardener. And Sabine, secretly wrestling with the society's huge deficit, had paid for that £400 from the proceeds derived from a single one of Douglas's introductions – a shrub now all the rage in England, Douglas's dazzling new red currant bush, *Ribes sanguineum*.

Douglas himself was occupied at first in tending his new plants at Chiswick. Unlike many plant explorers he had served a long apprenticeship as a gardener, and was now an expert at dealing with the requirements of small plants. If only he could have shown the same skill in dealing with the great and the good in London. In fact he found life as a hero in London difficult to bear. Physically he was not in good shape. Not yet thirty, he looked ten years older. His eyesight had begun to fail, and he was prey to bouts of rheumatism. And mentally, too, he bore wounds that were slow to heal.

Perhaps the life of an explorer is always difficult on his return from the wilds. Douglas had pushed himself, physically and mentally, beyond any normal limits of endurance. Now he had to pay the price. He was moody and even rude to the grandees of the Horticultural Society. Did he need a new role? Should he reach out to his admirers by writing a book on his travels? John Lindley, the distinguished botanist and the society's assistant secretary, had helped identify many of his new plants. Lindley now offered to help him with a book, and Sabine, with unusual generosity, told him he could keep the profits. But Douglas, ill and depressed, had no wish to become an author. (His journals were eventually published – but not till 1914.)

Perhaps his black mood reflected a resentment which he could hardly admit to himself. He had brought back a bonanza of new plants for the Horticultural Society, and had risked his life for them. And what had they done for him? They had paid him a pittance: less than the wage of the porter at their London office. And now they had left him without any form of employment.

In the event it was William Hooker, the Professor of Botany at Glasgow and Douglas's original friend and mentor, who solved the problem. He realised that Douglas could not reinvent himself as a professional botanist or bestselling author. He had only one role and it was staring everyone in the face. He was an explorer. Hooker told Sabine that, despite the society's need to economise, they must commission Douglas for a new expedition. Sabine – reluctantly perhaps – agreed. Douglas was once again to be a guest of the Hudson Bay Company. Once again he would sail on one of the company's ships. But this time Douglas planned to explore the country far to the south of the Columbia River. In fact he was aiming for the little-known heart of California, still nominally controlled by Mexico.

Before he sailed he had a number of congenial tasks to perform. The first was to learn the use of the scientific instruments needed for surveying and map-making: sextant, barometer, chronometer, hygrometer and compass. Fortunately Joseph Sabine's accomplished younger brother, Captain Edward Sabine, was an expert in this field. He agreed to give Douglas the basic instruction, and found him an impressively hard-working pupil. The staff of the Colonial Office, too, were impressed by Douglas. They agreed to pay his expenses on the understanding he would supply them with copies of the charts he produced.

The second task was to contact Dr Archibald Menzies, the pioneer of plant-hunting in the North-West Pacific. Douglas recognised the huge debt he owed his fellow Scotsman. Of course Menzies had blazed the trail that he had followed – and then dramatically extended. Menzies, now seventy-five and in retirement, had left the navy to become a family doctor in London. The two men met one evening, and no doubt exchanged many tales of high adventure. Menzies could have been forgiven if he had felt a twinge of jealousy. Douglas had succeeded in introducing the plants which Menzies had been first to discover – and would have himself introduced if Vancouver had not obstructed him. They were joined by a third Scotsman who had circumnavigated the globe, and had tramped along that wild, rain-swept coast of north-west America: Douglas's old friend from Glasgow, Dr John Scouler. He was rising fast in his profession, and would soon be a professor in Dublin.

It must have been an unusually convivial evening. The news that he could explore California had transformed Douglas. Gone was that oversensitive and prickly depressive who had insulted his friends and employers. Now he was the old Douglas, bounding through life like a teenager, the man who could inspire affection among even the most warlike tribal chief.

Douglas had one final task to perform before leaving. He must choose a reliable companion for his travels. He decided that a small, white Scotch terrier called Billy would be perfect for the job. Together they sailed for the Pacific in October 1829.

* * *

Meanwhile his employer, Joseph Sabine, was facing attacks from several different directions.

The first broadside came from the *Gardener's Magazine* and its remarkable founder and editor, the polymath and workaholic, John Claudius Loudon. He was reared on a Scottish farm, and apprenticed as a nurseryman. He studied at night and, like so many successful Scottish gardeners and nurserymen, Loudon had come south to make his fortune. He took the tenancy of a farm in Oxfordshire, farmed it efficiently and, and then sold it on for a profit of £15,000.

After a tour of the Continent in 1813–14 (when he witnessed the smoking ruins of Moscow soon after the retreat of Napoleon's army) he toyed with the idea of becoming an engineer or a landscape architect. Then he reinvented himself as an encyclopaedist. Before he was forty-five he had written and published two bestselling encyclopaedias – on gardening (1822), and on farming (1825) – and was editing and publishing two groundbreaking magazines: *Gardener's Magazine* (from 1826) and the *Magazine of Natural History* (from 1828). All this and more, when he was suffering acute pain from a botched operation on his right arm.

As a touchy newcomer from Scotland, largely self-made and self-educated, with many thousands of loyal readers, Loudon was a dangerous man to quarrel with. And Joseph Sabine was his enemy – or so he believed when he heard that the Horticultural Society was planning to launch a gardener's magazine to compete with his own. Loudon waited for the time to strike. Then, in May 1829, he launched his broadside against Sabine. It took the form of a devastating attack on the society's arboretum at Chiswick, created a few years earlier under the despotic control of Joseph Sabine. He mocked the society for the failure to lay out the beds artistically ('so tame and lumpish as to leave no striking or agreeable impression'); he derided the path system – or its absence, and the lack of gravel walks ('the dug clumps are surrounded by grass, which of course can only be walked on in fine weather'); he ridiculed the random arrangement of the genera ('as a scientific arboretum ... it is still more discreditable to the society'.)

And who was to blame for all these mistakes? They could only be explained by 'the preponderating influence ... of a gentleman, who ... is surpassed by none in describing paeonies, crocuses and chrysanthemums.' Of course Sabine was the gentleman and 'The evils to the Society which have attended placing so much power in the hands of this individual have been pointed out ...' And Loudon rubbed it in once more: 'when we reflect on this arboretum, we are astonished that such an absurdity could be produced in such an age and in such a country'.[3]

Loudon was certainly too hard on Sabine. He gave Sabine no credit for his real achievements after he took over as honorary secretary fourteen years earlier. The affairs of the society were then somewhat confused, but Sabine swiftly sorted them out. He was a bachelor with time on his hands. He had trained as a barrister, but had no need to practise, as he had a well-paid government job which was virtually a sinecure: he was inspector-general of assessed taxes. His ideas for developing the society had been dramatic, and in some respects highly successful. He had doubled the society's membership in his fourteen years as secretary, and achieved something even more important: he had made it fashionable. Loudon could mock him as a social climber. But the social success of the garden – and his own nimble ascent up the social ladder – were impossible to deny. The list of members, starting with the king, George IV, Tsar Nicholas of Russia, and numerous British dukes, read like a roll-call of the great and the good. And one of the highlights of the London season was now the annual fete in the society's exciting new 30-acre garden at Chiswick.

To call that garden an 'absurdity', as Loudon had called it, was itself somewhat absurd. What was nearer the mark was to say that its arboretum was a brave, pioneering experiment – with some obvious defects. Of course the arboretum needed a better path system, the beds were 'tame and lumpish' and the placing of the genera was more or less at random. But where else in England (apart from one or two specialised plant nurseries, like Loddiges of Hackney) could tree lovers find such a complete collection of trees? According to the plan of the arboretum, published in the *Gardener's Magazine* to illustrate Loudon's broadside, there were ninety-nine separate beds, divided by a fashionable serpentine canal. Roughly half of these beds were filled with genera of trees, the other half with genera of shrubs.

You started your tree tour inspecting magnolias on the left of the entrance. You then followed the trail of nyssas, thuyas, junipers, sweet chestnuts, thorn trees and horse chestnuts. Soon you were facing the serpentine canal, with cherries and other fruit trees ahead. Taking one of the bridges across the canal, you came to the main clumps of European forest trees – oak, beech, elm, ash, pine and lime – and their American and Asian counterparts. There were also numerous exotic immigrants from America: tulip trees, robinias and liquidambars. Oriental exotics included plane trees from Turkey, ginkgos from China and pines from the Himalayas. In all there were more than forty genera and hundreds of species of trees and other plants. Many were exciting new introductions – including presumably the first of Douglas's collections sent as seed from America, and soon to be showpieces of the arboretum.

If Sabine had a simple argument in his defence against Loudon's broadside, it was there in the arboretum in the shape of one of Douglas's new trees and plants. Sabine had chosen Douglas to search America for treasures, and Douglas had succeeded better than anyone could have dared to hope. But it was too late for argument. Nothing could now save Joseph Sabine. His enemies were closing in, and only humiliation lay ahead.

The crisis came in January 1831, three months after Douglas had set sail for the north-west. It was triggered by a minor, and somewhat ridiculous, incident. A member of the society called Henry Kerr was reported to have privately criticised Sabine's plans for the head gardener's house from which Sabine would have made a personal profit. 'I consider this sort of jobbing,' Kerr explained, 'as to the houses, that is, getting a good house for the Secretary, under the pretence of its being for the gardener, one of the greatest grievances'. Sabine retaliated by telling Kerr he was expelled. A letter of protest followed in *The Times* – and all hell broke loose.[4]

A committee of thirteen, led by Mr Gordon, MP for Lechlade, was appointed to enquire into the society's 'general expenditure and management'. By 2 March their report was ready, and it was devastating on two counts. Sabine was guilty of gross mismanagement over many years. Worse, he had wilfully deceived the council, the garden committee and the auditors, about the disastrous state of the society's finances.

The most damaging witness against him was John Lindley, his own second-in-command, and since 1828 the distinguished Professor of Botany at University College, London. Stung by Sabine's attempt to implicate him in these 'miserable proceedings', he lashed out at the man he had once thought was his friend. First, Sabine was a despot (a 'control freak' he would be called today). The head gardener had no power 'to hire or dismiss, to promote or degrade, to punish or reward his labourers'. All these things were done by Sabine. It was substantially true that 'not a tree can be moved, or a border dug, without a *written order* from the Secretary'. The result was that many of the most important operations were delayed for weeks, and even when it was too late to execute them. So the flower garden was in such a 'disgraceful' state that Lindley had been for a long time too 'ashamed to show the garden to any of my friends'.[5]

Second, Sabine's obsession with having all reports put in writing – for even the most trivial occurrence – gave him the power of espionage towards both his own staff and visitors. Sabine's aim was to root out and punish his critics, like the unfortunate Henry Kerr. But of course his staff resented being used as spies. Third, a great deal of money was wasted in using the ordinary labourers to show visitors around the garden. The visitors disliked the system, and the men could only mislead them with inaccurate information. It was a much better idea to put labels on the trees and plants. Lindley himself had begun this task. He was stopped by Sabine, 'who appeared to consider it an improper interference with his authority'.[6]

These were all serious charges from a highly reliable witness – charges of gross mismanagement by Sabine. (Of course it was a wonder that Lindley had not resigned.) But there was worse to come. When the committee of thirteen examined the books they found that Sabine had lied about the society's debts to the council, the garden committee and the auditors. The audit sheets he produced in May 1826 showed net debts of £3,350. The total of debts was 'in reality the . . . enormous amount of £18,397.'[7] Sabine was exposed as a liar and a cheat who had led the society down a path of reckless extravagance by falsifying the accounts.

However, as one would expect, the report of the committee of thirteen, published in early March, dealt with the scandal as

diplomatically as possible. They concluded that 'the embarrass-
ments of the society' were largely the result of 'the imprudence
of the Council in taking a garden on so large a scale, without
having secured adequate funds either for its formation or its
maintenance'. They 'disapproved' of the way the accounts were
prepared – as well they might – and 'complained' about 'negligent
management, of profuse expenditure, and of injudicious engage-
ments'.

But the report seemed to lay less blame on Sabine for cooking
the books than on the council for believing him. Their final conclusion was reassuring, indeed almost Panglossian: 'many objects
of the society had been substantially fulfilled'. They singled out
Douglas's successful mission to collect plants in America. And
they were 'highly gratified' to say of Sabine's role that there was
not 'the slightest reason for suspecting any of the present officers
of fraud'. Whatever errors might have been committed had arisen
from 'mistaken judgment, rather than from any want of zeal'.[8]

Of course many of the members took a very different view.
They were simply outraged by Sabine's behaviour. In due course
he was forced to resign. There was talk of a formal motion to
censure him, but it was decided that this might not go down well
with either the public or the society's creditors.

In the event it was left to Loudon to put the boot in. He wrote
that the 'evil days which may be said to have fallen on Mr Sabine
are the result of his making these societies (the Horticultural and
Zoological Societies) stepping stones to his intercourse for men of
rank'. And Loudon couldn't resist a final kick at his old adversary.
How would he console himself now, 'driven, like Adam, from the
garden to the field'? He would survive, Loudon thought, because
'Nature, ever kind, has a provision for everything' and in Sabine's
case he would be protected by his 'Ignorance, or indifference, or
vanity, or self-conceit.'[9]

* * *

Meanwhile, Sabine's celebrated protégé, David Douglas, 6,000 miles away on the Pacific coast of America, was blissfully unaware of Sabine's downfall. He had reached the Columbia River in April 1831, hoping to head south to California by way of his favourite trees, the sugar pines. But the country was too disturbed for safe travel, as even Douglas recognised. He decided to wait for a boat to take him to Monterey, the headquarters of the Mexican government which nominally controlled California. Meanwhile he could revisit his old haunts, including various tributaries of the Columbia River and the hospitable forts of the Hudson Bay Company.

What Douglas could not have anticipated was that a tsunami of disease – apparently a lethal form of influenza – had suddenly swept through these valleys, killing Europeans and Indians alike. Twenty-four of the staff of the Hudson Bay Company died in a few weeks. Fort Vancouver was paralysed. Native villages, which Douglas had known to have 100 to 200 active warriors, were now 'totally gone; not a soul remains', as Douglas reported to his friend and mentor in Glasgow, Professor William Hooker. 'The houses are empty, and flocks of famished dogs are howling about, while the dead bodies lie strewed in every direction on the strands of the river'.[10]

Fortunately for Douglas he was upriver during the worst of the epidemic. In fact he found time that summer to send home seeds of two of his most important discoveries: the noble fir (*Abies procera*) and the grand fir (*Abies grandis*). Both trees had escaped the notice of Menzies thirty-five years earlier, as they grew in the mountains several hundred miles inland. Douglas had spotted them on his first trip, but failed to send seeds – or perhaps the seeds had been lost in transit. Now he was delighted to be able to grab a second chance. With its glaucous leaves, enormous cones and towering silver trunk, the noble fir was the most elegant of all the numerous species of silver firs. By contrast the grand fir was a brutal and irrepressible giant: a 300-foot-tall giant that appeared to think nothing of growing a spiky new head after losing the first one in a storm.

That autumn Douglas at last reached California, only to find the Mexican authorities suspected his talk of plant-hunting was a cover for spying. It took him till April to persuade them to grant him a passport. He was finally free to explore the delightful coast to the north and south of Monterey. And what a treasure chest of new trees he found there only waiting to be revealed to the world. His most spectacular new discovery, strange to say, proved to be a species of pine tree that grew in two insignificant groves on the cliffs south of Monterey. Menzies had failed to spot them. None of the trees were large – the tallest barely reached 50 feet – and the oldest were gnarled and twisted by the wind from the Pacific. But when Douglas's seeds reached England it became clear that this new pine (eventually called *Pinus radiata*) not only flourished in the British climate; it was also the fastest growing pine tree known to science. In due course it spread to all parts of the temperate world, welcomed both as a rampant giant for the arboretum, and as the most productive pine for forestry. With its mass of large fir cones and a huge rugged trunk it now dominates many old gardens and arboretums. As a timber tree it has swept the board in New Zealand, and parts of South Africa and South America.

And all this from Douglas's seeds taken from a handful of miserable-looking trees on the cliffs of Monterey.

Why does this miraculous species grow so well in so many countries but so badly at home? Botanists believe it moved south during the last ice age and took refuge at Monterey. When the ice melted it found itself blocked by other species, and spent the next ten thousand years trapped at Monterey – until Douglas rescued it.

Another spectacular discovery in this area, of a very different sort, had been made by Menzies in the 1790s. It was now followed up by Douglas with his usual energy. At Santa Cruz, where Spanish missionaries had built a mission, there was a gigantic grove of what Douglas took to be an evergreen Californian version of the deciduous swamp cypress (*Taxodium distichum*) In due course it turned out to be a new genus, the coast redwood (*Sequoia sempervirens*), which proved to include the tallest trees in the world. Douglas was awestruck when he walked in this forest. As he wrote to his mentor, William Hooker: 'the great beauty of the Californian vegetation is a species of *Taxodium* [sequoia] which gives the mountains a most peculiar, I was going to say awful, appearance – something that plainly tells that we are not in Europe... Some few I saw upwards of 300 feet high... I possess fine specimens and seeds also'.[11]

Sad to say, those precious seeds never reached London, or failed to germinate. And it was not until 1843, in a consignment of seeds from Russia, that the genus was finally introduced to Britain and Europe. Douglas had better luck with other trees that he had discovered. He successfully introduced two more pines from California: the digger pine (*Pinus sabiniana*) named after his patron, Joseph Sabine; and the big-cone pine (*P. coulteri*) named after his friend and travelling companion, Dr Thomas Coulter.

But one mystery remains. Douglas failed to introduce two of the most important conifers growing in the 2,000-mile-long coastal strip, stretching from Alaska and north-west Canada to Oregon and northern California. He knew these trees, yet apparently didn't choose to send their seeds back to England. The first was the western red cedar (*Thuya plicata*). This was an iconic tree for the indigenous people of the region: given a new life as a gigantic totem pole, or a war-canoe paddled by a hundred warriors. The second was the western hemlock (*Tsuga heterophyla*), not the largest but certainly the most elegant of all the conifers from the north-west. Today they are important for forestry and are the crowning glory of many European gardens. But why did Douglas scorn to send home their seeds – and leave the honour to later generations of plant explorers? Apparently he was confused by two different species of thuya and tsuga, native to *eastern* America. These had already been introduced to Europe. But they were quite separate from, and much inferior to, the two majestic species of the north-west.

Douglas enjoyed his stay in California. After so many years of privations and hardships, it must have seemed like the Garden of Eden. Despite his Presbyterian origins, he had no hang-ups about religion. He was delighted to be the guest of the Catholic monks who had established missions on the coast. He roamed the mountains of the interior with his new friend, Dr Thomas Coulter, and his small dog, Billy the terrier. By the autumn of 1831 he was ready to return to his friends at Fort Vancouver on the Columbia River. But it took him a year before he could find a boat. In the meantime he had travelled to the Sandwich Islands. It was there, at Honolulu, that he received news from London that greatly shocked him. Joseph Sabine, his employer and patron and friend, had been forced to resign – drummed out from – the Horticultural Society. Douglas panicked. Perhaps he thought that he too would be sacked – or he wished to protest at the treatment of Sabine. In September he wrote to say he was resigning his membership. From now on he would be a freelance plant hunter, relying on the network of friends (and admirers) whose hospitality he had enjoyed in recent years.

He returned to Fort Vancouver in late 1832, welcomed by his

old friend, the chief factor, John McLoughlin. He was as restless as usual. Next year he planned a daring trip to Alaska and the north-west, hoping to return to Europe by an overland route by way of eastern Siberia. But it was a vain hope. For years he had led a charmed life. Now his guardian angel seemed finally to have deserted him.

The first disaster occurred on 13 June 1833. Douglas had given up the attempt to reach Alaska by way of a network of wild mountain rivers. He was now returning from Fort George south down the Fraser River, with a servant and personal assistant, a former sailor called William Johnson, and his own terrier, Billy. At the canyon south of Fort George their small birch-bark canoe was caught and overturned in the rapids. Douglas himself was first trapped in a whirlpool, then swept downstream for an hour and forty minutes. Astonishingly, both men and Billy the terrier survived. So did most of the scientific instruments (barometer, chronometer, thermometer and so on) and the notes and charts to accompany them. But everything else was lost: food, blankets, clothes and – crucially – his diaries for the last few years, as well the seeds of 400 species of trees and plants.

The brush with death, and the loss of so much that was irreplaceable, dealt a cruel blow to Douglas. He wrote sadly to Hooker: 'This disastrous occurrence has much broken my strength and spirits'.[12] Although his good spirits soon returned, he was physically in poor shape for a man of barely thirty-four. He was blind in his right eye, with blurring in the left; he was also subject to increasingly frequent bouts of rheumatism. Nonetheless he planned to return once more to the Sandwich Islands before finding a Hudson Bay Company boat bound for England. He was fascinated by the islands. Isolation in the Pacific had given them a unique legacy of trees and other plants. And Mauna Kea, snow-covered and nearly 14,000 feet high, and the tallest of the three volcanoes, beckoned irresistibly to mountaineers.

In the event Douglas climbed all three volcanoes in a single month (January 1834), a feat probably never attempted before. On Kilauea, then the largest active volcano in the world, he climbed down into the sulphurous crater, recording a temperature of 124 °F on the surface of the lava – and burning the soles of his shoes in the process. By April he was back in Honolulu, the capital, where he had been hospitably received by the British consul, Richard Charlton. He had also made friends with a clergyman, John Diell, chaplain from a seamen's mission. Diell was anxious to see something of the volcanoes in the south of the islands, and Douglas agreed to return with him to Kilauea.

And then, for the second time, disaster struck.

Douglas was by now alone (apart from his faithful companion, Billy); Diell had stopped to see friends on the journey south. What happened on the morning of 12 July will never be known for certain. According to a cattle hunter called Ned Gurney, Douglas shared breakfast with him, and then he showed Douglas the track leading to the town of Hilo past the volcano. Gurney was a former convict, transported to Australia for stealing, and now making a career trapping wild cattle on the flanks of Kilauea, and selling the meat to the crews of passing ships. That morning, according to his story, he had warned Douglas that he had recently dug three pits to trap cattle, and these pits were close to the track. About two hours later some natives, inspecting one of the pits, were horrified to find Douglas's body inside. Apparently he had been trampled to death by an infuriated bull, which was trapped in the pit and still alive. They rushed to find Gurney, who shot the bull and rescued Douglas's body. Billy the terrier was still waiting on the track nearby, guarding his master's bundle. The corpse, wrapped in skins, was carried to the small town of Hilo, where its arrival shocked John Diell and the local missionaries. Then, partially decomposed, it was sent to the care of Richard Charlton, the British consul in Honolulu, who reported to London the news of the tragic accident.

But *was* it an accident? Had Douglas really slipped and fallen into the cattle pit? Or was he pushed? Or had he first been murdered, then dumped in the pit? Gurney was the obvious suspect. Locals believed he had murdered Douglas to get his purse, reputed to be full of dollars. The purse, if it existed, was never found. Gurney claimed that he had seen Douglas's footprints beside each of the three pits, but heavy rain had washed them away. What about the ten hideous gashes on Douglas's head? Could an elderly wild bull really have inflicted them? Before Douglas was buried in the churchyard at Honolulu, Richard Charlton arranged for a post-mortem. It was conducted by four doctors from HMS *Challenger*, anchored in the harbour at Honolulu. Their verdict: these injuries did not suggest foul play.

The belief that Douglas was murdered has persisted to this day in Hawaii, and beyond. My own view is that I think Gurney should be given the benefit of the doubt. If he had been tried for murder there would have been some powerful arguments in his defence. Cattle pits were designed to be concealed with soil and grass, and sometimes people slipped and fell into them. Douglas had notoriously poor eyesight. He was also famously curious about everything to do with nature. Perhaps, like the cat in the saying, he was the victim of his own curiosity. And there was one key witness for the defence who might have been called: Billy the terrier. Would he really have sat by the track, patiently guarding his master's bundle, while his master was murdered nearby?

* * *

Naturally the news of Douglas's death shocked his friends and admirers in Britain and America. Of course plant-hunting was known to be dangerous. But who could have dreamt that he would die like that – mangled by a wild bull, or murdered by an ex-convict? (Some people remembered that another heroic explorer, Captain Cook, had also died a cruel death in Hawaii – killed in a fracas with the natives in February 1779.) There were effusive tributes to Douglas. In 1841 a monument was erected to his memory in the churchyard of the Old Kirk at Scone; subscriptions came from many parts of the world. A brief memoir of his life was later published in an appendix to his journals. It called him 'one of our greatest and most successful exploring Botanists, to whom the whole world is deeply indebted'.[13] This theme, of how much the world's gardens owed Douglas, was repeated in the *Gardener's Chronicle* nearly a century after his death. 'There is scarcely a spot deserving the name of garden, either in Europe or in the United States, in which the discoveries of David Douglas do not form a major attraction'.

Already, in the 1830s, his discoveries and introductions were beginning to transform the character of British gardens. Nurseries, supplied with Douglas's seeds, competed to supply a new generation of collectors. And competition between collectors added a spur. The new buzzword was 'arboretum', meaning a garden of trees. The arboretums themselves took many forms. But there was no doubt who led the movement to create them: three pampered dukes, and one working man of genius.

BRANCHES

CHAPTER 12

Duke Micawber's Arboretum

To call John Loudon a 'flawed genius' may be a compliment too far. His character was certainly flawed. He was touchy and combative, unable to compromise when compromise was unavoidable. Was he a genius? He was certainly gifted with an extraordinary range of talents: a successful farmer; a pioneering landscape architect; patentee of new roof design; creator of the 'gardenesque' style; designer, conductor and publisher of numerous groundbreaking magazines and encyclopaedias. And, like his compatriot David Douglas, he pushed himself to the very limit – and beyond. For days he would work from early morning to evening, without a break, dictating the text of his latest book or magazine. His right arm had to be amputated after a botched operation, and he was in constant pain. To cope with the pain he had become addicted to laudanum, and then managed to kick the habit.

By 1830 he was on the crest of the wave. His voluminous new brainchild, the *Gardener's Magazine*, had proved a popular and commercial success. It was the first gardening magazine to reach out to the new middle class: head gardeners and hobby gardeners, wives as well as husbands, all hungry for information, and eager to exchange ideas with fellow enthusiasts.

And 1830 was the year he fell in love twice over. He made a

happy marrage with a young writer called Jane Webb. He had reviewed her novel, *The Mummy*, an early work of science fiction. (Loudon spotted her because she had invented a steam plough years before anyone else.) He also fell in love with an idea. And it was this idea which would dominate the rest of his life – and bring him to the brink of disaster. He became obsessed with arboretums.

To trace this love affair to its roots would be to follow Loudon back to his first commissions as an aspiring landscape architect. He was an admirer of the work of Humphry Repton, and Repton had pioneered the design of a small 'Arboretum of exotic trees' at Ashridge.[1] In due course Loudon was employed by Lord Mansfield at his palace of Scone in Scotland and by Lord Tullamore at his new castle at Charleville in Ireland. Loudon's ideas for Scone may have included a small arboretum, but nothing came of these ideas; at Charleville his employers adopted his plans for laying out a collection of trees, but the trees made little impact.

Perhaps Loudon became disheartened. By 1822, at any rate, he showed no interest in pursuing the subject. His masterly *Encyclopaedia of Gardening*, published that year, runs to 1,469 pages, and covers an astonishing range of subjects. There is no mention of arboretums. But something extraordinary happened to change his mind.

Perhaps it was during the affair of Sabine and the society's disastrous arboretum at Chiswick, when Loudon had his Pauline moment – when he first realised the potential of a collection of rare and exotic trees correctly arranged. Or perhaps the idea for the book came to him during a visit to Conrad Loddiges's remarkable arboretum and plant nursery at Hackney Wick. Assembled there, in alphabetical order, and compressed into barely 8 acres, were several thousand species of trees and shrubs. Most were exotics, meaning they had originated abroad; and many had only recently been introduced into Britain.

But how many landowners and gardeners had any notion of the magnificent specimens now available for planting? It was true that many were expensive to buy in plant nurseries like Loddiges. But once the fashion for exotics had spread to a wider public the price would fall rapidly. In fact Loudon was now launching a planting campaign that echoed Evelyn's campaign nearly 200 years earlier. Of course Evelyn's call was a call to *arms*: to plant trees to provide timber for the all-important navy. Loudon's aims were gentler: to use trees to make Britain a paradise.

At any rate by 1830 he was passionately committed to the idea, and had set his heart on the means to achieve it. He proposed to publish an ambitious new book entitled *Arboretum Britannicum*. This magnum opus, to be published at first in sixty-three parts, and then as a series of volumes, would involve unprecedented expense. It would cover every aspect of the life of trees in Britain, including their 'history, geography, uses, appearance, culture and propagation'. He would commission artists to draw ten-year-old specimens from the arboretum of Messrs Loddiges of Hackney. Other artists would draw portraits of full-grown trees on estates like the Duke of Northumberland's at Syon, only a few miles from London. There was only one, somewhat puritanical, limitation. No trees would be depicted if 'remarkable for their age or peculiarity of growth'.[2] In other words, ancient and beautiful trees would be banned. They could only be a dangerous distraction.

Next year, readers of the *Gardener's Magazine* were full of helpful advice for Loudon. The rector at Allesley, near Coventry, wrote to warn him that the new book would be very 'laborious' to create. To represent the character of every species of tree would be 'enormously expensive'. Other readers were more encouraging. And the best news for Loudon was that the new horticultural society at Birmingham had chosen him as the designer of a botanic garden and arboretum planned for the suburbs at Edgbaston, a couple of miles from the centre of the city.

Here was an alluring project indeed – and Loudon's opportunity at last to prove he was a landscape architect as well as a magazine editor.

In May 1831 he began the design. The trees in the arboretum were to be laid out according to the 'natural' system of Bernard de Jussieu, the French botanist whose idea for classifying trees and other plants in families was gradually supplanting the 'sexual system' (counting the 'male' stamens and 'female' pistils) created by Linnaeus. Visitors would begin their tour with the magnolia family, and then follow a circular walk by way of the limes, the maples, the horse chestnuts, the conifers and so on. The design was dominated by an enormous curvilinear-roofed glasshouse, using a cast-iron framework instead of the usual wooden one. (Loudon had in fact created a patent for a flexible cast-iron rib, an ingenious invention which he had sold to a building firm.)

And then a blow fell which sent him reeling. In September news reached Loudon that, without telling him, the Birmingham Horticultural Society had dumped his project for the circular glasshouse. It would have cost too much and might have bankrupted them. Instead they had chosen to build conventional greenhouses arranged in a straight line. Loudon was furious. He decided that 'the whole of our design [was] spoiled'. Unable to compromise, and concede that his plan vastly exceeded the budget, he insisted on washing his hands of the whole affair. His only regret was that the society had chosen to adopt his idea for a circular walk around the arboretum. He disliked 'exceedingly the idea of having our name associated in any degree, however slight, with a garden which, though it might have been one of the most perfect of it kind existing anywhere, is now bungled...'

John Tradescant the Younger. Like his father of the same name, he was gardener to Charles I and an accomplished tree hunter. Fortunately, he had green fingers without his father's daredevil streak. From America he introduced astonishing new species including the red maple, the swamp cypress and the tulip tree.

nother of Tradescant's American discoveries was the false acacia (*Robinia pseudoacacia*). This ancient specimen, with limbs held together by a corset of iron, was planted in Princess Augusta's gardens at Kew c.1760.

Mocked by Horace Walpole (who preferred the Gothic style), this ten-storey pagoda at Kew gardens was commissioned by Princess Augusta and built by Sir William Chambers in 1762. It was recently restored and re-opened to the public, complete with its eighty golden dragons.

Bishop Compton's memorial on the lawn at Fulham Palace: the corpse of a giant tree.

This great ginkgo planted in Kew gardens in 1762 as the first of this ancient species to be introduced to Britain from China or Japan. It's now known as one of Princess Augusta's 'old lions'.

Sir Joseph Banks, unofficial director of the royal gardens at Kew for forty years, and the irrepressible promoter of expeditions to discover new species in all parts of the world.

Lord Macartney, leader of the ill-fated British mission to China of 1792-1794. Organised by Sir Joseph Banks, it was supposed to secure a trade agreement and make new botanical discoveries. But all it achieved was a slap in the face from the Emperor of China.

Monkey puzzles dominating the cliffs of a valley in Patagonia. This extraordinary new species was first introduced in 1795 by Dr Archibald Menzies, the surgeon-naturalist on Captain Vancouver's expedition to the Pacific coast of north and south America. Unfortunately the two men quarrelled, and the rest of Menzies' specimens were lost

David Douglas (1799-1834), the most daring and the most successful of all plant hunters in America. But his career as an explorer ended in tragedy.

The Douglas fir, most picturesque of the giant conifers introduced by David Douglas from Canada and north-west America.

John Claudius Loudon: farmer, inventor, editor and high priest of the cult of the arboretum. Unfortunately his eight-volume masterpiece – *Arboretum et Fruticetum Britannicum* – brought him to the verge of bankruptcy.

Young Joseph Hooker with a bevy of admirers in the Sikkim Himalayas. He brought back the seeds of more than a dozen new species of rhododendrons and made the genus all the rage for British gardens and arboretums.

In 1855 Hooker named this new species *Magnolia campbellii* as a compliment to a friend, Archibald Campbell, with whom he had risked his life in the wilds of Sikkim. It's the queen of the magnolias; the largest and the most magnificent.

A picture of a party of hunters at the foot of a giant redwood (*Sequoiadendron giganteum*) discovered in 1852 in the Sierra Nevada of California. Who would be first to bring seeds back to England? The race was won by a young Cornish tree hunter, William Lobb.

The elusive 'golden larch' (*Pseudolarix amabilis*) finally collected by Robert Fortune in eastern China in 1855. 'I look upon this tree', he wrote,' as the most important of all my introductions.' It's certainly the most beautiful of the deciduous conifers.

Right & below: The bachelor Duke of Devonshire's masterly arboretum at Chatsworth in Derbyshire. It was designed and built in 1833 by his young gardener (and protégé) Joseph Paxton. Many of the trees were new species of giants introduced by David Douglas from the north-west of America.

And, to make sure they got the message, he denounced the bunglers of Birmingham in the *Gardener's Magazine*.

Fortunately for Loudon his bevy of publishing ventures gave him a decent income, although the project for the *Arboretum Britannicum* was beginning to deluge him with bills. The first step was to commission the main illustrator. He chose J. C. Sowerby, whose father had illustrated *Curtis's Botanical Magazine* and dominated English botanical illustration since the late eighteenth century. He also commissioned specialised draughtsmen to turn several thousand botanical drawings into engravings. Costs were daunting. But Loudon overcame all the obstacles like a man on a runaway horse (or like David Douglas hunting the sugar pine).

In 1833 he published a new clarion call to his readers – to the women as well as the men. In June he had revisited the arboretum of Conrad Loddiges at Hackney Wick:

To us it is perfectly astonishing that thinking men among gardeners, who know the contents of these eight acres as well as we do, should continue to plant the commonplace and monotonous mixtures in shrubberies which they now do. We wish the ladies of gentlemen's families would visit this arboretum. We should like to see mothers who have a taste for plants take up the subject; for with mothers, we are persuaded, must commence all great and lasting improvements, not only in human conduct, but in matters of taste.

Let the panorama of Niagara, now exhibiting in London, be examined, and then let those who set any value on the rich colours of the trees constituting the woods in the background of that picture say whether they would not desire to have such trees in their parks and pleasure grounds. These trees consist of oaks, birches, liquidambars, acers and a few others . . . What a treasure to those who are capable of estimating the opportunity of such a collection!... what a *paradise* this island will become, displaying, as it will do, all the trees and shrubs in the world which will grow in temperate climates.[3]

What a paradise indeed! But not just remarkable for its beauty. Loudon was passionately keen that all the great London parks – Regent's Park, Hyde Park and Greenwich Park – should be replanted as arboretums. Once this had been achieved 'these scenes of rural enjoyment... might thus be made schools of botany and gardening, and serve to encourage a taste for both subjects in the rising generation'.[4]

Two years later, in 1835, Loudon took the next expensive step before the launch of the great *Arboretum Britannicum*. He wrote personally to three thousand landowners, secretaries of horticultural societies, nurserymen and so on – to anyone in fact he believed to have arboretums or interesting collections of trees and shrubs. They were asked to fill in a form giving details of what they had planted. The preliminary results were astonishing. In 1800 there were barely half a dozen arboretums in Britain and Ireland, taking a broad definition of the term, and all of these were merely parts of a botanical garden. By 1835, according to the returns supplied to Loudon, there were no fewer than thirty-one arboretums: of which twenty-three were in England, six in Scotland and two were in Ireland. (Sadly, none were in Wales.) In addition there were sixty-nine residences which 'appeared to have extensive collections', and over two hundred had trees and shrubs which seemed 'more or less remarkable'.[5]

Why had arboretums and tree collections suddenly become all the rage? It was a question that Loudon must have asked himself. And he himself was certainly not part of the answer; he had joined the movement himself too late for that. What of the pioneers who collected trees: from Bishop Compton at Fulham

Palace in the seventeenth century to George III at Kew in the eighteenth? Of course they had been influential at the time. But Fulham's trees had long gone, and Kew's were now in a state of rapid decline. The craze for tree-collecting had arisen, it would seem, from new causes.

The first was a shift in the aesthetic demands of landowners: that is, what they expected to get from the landscape around their houses. Capability Brown had redesigned hundreds of their estates in the second half of the eighteenth century. But his smooth formulas for the new 'natural' landscape – clumps of beech and oak with a stream turned into a lake – might sooth the senses but could not excite the eye. His successor, Humphry Repton, had backed the Picturesque school of landscape, which insisted on provoking the eye with variety. This meant much more contrast in the range of trees, especially colourful trees from abroad. Hence the red oaks and scarlet maples, the purple liquidambars, the yellow-barked willows, and the glaucous pines that lit up the new landscape.

The second cause was quite simply a boom in the growth of plant nurseries, and a huge increase in the variety of trees they put on sale. Once Napoleon had been packed off to St Helena, and the endless war with France was finally ended, the world's trade in exotic seeds and plants was free to blossom. And blossom it did, expanding in leaps and bounds, with pushy new firms like Veitch of Exeter and Lawson of Edinburgh competing with the long-established firms like Lee and Kennedy of Hammersmith and Loddiges of Hackney Wick.

The third cause was the rise of the horticultural societies in many parts of Britain. And the man who deserves most credit for this was Joseph Sabine. Over his twenty-year rule as secretary he had transformed the Horticultural Society of London. Of course he eventually brought the society to the brink of bankruptcy, but at the same time he had made the society a mecca for the great and the good – and a template for new horticultural societies from Birmingham to Ireland.

Whatever the cause, Britain, Scotland and Ireland were now leading the world in the craze for collecting trees and creating arboretums.

As one would expect, private arboretums dominated the field, with nineteen out of the thirty-one arboretums recorded by Loudon. Next came those created by botanic gardens (and a single zoo, in Surrey): a total of nine, ranging from the botanic garden at Oxford, founded in the seventeenth century, to newcomers at Glasgow and Hull. Commercial nurseries completed the list: Buchanan's at Camberwell in London, Goldsworth's at Epsom and Lawson's in Edinburgh. (Loudon's favourite, Loddiges, was only reckoned a 'collection'.)

As for their layouts, the trees and shrubs in the botanic gardens were laid out systematically: that is, according to either Linnaeus's system – or the less artificial systems that followed. Most of the commercial nurseries presumably followed suit. It was the private arboretums which displayed the most exciting layouts, partly because of their much bigger scale, and partly because of the reckless ambitions of their owners.

Which brings us to the trio of tree-hungry dukes who led the pack in the first decades of the nineteenth century.

The first and most talented was George Spencer Churchill, styled the Marquis of Blandford, and from 1817 the 5th Duke of Marlborough. From his Spencer forebears he had inherited a trio of artistic gifts. He was an accomplished flute player and published one of his compositions for the harpsichord. His paintings in watercolour showed decided promise. He was happy to join his brothers and sisters in the amateur theatricals that were a feature of Christmas at Blenheim; this was the family's vast baroque palace presented to the 1st Duke of Marlborough by a grateful nation. But, despite his unusual talents, George was a sad disappointment to his parents. Of course his father, the 4th Duke, understood and may have even respected George's passion for trees and other plants. As a young man, the 4th Duke had himself commissioned Capability Brown to sweep away the great baroque gardens at Blenheim and turn a humble stream into a lake fit for an emperor. But the 4th Duke was one of Britain's greatest landowners and richest men. George was a mere eldest son – a duke-in-waiting, so to speak – and his only income was a modest allowance paid by his father.

What shocked and alienated both his parents was George's wild extravagance. He combined the collecting fever of a Renaissance prince with the self-destructive delusions of a Micawber. Collecting, like gambling, was a common addiction in the set in which he grew up. For George it was an insatiable appetite – a form of mania.

His collection of books was famous for the high prices he had paid. He had splashed out £2,260 for a 1471 edition of Boccaccio's *Decameron* – the only known copy that had escaped the bonfires in Florence lit by Savaranola. (Napoleon Bonaparte, then at the height of his power in Europe, was an unsuccessful bidder. For 170 years this was to be a highest price ever paid for a single volume.) Another irresistible trophy for his collection was the famous Bedford Missal, executed for the Duke of Bedford in 1422; it was knocked down to George for the record price of £698 5s.

He was no less extravagant in the price he paid for his trees. According to Loudon, in 1804 he owed Lee and Kennedy £15,000 for trees and shrubs – equivalent to a million and a half in today's money. Apparently this huge sum was only a small part of what he spent on his newly acquired country estate at Whiteknights near Reading.

In 1798 his father, the 4th Duke, had bought Whiteknights and leased it to George. And there he settled for much of the next two decades with his long-suffering wife, Susan, and an energetic family of five children. From the family's point of view the purchase was probably a mistake, as George was already up to his ears in debt. Worse still, he was involved in a court case which exposed him, and his family, to ridicule. He was sued for 'criminal conversation' by a close friend, Charles Sturt, who claimed £20,000 in damages. Sturt had discovered that George was having a passionate affair with Mary Anne, Sturt's wife, and was the father of Emilia, her latest baby. Sturt won the case but the jury couldn't take his claim seriously; he was only awarded £100 damages. George suffered the ignominy of having his mawkish love letters splashed across the London papers.

But the garden and park at Whiteknights blossomed; in fact they soon became famous for their exotic design. George proved to be brimming with new ideas for the place. He was an admirer of Humphry Repton, and planted his expensive collection of trees in a heightened version of the Picturesque style. Was this an arboretum? It certainly extended its meaning, and pushed out the frontiers. The novel design took the form of three separate groups of trees and other plants in the landscaped park. But that understates the complexity and exotic character of each group.

In the first, in startling contrast to the plain, classical house, were the so-called Botanic Gardens. These seemed more like a stage set for an oriental romance. Behind a screen of cedars of Lebanon and umbrella pines were a series of arches, surmounted with crescents and decorated with jasmine and *Kerria japonica*. The gardens themselves were divided into bizarre shapes: lawns and groves cut into squares and circles. Baskets of sage and begonia jostled for space with Gothic and oriental bowers. There was a 'Linnaean garden', described as a veritable 'scientific museum'. There was a magnificent fountain, in which dolphins spouted water and lizards drank it. (This was based on a design by Lady Diana Beauclerk, George's artistic – and scandalous – aunt.) And the gardens were encircled by many of George's collection of American trees and shrubs, including azaleas and rhododendrons, and two fragrant magnolias: *M. fraseri* and *M. virginiana*. Still more fragrant was their evergreen cousin, *M. grandiflora*, planted as a 'Magnolia Wall': a prodigy consisting of twelve plants, already 20 feet high and 140 feet long, which had cost £120 to buy from a dealer.

The second group, in the New Gardens, was reached by an elegant, 110-foot iron bridge across the end of the lake. At first sight it might have seemed like a woodland walk in a typically relaxed Picturesque style. Gone were the Gothic fantasies and the Chinese puzzles. The scenery seemed closer to the scenery of the English Lake District. There were groves of native trees, oaks and elm and beech. But along the sinuous trail were lurking many exotic immigrants: manna ash and chestnuts and larch from Europe, cedars from the Lebanon, trees of heaven from China, and no doubt tulip trees and hickories and gleditschias and clumps of azaleas and other trees and shrubs from eastern America.

The third group, termed the Wilderness, and dominating the south-west corner of the park, had once been as bare as the name suggested. Now it was described as embellished by 'beautiful walks, velvet lawns, exotic plantations, flowery arcades and gay pavilions.' In fact George, romantic that he was, had had his fill of the Picturesque. He found the exotic irresistible. Behind a whimsical fence of grey boulders (called the 'wethers' because the stones looked like sheep) he had created a new series of lawns and bowers and rustic seats and summer houses, with a grotto at the end of the walk. The climax was provided by an astonishing tunnel of laburnum 1,200 feet long (a fantastic feature which was to be copied many times by the garden designers of later generations). And once again he relied on his collection of American trees, like catalpas, to provide a framework for the whole design.

What is one to make of this new kind of arboretum, if indeed it was one? Contemporary opinion was sharply divided. In January 1821, four years after George had inherited his dukedom, he was visited by his neighbour the Duke of Wellington and Wellington's intimate friend Mrs Arbuthnot. The latter wrote a glowing account in her diary:

> ... we rode a large party from Stratfield Saye to see White Knights, a place belonging to the Duke of Marlborough, where there is the finest garden in England, quite beautiful. It consists of 36 acres, laid out with the greatest taste. From the profusion of evergreens the place looked quite like summer, & it is impossible to express the beauty of the American plants.[6]

Rather different views were expressed by Mary Russell Mitford, who lived nearby. She visited the garden twice: in 1807 (when the trees and shrubs were small, and much of the work was still unfinished) and in 1817 when many plants were mature. After the first visit she wrote:

> The park, as they call it ... is level, flat and uninteresting; the trees are ill-clumped; the walk round it is entirely *unvaried*, and the piece of water looks like a large duck pond, from the termination not being concealed ... the contents [of the hothouse] might be interesting to a botanist, but gave me no great pleasure. The thing I best liked was the garden in which

the conservatory is situated; the shrubs there are really very fine, particularly the azaleas, and the American honeysuckles both pink and yellow; the rhododendrons are superb...[7]

After the second visit she wrote scathingly that the 'notable fool' the Duke of Marlborough was employing Mr Hofland to 'take views at Whiteknights – where there are no views' and employing Mrs Hofland to 'write a description of Whiteknights – where there is nothing to describe'. She went on to say that the Wilderness was now closed to visitors and it was

a perfect Bluebeard's chamber; and of course all our pretty Fatimas would give their heads to get in. Well, thither have I been, and it is the very palace of False Taste – a bad French garden with staring gravel walks, make-believe bridges, stunted vine-yards, and vistas through which you see nothing. [8]

Perhaps one should not take Mary Mitford's strictures too seriously. Later she wrote a sentimental poem eulogising the garden; this was published in the Hoflands' magnum opus. She then explained herself, in a letter to a friend; 'to make myself amends for flattering the scenery in verse, I comfort myself by abusing it in prose...'[9]

A more balanced critic was John Loudon, now the high priest of the arboretum movement, who visited Whiteknights on a number of occasions. By the time of Loudon's final two visits – in 1833 and 1835 – George had inherited Blenheim Palace from his father, and Whiteknights had already passed into new ownership. Loudon noticed that many of the more exotic elements, including aquariums and hothouses, had been removed since George's time:

leaving only the shrubs and trees . . . The walks remain as they were, as do a few of the flower-beds which are left unturfed, and the whole of the beds in the botanic garden. The interest excited by the garden, notwithstanding all these changes, is still almost as great as ever; because the rare trees and shrubs which were at all times the only objects of permanent value, still remain.[10]

Loudon confirmed this tribute to George's pioneering work when Loudon returned to Whitenights two years later. Everything was now in excellent order. And George should not be blamed for some of the mistakes he had made in the choice of sites for trees and shrubs. 'Such errors in the progress of an art are unavoidable'. Thirty years before, when George had begun the arboretum, very little was known about the requirements of the rare specimens he had planted. Did they need acid or alkaline soil? Did they need shade or exposure? Despite some casualties, the great majority of George's trees were heading for a triumphant maturity.

If only the same could have been said about George himself. Whiteknights had been twice mortgaged: first for £45,000 in 1812 by his father's trustees, to pay off George's spiralling debts; and then for £50,000 in 1816 by George himself, in the expectation that he would soon inherit the Blenheim estate. By next year he was indeed the 5th Duke of Marlborough, but Blenheim couldn't save him. The ducal estates were entailed, and its trustees naturally regarded him with suspicion. He continued to spend thousands – on books and pictures and a doomed £50,000 investment in the Pantheon, as well as on Whiteknights – as if there was to be no tomorrow.

To add to his eccentric reputation, he now started an affair with an uneducated local girl of fifteen called Matilda Glover. She was installed as his mistress in the home lodge at Blenheim, and soon he was father to a thriving second family. For his own long-suffering wife, Susan (now the 5th Duchess) this was the last straw. She left Blenheim in 1819, never to return.

Meanwhile the duns and bailiffs were closing in on Duke Micawber. First to be sold at auction was his precious collection of books and pictures; many only fetched a fraction of their original cost. (Fortunately some of the most important were rescued: the delightful Bedford *Book of Hours* ended in the British Library). As for Whiteknights, in 1821 one of his creditors, the Indian nabob Sir Richard Cockerell, took formal possession of the house and estate. Sir Richard lived there for several years. Later the estate passed back to a descendant of the Englefields, the modest Catholic family who had built the house and laid out the first version of the park and garden. More than a century later the estate became the campus for the University of Reading. A few of George's magnificent trees – cedars and tulip trees and larches – still flourish there today.

George spent his last two decades living quietly with Matilda at Blenheim, alienated from his wife and legal children, but apparently proud of his second family. He had a small pension, inherited from the 1st Duke, which his creditors couldn't touch. George promised Matilda that he would marry her if his wife Susan predeceased him. But George died first – at Blenheim in 1840. One hopes that he had finally come to terms with reality. Did he find comfort in the thought of his achievements – and that, despite all his debts to his creditors, the world owed him still more for his pioneering work at Whiteknights?

But now we must leave the 'profligate duke', as he later became known, and pass to a man different from him in almost every way, except that he, too, was a duke and he, too, had created a fine arboretum.

CHAPTER 13

A Tale of Two Dukes

No one could have guessed that John Russell would, one day, create a great ducal garden. He seemed to lack the qualities needed to make a successful squire, let alone a successful duke. He was shy and somewhat withdrawn. Much could be explained by a difficult childhood. He was the second son of parents who died tragically young, his father from a fall from a horse, his mother from consumption. So he was an orphan before he was two. He was brought up by his paternal grandparents, the 4th Duke and Duchess of Bedford, who had little time for him and his elder brother. At first they expected he would follow a military career. But he married before he was twenty – to Lord Torrington's daughter, Georgiana Byng – and was then installed as MP for Tavistock, one of his family's rotten boroughs.

Like most dukes, and their families, Bedford was a loyal Whig. And he was more. He voted in the Commons with the radical Whigs led by Charles James Fox. He joined the Society of the Friends of the People, and was an unselfish advocate for parliamentary reform (which could have meant the end of rotten boroughs like his own – but didn't). Like other leading Foxites, he opposed the Peninsular War, and argued for peace with Napoleon. But the war continued, and it seemed it would never end.

In 1801 Georgiana had died suddenly, leaving him with three

young sons. Her death was followed the next year by that of his elder brother, Francis, the 5th Duke of Bedford, who died un-married. So the dukedom fell, unexpectedly, into John's lap. And with the dukedom, and a seat in the Lords, came a cornucopia of possessions, with income to match: bricks and mortar in London, like the great Bedford estates in Bloomsbury and Covent Garden, agricultural estates in Devonshire and other counties, and above all the Woburn estate in Bedfordshire, with acres galore, including the famous abbey with its romantic garden and parkland.

Four years later John Bedford was chosen by Lord Grenville to serve as Irish lord lieutenant in the short-lived 'ministry of all the talents'. Although clearly a lightweight, Bedford knew how to make friends in Ireland; he persuaded Grenville to take steps to conciliate Catholics by ending discrimination against Catholic of-ficers in the army. But the king said no – and Grenville's ministry collapsed.

Meanwhile Fox had died at the age of fifty-seven, his bloated face and figure mocked by every cartoonist. And the years ahead were to offer no joy to the Whigs but two decades in the wilder-ness. If John Bedford had been keen to succeed in politics, he had backed the wrong horse.

The truth was that, in middle age, he was much more suited to life as a country gentleman. He enjoyed collecting pictures and statues. He loved trees and plants and was an amateur student of botany. By now he had married again – a second Georgiana, daughter of the Duke of Gordon – and his high-spirited new duchess had extravagant tastes. She hatched a second family of ten children. The shy, rather lonely duke was soon a family man, well reconciled to pillow fights and games of blind man's buff. At parties the duchess pelted her guests with apples and oranges. When the shooting season opened, she organised spectacular *battues.* In 1820 Charles Greville recorded in his diary 'the *chasse* was brilliant, in five days we killed 835 pheasants'.[1]

John Bedford himself was not a great shot. (He had once fought a duel with the enormously fat Duke of Buckingham, but somehow missed even that target.)

In fact he was a man of peace, probably happiest when talking to his head gardener. By the late 1820s he was devoting more and more of his time – and money – to redesigning the garden at Woburn.

What had inspired him? Of course there was the new fashion for collecting trees, promoted by Loudon in his *Gardener's Magazine* from the mid-1820s. Rivalry is always a spur to collectors. John Bedford had numerous dukes to compete with, including the 'Bachelor Duke' – the 4th Duke of Devonshire – who owned Chatsworth and other great estates in Britain and Ireland. There was also the boom in plant nurseries, and the corresponding bonanza of new trees and plants now on the market, mostly introductions from America.

Now John Bedford had inherited an estate at Woburn once famous for its evergreens. Two generations earlier, in the heyday of Capability Brown, his grandfather, the 4th Duke, had created a new kind of landscape. This differed radically from the ones designed by Brown. Instead of polished clumps of beech and oak, the duke had created an early version of a pinetum. A series of grassy rides criss-crossed 100 acres of Scots pines either side of a new lake. The rides led to a collection of spiky, exotic conifers: Weymouth pines, Norway spruce, cedars of Lebanon, silver firs from the Alps, cypresses from the Mediterranean, as well as well-known evergreens like arbutus, holly and ilex. Later in the century Humphry Repton had tidied up this precursor of the pinetum, and improved the shape of the lake. So this was now the challenge for John Russell, the 6th Duke. Could he redesign the pleasure ground beside the house with as bold and original a scheme as his grandfather's scheme for the Evergreens in the 1750s?

The Duke's new plans were not short of novelties: a camellia house, a Chinese dairy, a greenhouse for pelargoniums, a menagerie and so on. But the most spectacular feature was to be the new arboretum, which formed a twisting, two-mile circuit around the pleasure ground.

Fortunately the duke himself, and his remarkably accomplished head gardener, James Forbes, have left us a very complete account. Forbes was born in Scotland, like so many of the more enterprising head gardeners, and took over the garden at Woburn in the late 1820s. By 1832 his expertise was rewarded by his election to a fellowship of the prestigious Linnean Society. Next year he produced a masterwork: a 440-page, leather-bound book (complete with seventeen pages of index) entitled *Hortus Woburnensis*. This trumped all previous attempts to describe a British garden – even multi-volume works like W. T. Aiton's latest edition of *Hortus Kewensis*. Forbes catalogued 'upwards of Six Thousand Ornamental Plants Cultivated at Woburn Abbey'. Each plant was allotted one of twenty-four abbreviations to describe it, including 'H.S.' for 'Hardy Shrub, or small Tree' and 'H.T.' for 'Hardy Tree, which attains a considerable height'.[2] Of course the trees represented only a small proportion of the plants: about 330, according to a rough count, concentrated in thirteen separate genera. But these included some of the finest and rarest specimens in the country. Forbes not only listed the current Latin names for each of the 6,000 plants, identified by genus and species; he also listed, in abbreviated form, an astonishing amount of botanical information: the common name, the form of leaves, the colour of the flowers, the country of origin, the year of introduction and the type of soil required.

And Forbes did very much more. With twenty-six maps and illustrated plates, he conducted readers around the novelties that the duke and head gardener were now in process of creating. Let him guide us to the new arboretum:

> The main walk, which sweeps round the greater part of the Pleasure Ground, is nearly two miles in length... The American Banks cover upwards of an acre of ground, the whole being richly planted with the numerous species and varieties of Rhododendrons, Azaleas etc. Along the centre are planted various sorts of holly, always pleasingly conspicuous by its glossy foliage. Opposite this bank is the collection of *Pines* and other *genera*, belonging to the *Coniferae tribe*, among which may be seen the *Pinus Douglassii* [*Pseudotsuga menziesii* or Douglas fir], *lambertiana* [sugar pine], *ponderosa* (western American pine), *Gerardii, and Araucaria imbricaria* [monkey puzzle], *Araucaria brasiliana* [Brazilian monkey puzzle], *Cedrus deodara* [deodar cedar] *etc*... Adjoining the collection of Pines is situated the *Salictum* [willow garden], consisting of the most numerous species and varieties of *Salices*... At a short distance from the Willow Garden is a clump of Cedars, one of which measures 62 feet in length of clear straight timber, and is certainly one of the handsomest timber trees of the kind in the country... In a clump, towards the top of the Pleasure Ground, is the collection of American Oaks... From this part of the grounds there is a beautiful view of nearly twenty miles extent, finely varied with wood, hill, dale and other elements of the Picturesque. Hence the walk winds towards the Menagerie, passing through different groups of Forest Trees... with the species of each genus grouped together, whereby they are much more readily distinguished from each other.[3]

What did John Loudon make of all this – Loudon who was the high priest and arbiter of taste in this new world of arboretums? It's clear from Forbes's account that his and the duke's plan for the arboretum followed Loudon's own recommendations in two important ways. First, it was laid out as a 2-mile *circuit* of the pleasure ground. Second, the trees and shrubs were arranged by genus, and not laid out merely artistically, as you might lay out a woodland garden. Loudon had denounced Joseph Sabine for failing on both counts when Sabine laid out the Horticultural Society's arboretum at Chiswick. But, strange to say, Loudon himself is tantalisingly silent about this great new arboretum at Woburn. In 1836 he commended the duke's work, it must be said, with the generous words: 'the next greatest improvements made in private gardens are those at Woburn Abbey'.[4] But he gives no details of the arboretum. Could he have been a trifle jealous? Perhaps his silence was a mere accident; the *Gardener's Magazine* covered a vast range of subjects at home and abroad. But probably the main reason for not mentioning Woburn's arboretum was simple enough. Loudon had decided to use another duke and another arboretum to promote his passion for arboretums. The duke was John Bedford's rival, the 'Bachelor Duke', alias the 6th Duke of Devonshire, and his new arboretum at Chatsworth was, according to Loudon, the model for the world to copy.

Loudon's admiration for Chatsworth was, it must be said, of very recent origin. It followed an unexpectedly friendly letter to the duke in 1836, inviting his gardener to write an account of the new arboretum at Chatsworth and send it for publication in the *Gardener's Magazine*. Earlier he had mocked the duke and all his works in the pages of the same magazine. His motives for denouncing him were straightforward enough.

In 1831 the duke's gardener, Joseph Paxton, had launched a new gardening magazine of his own, called the *Horticultural*

Register. Paxton aimed to take a bite out of the same market as Loudon had exploited with his now well established *Gardener's Magazine*, although the new magazine was cheaper and more limited in scope. Loudon lost no time in attacking this interloper who cut into his own profits. He hit Paxton where it would hurt most: in the design and management of Chatsworth. The place had 'always appeared to us as unsatisfactory'.[5] He disapproved of the squareness of the building (today recognised as a baroque masterpiece), and the way the waterworks were scattered in the pleasure ground. The baroque cascade should be converted into a waterfall. As for Paxton's own contribution, Loudon mocked the way Paxton had mixed ornamental plants with fruit and vegetables in the kitchen garden, and denounced the ragged box hedges and the rotten wood in the forcing houses.

Paxton made a dignified reply in the next issue of the *Register*. He reproved Loudon. 'Did you not say to the young man who accompanied you round, that Chatsworth was altogether the finest place you had seen on your travels? How then is Chatsworth so unsatisfactory a place?'[6]

Two years later Paxton took another bite out of Loudon's market. He launched a new botanical monthly, the *Magazine of Botany and Register of Flowering Plants*. Predictably, Loudon damned it in his own magazine. 'To botanists it is of no use, as the plants are neither new, nor described with scientific accuracy.'[7] But the new monthly was a commercial success, and, like its sister magazine, continued to cut into Loudon's profits.

Who was this thorn in Loudon's side – young, energetic, brilliant, Joseph Paxton? And how did he become the Duke of Devonshire's closest friend? The story is an odd one.[8]

In 1826 one of the young gardeners working in the arboretum of the Horticultural Society at Chiswick had a chance encounter with the owner of the house next door. The owner was William

Spencer Cavendish, 6th Duke of Devonshire, one of the richest landowners in Europe. One of his London houses, the magnificent villa designed by William Kent, adjoined the society's gardens. The young gardener was twenty-three-year-old Joseph Paxton. He was largely self-educated, as his father, a farm labourer on the Woburn estate, had died when he was a child. The two men met, it appears, when the duke let himself into the society's gardens. The duke was swept off his feet by the young gardener; clearly they shared a passionate interest in plants. The duke needed a new head gardener at Chatsworth who would bring exceptional energy to the job. On the spur of the moment he offered the job to Paxton.

The partnership that ensued was to transform the lives of both men – as well as the landscape at Chatsworth. Indeed Paxton, the working-class hero who was to be the master-builder of the Great Exhibition, ended his career even better known than the duke. (Today he might be called a hero from zero.) For the next fifteen years, however, Paxton focused all his energy on redesigning the gardens at Chatsworth.

His first, pioneering scheme meant creating an 8-acre pinetum beside the pond on the upper terrace of the pleasure ground. This was, in a sense, merely a dress rehearsal for the still more ambitious plan for an arboretum; the pinetum would be one piece in that jigsaw. It certainly delighted the duke. To collect a full range of pines and other conifers, Paxton scoured the London nurseries, and the gardens of his former employers, the Horticultural Society. The cost was of little concern to the duke, who was spending a fortune on classical statues, old master pictures and Sir Jeffry Wyattville's additions to the house. What was important to him was to acquire rarities. Like his rival, the Duke of Bedford, he had managed to get some of the latest conifers introduced from the north-west coast of America by that daredevil David Douglas. These included the Douglas fir itself (*Pseudotsuga menziesii*), the sugar pine and the western yellow pine (*Pinus lambertiana* and *P. ponderosa*). In America they were giants; at Chatsworth a few feet tall at the very most. Some were bought as seeds; others as seedlings barely a foot high. Indeed the duke recorded that the Douglas fir had come up from London 'in Mr. Paxton's hat'. But it was a beginning.

About the same time Paxton was given another project by the duke which would have defeated a lesser man. The duke had bought a large weeping ash from a plant nursery near Derby, 28 miles north of Chatsworth. The tree's roots were 28 feet in diameter and its pendulous branches radiated 38 feet from one side of the trunk to the other. It weighed about 8 tons. Could he dig it up and move it to Chatsworth? Paxton was certain that he could. Others were equally certain he would fail. Paxton took an army of labourers from Chatsworth – about forty men with a team of horses – and a new tree-moving machine specially designed for the job. At the first attempt the chains snapped. Paxton added stronger ones. The tree began its journey south, squeezing through the toll gates in its path. The Duke waited at Chatsworth in a state of high excitement. After four days it reached the park gates, which had to be lifted from their hinges to allow the tree to proceed. The duke met the tree by the new north entrance built by Wyattville. He declared that Paxton had performed a miracle. With the help of no fewer than 450 labourers, a huge hole was dug and the tree's roots bedded down in its new home in the courtyard facing the original house. It has stood there, apparently content enough, to the present day.

Incongruous as it might appear, the two men – millionaire duke and the gardener he employed for a modest wage – had now formed a kind of partnership. They shared much more than a passionate interest in gardening and landscape. They had become extremely close friends. Of course each had a private life of their own. The duke had a mistress, Eliza Warwick (although the affair was near its end) and a busy social life in London as well as at Chatsworth. Paxton was happily married to Sarah, the housekeeper's clever niece, and soon they had a family of three girls and a boy. But the duke was often depressed, and a prey to hypochondria. Paxton's infectious high spirits and seemingly inexhaustible energy transformed the duke's life. He was captivated. Paxton taught him to be fascinated by his own garden. For his part he was delighted to show Paxton the world.

In 1833 he took him on a coach tour of great gardens of England: Lady Grenville's at Dropmore, Earl Spencer's at Althorp, the royal gardens at Windsor and so on. (This ended rather suddenly when the duke sprained his knee.) Next year Paxton was whisked off to Paris to see the Louvre and the Palais Royal, followed by a tour of the private gardens at Versailles and St Cloud. Paxton was overwhelmed by the glasshouses at the Jardin des Plantes; he had never seen glass used so imaginatively. But the famous waterworks at Versailles disappointed him. No doubt he thought he could do better at Chatsworth. Still, Paxton revelled in these foreign trips with the duke. He had left his wife Sarah to take over his role in his absence: calling in the men from the woods, making sure the gardens were clean and tidy, gravelling the new east front of the house. He was bursting with the news of what he had seen. 'I have come so far,' he wrote to her, 'and seen so much that it seems an age since I left home'.[9]

He had indeed come far. Perhaps it was this trip to Paris that inspired both Paxton and the duke to try their hands at making Chatsworth the English Versailles – or to go one better. Versailles was a great baroque garden, full of statues and other wonders, but the choice of trees was conventional. At Chatsworth, Paxton and the duke planned to make a giant arboretum full of rarities – in space enough to plant every species of tree that would grow in the British climate. The first step was to follow up the creation of that small pinetum by the pond on the upper terrace. They would build a mile of new roadway linking the seventy-five families, and the two thousand species and varieties of trees and shrubs that would form the arboretum.

Progress was made at breakneck speed. (Did they look over their shoulders at work on the Duke of Bedford's arboretum at Woburn?) In April 1835 an army of labourers descended on the terraces north of the formal gardens and great cascade. Most of the ground was occupied by a forest of veterans: centuries-old oak and other hardwoods. Few were spared. Paxton had decided to clear 40 acres for the new arboretum, and the timber from these veterans was worth good money. Soon the hillside was a mass of tree stumps and mud – but the duke was in his element. 'I don't mind in the least how dirty it may be, I shall be glad to find the pleasure ground up to my neck in mud all over'.[10]

Meanwhile Paxton was faced by the exhausting task of collecting up the two thousand species and varieties of trees and shrubs needed for planting, many of which were extremely rare. Some of them came from the Horticultural Society's garden in Chiswick; others, no doubt, from the duke's own garden next door. Loddiges and the other London nurseries had a bonanza of sales to the duke. And fortunately Paxton had many friends and admirers. William Hooker, the Professor of Botany at Glasgow, promised to write to his far-flung correspondents to ask them to send plants to Chatsworth. By early June the vast arboretum had taken shape. Predictably, the duke was overwhelmed. 'It is transcendent', he wrote in his diary.[11] He had never doubted his faith in Paxton's abilities. But this was extraordinary. Paxton explained that the entire arboretum – roadway, plants and planting – had cost nothing to create. The timber from the felling of the veteran oaks had paid for the lot.

Which brings us back to that unexpectedly friendly letter from Loudon in 1836, inviting his old enemy Paxton to write a piece on the arboretum in the *Gardener's Magazine*.

Somehow a rapprochement had been arranged. No doubt Loudon had finally realised that they must bury the hatchet, as the millionaire Duke of Devonshire and his remarkable young gardener were unbeatable. But the main reason for Loudon's volte-face was that in 1836 he learnt that the new arboretum at Chatsworth was the most complete and comprehensive in Britain. The Duke of Bedford's at Woburn followed the principles specified by Loudon – but only up to a point. His arboretum included a mere thirteen genera of trees, and the trees were arranged in scattered groups, obedient to the demands of the Picturesque rather than given space as individual specimens. His rival the Duke of Devonshire had planted no fewer than fifty genera of trees, and included more than five hundred species. These trees were laid out as individual specimens, exactly as Loudon had prescribed. All this was made clear when Paxton submitted his article to the *Gardener's Magazine*, complete with a map showing the position of every individual species.

Paxton's article and map were milestones in the history of landscape and garden design. The reader was invited to follow in his footsteps the twisting, mile-long trail through the new arboretum. Small trees and shrubs hugged the trail; big trees were given plenty of elbow room. First on the left was the small group of *Magnoliaceae* (the magnolia family, which includes the tulip tree). There were nine species in the family, mainly from America, and some exciting varieties, especially the newly created oriental hybrid, *Magnolia x soulangeana* (today the best known of all magnolias). *Tiliaceae* (the lime family) straddled the path ahead: only two species, big-leaved and small-leaved, with twelve varieties. Next came one of the largest and most decorative of all families: *Aceraceae*, the maple family, a rich haul of thirty-one species mainly from Europe.

But the most colourful members were two Americans, the red maple (*Acer rubrum*) and the silver maple (*Acer saccharinum*) And two more had recently arrived from the north-west coast of America, introduced by David Douglas: that future giant, the big-leaved maple (*Acer macrophyllum*) and its delicate companion, the wine-dark vine maple (*Acer circinatum*). Up the slope to the pond and the 55-strong 'pine' collection either side (many of which are now allocated to other genera). This was the home of the original pinetum, enlarged as new plants became available. It now included four remarkable species introduced by David Douglas shortly before his death – the bright green Monterey pine (*Pinus radiata*) the glaucous noble fir (*Abies procera*), the pushy grand fir (*Abies grandis*) and the spiky Sitka spruce (*Picea sitchensis*). All four species were soon to be recognised as the superstars of the world's forests. But at Chatsworth in 1836 they were barely taller than a child.

On across the upper terrace, past the sophoras and the cherries and the service trees, to the boomerang-shaped plantation of ash, credited with thirty-three species, making it one of the largest genera on the trail. Beyond were the oaks, forty-six species of them, many from America, including those collected by the unfortunate John Banister when he was working for Bishop Compton. The walk ended with a series of genera that could only claim a single species: the American swamp cypress (*Taxodium distichum*) with its feathery, pale green plumage; the mournful silver birch (*Betula pendula*) from Britain and Europe; and finally the miraculous ginkgo snatched from the gardens of China – the tree with leaves shaped like a butterfly's wing, and a pedigree that stretched back millions of years before the age of the dinosaur.

This was the arboretum – the most comprehensive and ambitious in Europe, and nearly complete after only four months' work – the model arboretum that Loudon was now recommending to the readers of the *Gardener's Magazine*. He had a further reason for admiring the project. Paxton had explained that the garden at Chatsworth, unlike the garden at Woburn, was open to the public every day of the year.

For Loudon, with his radical views on society, this was decisive. Now he could 'rejoice in the idea of an arboretum... at such a place as Chatsworth, one of the most magnificent in England... with a degree of liberality and impartiality that can never be sufficiently commended, open every day in the year, and shown to all persons, rich and poor, without exception'. He forecast that visitors to the arboretum, who might have gone there to see the famous waterworks, would come away with 'the first germs of a taste for trees' which would 'increase with every opportunity... for its gratification'.[12]

Paxton and the duke must have been delighted. They were both highly competitive, and felt they had inflicted a crushing defeat on their rival, the Duke of Bedford. Although the arboretum at Woburn had been started in 1833, it was apparently still half unfinished. As Paxton told his wife Sarah, 'I went to Woburn and what do you think old John Bedford has been at? Why, making an arboretum this winter in emulation of the one at Chatsworth, it will be a miserable failure... I suppose they are jealous of us...'[13] For his part, the Duke of Devonshire confided to his diary that Forbes, the gardener at Woburn was 'a very consequential stupid fellow – very different from my gardener I think'.[14] No doubt Paxton would have been of the same opinion.

When Loudon recommended Chatsworth as a model

arboretum, he must have recalled his own wretched experiences in designing an arboretum for Birmingham. Perhaps he had been too hasty in washing his hands of the whole business. (Without a word, they had rejected his revolutionary plan for a conservatory with a curved glass roof. The cost, they later claimed, would have been prohibitive.) But the chance was not lost for ever: the chance that he, the high priest of the arboretum movement, should actually create one himself. In 1839 a wealthy factory owner and philanthropist in Derby, Joseph Strutt, invited Loudon to design a 'public garden of recreation for the general population of Derby.'[15] There was no mention of an arboretum in the brief. But Loudon lost no time in explaining its attractions to Mr Strutt.

A 'general botanic garden' would be too expensive to create and to manage. A 'mere composition of trees and shrubs with turf' like a common pleasure ground would become 'insipid after being seen two or three times'. An arboretum was the answer – meaning 'a collection of trees and shrubs, foreign and indigenous', hardy enough to endure life in Derby, 'with the names placed to each.'[16]

In short it would have all the 'ordinary beauties' of a pleasure ground. But each specimen would have its name, origins, date of introduction and so on, inscribed on a brick 'tally'. So the walkers in the garden would be induced to study the history of each species, its uses here and abroad, its appearance in the different seasons, and the various inspiring associations connected with it.

The site that Strutt was offering to give to the town had several advantages. It was very central (a few hundred yards from the new station), it was sheltered by a belt of healthy trees, and the soil was fertile and reasonably well drained. It was about half a mile long and shaped like a leg of mutton. But it was small and rather cramped – a mere 11 acres including the shelter belt – the air (like the air of all industrial towns at that date) was heavy with soot, and the water table was too near the surface to risk any serious landscaping.

Still Loudon grabbed the chance with both hands. As a man of the people, Loudon was delighted with Strutt's insistence that there would be no entry charge for those who came on Sunday (and one weekday). On other days charges would be minimal. Strutt was also keen that parts of the ground should be left unplanted so that 'tents may be fixed, or parties may dance etc'.[17] Loudon had no problem with that – indeed he welcomed the idea that an arboretum could be the place where people would go to enjoy themselves. Of course the new curator and his staff would have to ensure people behaved responsibly. And he had commissioned two picturesque Tudor Revival lodges, one at either end of the arboretum, where the public could sit and relax, unpack their picnic, read a copy of *Arboretum Britannicum* – or simply head for the public conveniences.

Loudon completed his new arboretum with astonishing speed. Nearly eight hundred trees and shrubs, costing a mere £79 18s, were planted that first season 1839–40, mainly acquired from a single plant nursery, with additions from a Canterbury nursery and the Royal Horticultural Society in Chiswick. There were no duplicates; that would have suited the Picturesque style and a mere woodland garden. Each of the twenty-six families of trees and shrubs was represented by one or more of the 180 genera, and each genus by one or more of the 913 species and varieties. And all were arranged 'scientifically': that is, in a specific order according to the 'natural system' of Bernard de Jussieu. This was the new convention promoted by Loudon and already followed by Paxton and the duke at Chatsworth.

Where Loudon broke new ground was in the way the trees were planted. He had always been shocked by the sight of trees buried so deep at planting that they looked like mere posts. It was the 'ramification' – the display of the surface roots joining the trunk – which gave young trees a 'very great beauty'. To prevent the 'monstrous and unnatural' practice of deep planting, Loudon instructed the gardeners at Derby to plant all the trees on little hills. He also laid out a network of gravel paths through the arboretum, with the main broad walk through the centre, with another broad walk intersecting it, and a sinuous path surrounding the whole garden. This circuit had been hidden behind a series of new ridges or mounds, made to look natural. The ridges would conceal walkers using the circuit from those on the broad walk, and make the small arboretum *feel* much larger than it was.

These were Loudon's plans, and they delighted not only Joseph Strutt but were received with acclamation by the good people of Derby. Thousands came to celebrate the inauguration. One feature, however, of Loudon's grand design was already controversial. He had made the arboretum 'comprehensive': to include not only all the species of trees and shrubs hardy in Derby's climate, but hundreds of *varieties* of those species. Could the 11 acres really provide enough room for all these 1,013 plants? At Chatsworth Paxton had needed 40 acres for a similar number of plants – with acres more ready for future expansion. Would the Derby Arboretum soon be a victim of its success, choked with mighty oaks and towering elms? Loudon had crammed in sixteen species of oaks and six species of elms, not to speak of forty-one species of pines, spruce, firs and cedars. And what about the botanical discoveries of the future? How on earth could room be found for them?

Loudon's answer was blunt, and his ruthlessness must have shocked many of his new admirers. No tree should be allowed to exceed 40 or 50 feet in height. It should be felled forthwith. As for making room for new botanical discoveries, it would be best to avoid adding to the collection for the next fifteen or twenty years – and then 'take up the whole and re-plant'.[18] In other words he was recommending a massacre of the entire collection in order to start again with a 'tabula rasa' or clean sheet.

Ladies at the Derby arboretum

Of course Loudon had more pressing concerns. The publication in 1838 of his magnum opus, *Arboretum Britannicum*, had resulted in glowing reviews – and financial disaster. He had insisted on expanding the book to no less that eight volumes, of which four were complete with illustrations drawn and engraved for the project. This had raised the cost to £10 a set (£1,000 in today's money): enough to exclude all but the richest collectors. He now owed the printers £10,000.

Poor Loudon, and his dreams of perfection! To add to his

troubles, he was in constant pain. Lung cancer was diagnosed. By 1843 it was clear he was dying. Yet he still worked absurdly long hours on the *Gardener's Magazine*, with the help of his long-suffering family, his wife Jane and their daughter. By heroic efforts they reduced the debt to £2,000. In December of that year he dictated a final editorial – and died in Jane's arms.

Meanwhile the world that Loudon knew had been startled by a new and alarming crisis. The royal gardens at Kew, once the most celebrated in the kingdom, had been in decline for many years. Could they now be saved by an Act of Parliament? Or was this the end of the road?

CHAPTER 14

Sir William to the Rescue

Early in February 1840 John Lindley was invited to attend a crucial meeting of the Treasury: to hear the government's plans for the royal gardens at Kew.

The air in London was thick with rumour and innuendo. Lindley was Professor of Botany at London University and assistant secretary of the Royal Horticultural Society (and the man whose damning evidence had led to the sacking of Joseph Sabine a decade earlier). What he was now told by the Treasury spokesman must have confirmed his worst suspicions. In order to save money, the government was planning to abolish the Botanic Garden at Kew. They would demolish the glasshouses and dispose of the trees and other plants to some suitable 'public body' who would allow the public access to them at least two days a week. The Treasury favoured the Royal Horticultural Society, whose garden at Chiswick would make an admirable new home for the plants.

Of course Lindley was astounded. Only two years before he had been commissioned by the government to lead a working party to report on the management of all five royal gardens including Kew. Lindley's report on Kew seemed to have been welcomed by the government. Far from recommending its abolition, he had proposed it should be greatly expanded. Reborn as a national botanic garden, it would serve as the hub of a network of British botanic gardens stretching from Africa to Australia. (It had originated with Sir Joseph Banks, this idea for an imperial mission.) Lindley now showed his mettle. He warned Sir Robert Peel he would have the matter raised in Parliament. And he lobbied furiously against the Treasury's cost-cutting.

He soon forced the Treasury to climb down, and repelled the attempts by an ambitious rival, the Royal Botanic Society, to grab the Kew plants and create a national botanic garden in Regent's Park. But a big question remained. If Kew had been rescued, and was to be reborn as a jewel in the nation's crown, who was to be its director? Was it to be Lindley himself – or his old friend and new rival, Sir William Hooker, Professor of Botany at Glasgow?

It was now that the proverbial meanness of the Treasury proved an unexpected godsend to Hooker. Both men had been educated at Norwich Grammar School, and both were now distinguished professors who could match unchallenged scholarship with phenomenal energy. In one respect Hooker had the edge on Lindley; he was more diplomatic. People said he could charm birds out of trees (and perhaps trees out of the Treasury). But Lindley was the candidate with the most powerful backers. These included the MPs who had chosen him to write the report on Kew two years earlier, and the 'Bachelor Duke' from Chatsworth, the 6th Duke of Devonshire, who had the ear of Lord Melbourne, the current prime minister. Hooker's backers, by contrast, included Devonshire's rival, the current Duke of Bedford. But John Bedford cut little ice at Westminster. In any case, he died quite unexpectedly in October 1839, while the contest was still unresolved.

It turned out that the Treasury was only proposing to pay the new director a derisory salary of £300 a year – plus a housing allowance of £200. Lindley dug in his toes: he needed at least £1,000 a year. This tipped the balance decisively in favour of Hooker, and he was handed the keys of his new empire at Kew on 3 April 1841. But 'empire' was hardly the word.

Kew was more like a ghost from the past. Twenty years after the deaths of both Joseph Banks and George III, it was barely recognisable. The ten major glasshouses were coated in soot, and close to collapse. One of the palm trees had threatened to burst through the roof. The botanic garden, and the pioneering arboretum, once famous, were now mere shadows of themselves. There were few labels on the plants, no library, no herbarium, and even the records had vanished – cheekily removed by the last director, W. T. Aiton.

Fortunately Hooker was blessed with irrepressible optimism. And the Kew that was now reborn to Hooker's design is recognisably the Kew we know today.

First, and by far the most important, was the fight for more space. Every part of the 11-acre Botanic Garden was hopelessly cramped. The 5-acre arboretums was now a midget in comparison with the great ducal arboretums at Woburn and Chatsworth. It was also a jungle. Yet only the other side of a fence was a 200-acre pleasure ground, and the famous series of temples and other buildings designed by Chambers and Kent.

Second, was a desperate need for modern glasshouses, including a full-size palm house, like the magnificent 'Great Stove' designed and built by Paxton at Chatsworth. Other buildings – library, herbarium and so on – would have to wait their turn. But a new palm house could be the symbol Kew needed, and an icon that would attract the public from far and wide.

In 1844 Hooker succeeded in grabbing room enough for a large palm house in the pleasure ground close to the pond. But who would design it? One of Hooker's strengths was that he knew his own limitations. Somehow he induced the government to pay for Richard Turner, a young Irish ironmaster and engineer, to design and build the new palm house. Decimus Burton, the well-known architect, was invited to supervise the work; it was Burton who had supervised Paxton's work at Chatsworth. But the iconic qualities of the palm house came from Turner's pen – and Turner's ironworks. Here was a functionalist giant, its ribs carved from wrought iron, an inflated balloon of yellow glass, a hero before its time. (But, sad to say, it cost more than Turner had anticipated and left him close to bankruptcy.)

A new arboretum at Kew demanded even more space than a new palm house. In fact it meant Hooker needed to grab most of the rest of the original pleasure grounds. By 1845 Hooker had somehow succeeded. To design the new arboretum, he then hired a young landscape architect called William Nesfield, who would be supervised by Decimus Burton. Nesfield might have seemed an odd choice. He was a designer of formal gardens, which were now, after nearly a century, coming back into fashion. He knew about parterres and *pattes d'oie* and vistas and statuary – and, what was more important, he knew about Picturesque gardens. But he knew next to nothing about taxonomy, to which Hooker had devoted more than thirty years of his life.

Fortunately both men were in agreement about the need to link both projects, the new palm house and the new arboretum. At present there was an ugly wire fence running in a great arc from the Temple of Bellona to the path west of the Orangery. Once this fence had been removed, the palm house would be free to let loose three magnificent vistas. Of course many trees would have to be felled (or, like a forty-year-old Lucombe oak, laboriously re-sited) to create the vistas. Then the eye would leap across the parterres of the palm house to the new boundaries of the arboretum.

The first vista would lead to the famous pagoda built by Chambers eighty years earlier. The second would carry the eye across the Thames to the distant battlements of Syon House, the palatial estate of the Duke of Northumberland. (And Nesfield explained that an obelisk by the Thames path would add emphasis to this vista.) The third vista was shortest: barely half a mile long. Here the eye was to focus on one of the monumental trees planted by Capability Brown – a cedar of Lebanon only seventy years old and already a young giant.

In his design for the arrangement of the trees and shrubs in the new arboretum Nesfield was even more radical. His brief from Hooker was conventional enough. This was not to be a mere woodland garden. The trees and shrubs were to be individual specimens, with the species and genera grouped in families. They were to be displayed for their botanical interest as well as for their artistic value. This was the 'systematic' or 'scientific' arrangement that had been followed by James Forbes at Woburn, by Joseph Paxton at Chatsworth and John Loudon at Derby. But Nesfield believed that science could exact too heavy a price. Somehow a new way of reconciling art and science must be found. His solution: by all means group the trees by families, but first create a series of sinuous *glades* to provide a picturesque setting for each family, and arrange the plants accordingly.

To his credit, Hooker, backed by Decimus Burton, accepted this novel approach. Many of the existing parkland trees – fine beech and oak and elm – had to be felled in order to create the new glades or 'indentations', as Nesley called them. Then the planting could begin. Down the Pagoda vista there was room for three of the largest families: the hollies (*Aquifoliaceae*) planted nearest the palm house; the rose family (*Rosaceae*) on both sides of the walk, and the pea family (*Leguminaceae*) close to the pagoda. Down the Syon vista there was room for five more large families: the conifers (*Coniferae*), horse chestnuts (*Aesculaceae*), the oaks and beech and sweet chestnuts (*Cupuliferae*), the maples (*Aceraceae*), and the elms (*Ulmaceae*) beside the proposed obelisk. The third vista had space for a single huge family, the willows (*Saliceae*). And other families – for ash, birch, walnut and lime – were half hidden in more secluded parts of the arboretum. All this was shown on the small sketch map submitted to Hooker by Nesfield. (Presumably Nesfield also included many smaller families for which there was space in the glades – but not on his map.)

From an artistic point of view, Nesfield's plan for Kew was a great advance on John Bedford's at Woburn or Paxton's at Chatsworth or Loudon's at Derby. The key to the Picturesque was contrast, and contrast was what the glades could provide. Although prodigal in the space they required, they offered ample room for expansion. As the great trees advanced, the glades would progressively retreat. And even the most blinkered botanist would see one advantage from Nesfield's designs: Kew's trees would retain their identity as individual specimens long after Loudon's had coalesced into a jungle – or had fallen to the axe of his successors.

By 1848 Hooker's ambitious plans for the rebirth of Kew were close to completion. One important question was at first unanswered. Could Hooker find the right man to serve as a plant explorer, a man who could be sent out to hunt for plants in the temperate but largely unexplored mountains of the East? It was a dangerous job, hunting for plants – as had been made only too obvious in recent years. Most shocking perhaps was the gruesome death of David Douglas. But deaths from tropical disease were common, and fatal accidents alarmingly frequent; one had only to think of the two young gardeners, sent out to America from

Chatsworth, and drowned before they could even begin to hunt for plants.

In the event Hooker made the daring proposal. Why not send out his own second son, Joseph, to hunt for plants in one of the wildest and least-known parts of the Himalayas – the independent state of Sikkim, due north of British-controlled India?

Joseph Hooker

Joseph seemed an admirable choice. In his early twenties he had distinguished himself as the surgeon-botanist on the three-year expedition to the Antarctic in the *Erebus* and the *Terror*. This was the mission, led by Sir John Ross, to confirm the existence of the great Antarctic continent and discover the precise position of the magnetic South Pole. More than once the two ships had narrowly avoided being crushed by icebergs. On their return, Joseph had then been commissioned by the government to write a three-volume report on his discoveries and adventures. Now thirty-one, he was unusually versatile. He was not only an experienced explorer. He was a botanist (and palaeobotanist) with a medical training, and a gift for drawing; and he had proved a natural diplomat, as well as an entertaining companion for Ross during the long nights of the Antarctic winter. Sir William Hooker had no difficulty in persuading the government to pay for Joseph's new expedition. The East India Company was prepared to give him a free passage to Calcutta. And the newly appointed governor-general, Lord Dalhousie, declared himself delighted for Joseph to join his party. They sailed from London in a paddle steamer in late 1847. After changing ships at Suez, the party duly disembarked at Calcutta early in 1848. Then Joseph, after several weeks botanising in the steaming plains of Bengal, headed north on an elephant, bound for the British hill station at Darjeeling, in the cool, damp foothills of the Himalayas.

Hooker in the Himalayas

Darjeeling was the gateway to Sikkim. And one of the main reasons why Joseph had chosen to explore Sikkim, rather than some corner of the Andes, was that he had obtained (presumably through his father) some very promising contacts in Darjeeling. The first was an eccentric naturalist and orientalist called Brian Hodgson. Few European naturalists had ever made such a vast collection of Indian mammals and birds as Hodgson. His discoveries – 39 new species of mammals and 124 new species of birds – were immortalised in more than a dozen names, including Hodgson's hawk-eagle, Hodgson's flying squirrel and Hodgson's rat snake. His zoological collections alone, presented by him to the British Museum, totalled 10,499 specimens. And his bungalow at Darjeeling, where he welcomed Joseph in April 1848, was a cabinet of curiosities – a personal museum of Tibetan prayer wheels and Buddhist texts in Sanskrit, and paintings of plants and birds and animals by Indian artists.

No wonder Joseph was thrilled to be Hodgson's guest. And who could resist that heart-stopping view from the window of his bungalow: Kanchenjunga, then believed to be the highest mountain in the world? (In 1856 a team of British surveyors announced that 'Mountain XV' – yet to be christened 'Everest' – was actually 846 feet higher.) And Hodgson was keen to take Joseph – his 'accomplished and amiable guest', as Hodgson put it – to 'make nearer acquaintance of this king of the mountains' and then 'to slip over one of the passes into Tibet' to explore that unknown plateau and its mysterious plants and animals.

A dangerous idea of Hodgson's, one might have thought, to 'slip over' into Tibet, a country closed to foreigners. In the event Hodgson was too sensible to attempt it. It was Joseph's second contact in Darjeeling, Dr Archibald Campbell, who pursued this Tibetan venture with a recklessness that now seems hard to credit.

Campbell was the British Resident in Darjeeling, and the

man responsible for maintaining good relations with Sikkim and its rajah. Until recently Campbell's life had been easy enough. Sikkim was a small, weak and impoverished kingdom, with three large Himalayan states breathing down its neck: Nepal to the west, Bhutan to the east and Tibet (ultimately a dependency of China) to the north. By 1814 Nepal had invaded Sikkim, and tried to depose the rajah and grab his kingdom. The British then rescued the rajah and set him back on his impoverished throne. But there were a set of conditions, some of which the Sikkimese resented: the British took control of Darjeeling, across the border from India, as a 'gift' of the rajah. A small rent was also paid for the use of some adjoining territory. Soon Darjeeling became a bustling city and hill station of five thousand inhabitants, a respite from Calcutta and the burning plains of Bengal for British expatriates, and a counterpart of Simla in the Punjab.

By 1848, however, time had sharpened the resentment felt by many of the Sikkimese. There was a new Dewan (a sort of prime minister) at the rajah's court at Tumlong. He was a Tibetan who had married one of the rajah's natural children, and he was openly anti-British. He was opposed by Tchebu Lama (a sort of lord chamberlain) who was the leader of a rival faction, backed by many of the lamas in Sikkim. But the Dewan had the ear of the rajah, who was old and comparatively weak. In effect the Dewan now ran the country – and was quite as reckless as Dr Archibald Campbell.

This was the situation, a Himalayan can of worms, as Campbell and his protégé, Joseph Hooker, crossed the icy pass leading to Tibet in November 1849. Campbell had two diplomatic aims: to reassure the rajah and slap down the Dewan. But his plan to slip into Tibet without permission was highly provocative – both to the Sikkimese and the Tibetans. Neither Campbell nor Hooker seemed even remotely aware of the dangers that threatened them personally.

* * *

Back in London Sir William Hooker was enjoying packet after packet of delightful letters from his clever young son. Of course the post from Darjeeling to London, via Calcutta and Suez, could take up to three months. But Joseph was the most assiduous correspondent. His letters described some of the frustrations of travel in the Himalayas: thieving porters, hostile lamas, starvation rations, pitiless rain and leeches thirsty for blood. Yet Joseph was clearly having the time of his life. He was not only a scientist. He was an incurable romantic.

The perils of exploration only added to its attractions.

'One often progresses', he wrote to his friend George Bentham, 'spread-eagled against a cliff for some way and crosses narrow planks over profound abysses with no hold, but as my head never gets giddy, there is no more fear of falling than in the main roads'.[1]

At another time he stood, transfigured like the hero of one of Caspar David Friedrich's paintings, as he watched the sun set behind the 'dazzling mass' of Kangchenjunga. Then nothing was visible except an ocean of mist out of which rose, like capes and promontories and islands, the spurs of the mountains. 'As darkness came on,' he wrote in his journal,' and the stars arose, a light fog gathered round me, and I quitted with reluctance one of the most... magic scenes I ever beheld.'[2]

As for his botanical discoveries, he was proud to tell his father that he had discovered more than a hundred plants unknown to science: including new primulas, blue poppies, a giant rhubarb and numerous rhododendrons. In fact in the autumn of 1848 he had dispatched to London no fewer than eighty *loads* of dried specimens, living plants and seeds for appraisal at Kew. Most astonishing were Joseph's newly discovered rhododendrons. At this time there were only three species of rhododendrons common in European gardens. Two of these were east coast Americans: the two purple-violet rosebays (*Rh. catawbiense* and *Rh. maximum*) that grow in the Appalachians. The third species was the invasive Asiatic species, *Rh. ponticum*. (There were also hybrids from all three of these species.)

What Joseph had discovered in Sikkim was whole valleys of giant newcomers. Many were effectively trees, 40 or even 50 feet tall – more than three times the height of the shrubby rosebays – and both their flowers and their leaves were astonishing. Joseph lost no time in marking them with his personal stamp. He named half a dozen after his friends. The blood-red *Rhododendron hodgsonii* was named after his host, Brian Hodgson; the scarlet *Rhododendron thomsonii* after one of his oldest friends, Thomas Thomson, a fellow student of botany at Glasgow who was now working in India; the towering, creamy-flowered *Rhododendron falconeri* was named after Dr Hugh Falconer, the superintendent of the botanic garden at Calcutta and the father of the Indian tea industry. To the largest of all, *Rh. arboreum*, he added *campbelliae* to identify its subspecies in Sikkim. This was a new, high-altitude and so hardier form of the plant discovered earlier in the Indian Himalaya; the Latin ending *'ae'* was a compliment to the wife of his friend, Alexander Campbell.

These were four of the 40-foot-high giants whose seeds were now safely on their way back to Kew. But what of the safety of that daredevil, Joseph himself?

Early in December an alarming report reached the British authorities in Darjeeling. Joseph Hooker and Alexander Campbell had been arrested. They had been caught trying to cross into Tibet, and were now prisoners of the rajah and the Dewan. Still more alarming reports reached Calcutta and the Punjab, and in due course were relayed to Sir William Hooker in London.

The two men had vanished – and it was feared they had been murdered on orders from the Dewan.

What had happened was this. On 7 November the two men reached the Chola pass, a bleak, stony slice of gneiss hacked out by the glaciers 15,000 feet above sea level. Beyond lay the snow-covered spruce and birch forests of Tibet. Campbell's job was to negotiate with the Rajah of Sikkim. He had no permission to enter Tibet. But on he went down the other side of the pass until he was stopped by a group of about ninety Tibetan sepoys, a few of whom were armed with matchlocks, and the rest with bows and arrows. Their dingpun (or commander) was a 'short swarthy man' in a loose scarlet jacket with large brass buttons borrowed from an Indian naval uniform. He saluted Campbell politely, but explained that they must turn back.

Meanwhile a party of Sikkimese sepoys in red jackets had arrived and began to jostle and threaten Campbell, despite pro-tests from the dingpun. After Campbell and Joseph had crossed back into Sikkim they were led to a hut in a mountain village, seething with local tribesmen; it was here they planned to spend the night.

Neither man was prepared for what followed. Let Joseph tell the story:

> We went into the hut, and were resting ourselves on a log on one end of it, when, the evening being very cold, the people crowded in; on which Campbell went out, saying, that we had better leave the hut to them, and he would see the tents pitched. He had scarcely left, when I heard him calling loudly to me 'Hooker! Hooker! The savages are murdering me!' I rushed to the door, and caught sight of him striking out with his fists and struggling violently; being tall and powerful he had already prostrated a few, but a host of men bore him down

and appeared to be trampling on him; at the same moment I was myself seized by eight men, who forced me back into the hut... pressing me against the wall; here I spent a few moments of agony, as I heard my friend's stifled cries grow fainter and fainter.[3]

After a few minutes three of the Sikkimese came into the hut and told Joseph's captors to let go of him. They explained that Campbell was a prisoner 'by orders of the Rajah' who was 'dissatisfied with his conduct as a government officer, during the last 12 years'.[4] Joseph was told that Campbell had been tortured by someone twisting a cord round his wrist using a bamboo wrench. Then, tied hand and foot, Campbell was dragged off to his tent. He would now be taken to the rajah's headquarters at Toomlong and held captive until the British authorities in Calcutta agreed to the 'rajah's demands' on a number of issues. Of course the weak and elderly rajah had little to do with it. The Dewan was in charge, and the only man who could have opposed him, Tchebu Lama, the lord chamberlain, was afraid that he might be next to be arrested.

Three days later the captives reached Tumlong, where Campbell was imprisoned in a hut like a cage on a terrace a few hundred yards below the rajah's palace. Hooker was told that he was free to go if he chose, but decided to stay with his friend. He was interrogated in a local temple by a group of the rajah's (and Dewan's) counsellors, who explained some of their more contentious demands. The British must redraw the border with Nepal; they must modify the laws about slavery; and they must arrange for direct contact with Calcutta, bypassing Campbell. In return Hooker gave them a warning. It was an outrage to imprison the agent of a friendly power, and there would be serious consequences.

On 15 November their enemy, the Dewan, finally made his appearance. He was carried in an English chair – ironically given him by Campbell several years earlier – and wore an enormous straw hat with a red tassel and black velvet butterflies on the flapping brim. At first he feigned sickness, and refused to see his prisoners. He seemed oblivious to the crisis in which he had embroiled his country. It was true that Campbell and Joseph had broken the rules by crossing into Tibet. This could have embroiled the Sikkim rajah with the Chinese authorities. And this was more than a mere indiscretion. As that wise counsellor Brian Hodgson reported to Joseph's father: 'the real grievance is, that not merely your son, a traveller, but that a representative of government goes north, exploring the frontier and entering Thibet, against the wish and remonstrance of Sikkim'.[5]

But the Dewan had of course overreacted. Taking hostages was often practised in these Himalayan kingdoms. No doubt he had naively imagined that the British would cave in when they heard Campbell had been taken hostage and locked in a cage. After a week the Dewan agreed to see Campbell and the Dewan's illusions were bluntly dispelled. The British army in India was more than half a million strong. They could wipe Sikkim off the map any day they chose. And no negotiations were possible until Campbell and Hooker had been set free.

For three weeks Campbell was held captive in the hut at Tumlong, with Hooker at his side. They were woken each morning by the blare of trumpets and conches, and the crash of cymbals beaten by the priests in front of the numerous temples in the valley. It rained most of the time, and Joseph busied himself with his meteorological register. There was no one to entertain them except for a small Lepcha girl whom they christened 'Dolly'. She was a brilliant mimic, and gave Joseph a Tibetan Jew's harp and a Tibetan pipe, with which he 'whiled away the dark evenings, as my cheerful companion amused himself with an old harmonicum, to the enchantment of Dolly and our guards and neighbours.'[6]

It was not until early December that the Dewan was finally brought to heel. By now the rajah, under pressure from the local lamas and afraid that he might lose his kingdom, had lost faith in his prime minister. It was agreed that the Dewan would take the captives under guard to Darjeeling. Even then the Dewan dawdled, and to Campbell's astonishment tried to sell him hats and clothes and other trade goods he had bought in Tibet. A week later the two men finally reached the frontier – the bamboo bridge at the River Rungeet – and at 8 p.m. that night were delivered back to the safety of Darjeeling.

At first they were greeted like ghosts. Their friends had heard the rumours that they had been captured and later murdered. (Brian Hodgson was afraid Joseph would be taken in a cage to Lhasa or even to Peking.) Now they could celebrate. Joseph wrote numerous letters to confirm his escape, and a cheerful account of his ordeal which was later published in his *Himalayan Journals*. Then, with characteristic energy, he arranged for a new botanical foray. He would explore the Himalayas of Assam and the north-east borders of India.

But for Sikkim, its rajah and the Dewan, the hostage crisis proved, predictably, a disaster. The arrest and imprisonment and torture of a British diplomat was not to be taken lightly by the authorities in Calcutta. A line had been crossed, a taboo broken. Calcutta's revenge swiftly followed: the payment of £300 a year to the rajah for the 'gift' of Darjeeling was ended abruptly. What was even more humiliating, and damaging to the rajah's pocket, Britain grabbed the Terai – a large tract of lowland Sikkim – and annexed it to the empire. The rajah had to bite his lip and accept his punishment. As for the Dewan, his enemies in Sikkim were out for his blood. He was sacked by the rajah but warned not to try to escape to Tibet.

Meanwhile Joseph had spent an enjoyable six months in Assam, and then returned to a hero's welcome in London.

By this time Sir William Hooker, and his staff at Kew, had begun the laborious task of sorting the botanical treasure trove Joseph had sent back via Calcutta in the previous two years. There were more than a hundred new species of trees and shrubs and herbaceous plants. The most outstanding – and the most relevant for arboretums – were the twenty-five species of rhododendrons. Most of these were new to science: like *Rhododendron falconeri*, *Rh. thomsonii* and *Rh. hodgsonii*. Others, like *Rhododendron arboretums*, were introduced in a more hardy and therefore more useful form. The naming and identification of new species, based on dried specimens, was organised by Sir William Hooker at Kew. But how to give the wider public an idea of Joseph's amazing discoveries?

Long before Joseph's return to London, Sir William had actually launched a book celebrating Joseph's travels. Entitled *Rhododendrons of Sikkim-Himalaya*, it was published in three parts in 1849 to 1851. The strikingly bold illustrations by Walter Fitch, Kew's resident artist, were based on dried specimens or the sketches made by Joseph – both sent to Sir William from Sikkim. ('It is not every botanist,' came a snide comment from the *Athenaeum*, 'who has such a father at home as Sir W. Hooker'.) And not content with one book, Sir William encouraged Joseph to publish his journals as soon as he returned.

The campaign to publicise his achievements continued with yearly features of his new rhododendrons in *Curtis's Botanical Magazine*. At the same time Kew was busy making shrubs and trees from the seeds Joseph had sent back to London, and distributing them far and wide. The first flowers from a new rhododendron emerged after only three years. It was *Rh. dalhousiae*, named as a tribute from Joseph to the viceroy's wife, and its fragrance astounded gardeners. But it was no surprise that every ambitious nurseryman now wanted to stock their nurseries with Joseph's new plants, and rhododendron fever began to spread across England and beyond.

Of course the cult never reached the pitch of Dutch tulipomania of the seventeenth century. But it transformed British gardens and arboretums. A wall of Himalayan rhododendrons made the perfect background for the display of the flowers of deciduous trees like magnolias or cherries. And that wall was not a dull green – like a wall of yew or box or privet. In spring and summer it was overflowing with flowers. Every month the kaleidoscope changed: from the scarlet splashes of *Rhododendron barbatum* in March to the peach-coloured trusses of *Rh. falconeri* in May.

No wonder Joseph was saluted as a hero, and the new Rhododendron Dell, carved out of Kew's arboretum, was brimming with his trophies.

But Joseph's days as a daredevil were over. Other explorers were risking their lives in the hunt for new trees and plants. And their quarry lay thousands of miles east of the Himalayas – in the unknown hills of southern Japan and eastern China.

CHAPTER 15

Fortune Smiles

By the early 1840s the number of plant nurseries in Britain had continued to increase by leaps and bounds. Many had planted their own arboretums to show off their stock. Loudon listed no fewer than eighteen nurseries of this kind in his own monumental *Arboretum Britannicum*. The best known were the big four in London: Loddiges of Hackney (his favourite), Lee and Kennedy of Hammersmith, Osborne of Fulham and Knight's Exotic Nursery of Chelsea. But the others were well scattered over Britain. Two of the most successful were Lawsons of Edinburgh and Veitch of Exeter. For fifteen years the art and science of gardening had been eloquently promoted by Loudon in his *Gardener's Magazine*. And now it was a fashion, if not a craze, for a new middle class. Commercial plant nurseries found it hard to keep up with the demand. For there was no regular supply of new introductions from the temperate corners of the world like China, the Himalayas and western America.

The leading sponsor of plant-hunting at this period, however, was not a commercial nursery. It was the London Horticultural Society. Before his tragic death in Hawaii, David Douglas had done the society proud. Many of the small plants and seeds that he had sent back from California, Oregon and the north-west of America, had adapted perfectly to a new soil and a new climate.

Some of the Douglas firs he had introduced could grow three feet a year. Douglas's trees and other plants were snapped up by the members of the society, commercial nurseries and the general public. All this meant a handsome dividend for the society.

But could they afford to send out a new plant explorer? By 1842 the moment had come, according to Professor John Linley, who had served as the masterful vice-secretary of the society ever since the downfall of Joseph Sabine. Lindley recommended a young Scottish gardener called Robert Fortune to be the Society's man in China. He had been trained (like David Douglas) at the Edinburgh botanic garden, and then come south to work as a superintendent in the Society's hothouse at Chiswick. He was now prepared to go out to China, on the extremely modest salary of £100 a year, to search the country for new trees and other plants.

Reluctantly China was now opening its borders to foreigners. That year, 1842, the British government had ended the First Opium War with the Treaty of Nangking which forced the Chinese to make humiliating concessions to British merchants and British trade. These included the cession of Hong Kong, so that it became a British colony, and the opening of five treaty ports to international trade: Canton, Amoy (Xiamen), Foochow (Fuzhou), Ningpo (Ningbo) and Shanghai. A shameful part of this agreement, extorted by the British, was to legalise the export of opium from British India to the Chinese empire.

Thirty-one-year-old Robert Fortune had had no formal training in botany. But he had impressed Lindley with his desire to learn, and Lindley had shown him how to prepare dried specimens of plants for identification and study in the herbarium. Fortune was energetic and charming, and he had had ten years' practical experience of growing plants. In February 1843 he sailed from London on board the *Emu*, bound for Hong Kong, which was reached after a voyage of four months. He had been instructed to bring various pieces of equipment: spades and trowels, a number of Wardian cases (sealed and glazed containers for plants that served as miniature greenhouses), a thermometer, a geological hammer, and a so-called 'life preserver' – a glorified walking stick. His request to bring firearms had initially been rejected by the society. But old China hands must have warned him of the dangers he faced. He insisted that he should be allowed to bring a 'fowling piece' (shotgun) and a pistol. Lindley persuaded the Society's planning committee to change their mind and make this concession – luckily for Fortune, as events would soon show.

Robert Fortune

The formal contract with the society, inscribed in an elegant copperplate hand, ran to five pages. But it boiled down to three points. First, he was to 'collect seeds and plants of an ornamental or useful kind, not already cultivated in Great Britain'. In making this collection he was to concentrate on hardy trees and other plants suitable for planting outdoors in Britain. Second, the society claimed the exclusive rights to 'all collections of living plants and seed'. He was also instructed to prepare one set of dried specimens 'of all plants you meet with and have an opportunity of so preserving'. However, there was an important concession: 'any other collections' of dried specimens would be his own private property, for him to sell to other collectors and nurserymen if he chose. Third, he must keep a detailed journal.[1] But the society had no claim to anything he might publish about his adventures (or misadventures) in China. So here again there was room for Fortune to make money on his own account, which might compensate him for his meagre salary of £100 a year.

At first sight Fortune was not impressed by the new British colony of Hong Kong. Viewed from the sea, the coastal hills, he later wrote, 'had a scorched appearance... the trees are few, and stunted in their appearance, being perfectly useless for anything but firewood... Was this then the "flowery land", the land of camellias, azaleas and roses, of which I had heard so much in England?'[2]

Fortune soon recovered his spirits. He had arrived well briefed; he had few illusions about modern China. It was no 'fairyland' as he put it. He knew that violence was endemic, and the emperor in Peking had little control over what happened in the provinces of his enormous empire. Besides, feelings in the coastal towns still ran high as a result of the humiliations – and bloodshed – in the Opium War. But he found a ready welcome from the large British community in the process of building a new town on the north of the barren island of Hong Kong. In preparing his trip, the society had provided him with no fewer than twenty-three letters of introduction from the great and the good; these even included one from the foreign secretary, Lord Aberdeen. The recipients were the new British rulers of Hong Kong: the governor, Sir Henry Pottinger, who had negotiated the Treaty of Nangking; the commander-in-chief of the British troops, Lord Saltoun; and (most useful) the British merchants with a finger in every pie, the firm of Jardine and Matheson.

For several weeks he explored Hong Kong and its neighbouring island, Macao, as well as the principal port of Canton, at the head of the Pearl River. But his instructions, as we saw, were to concentrate on collecting hardy plants. This meant leaving the tropics and heading north to the treaty ports of Ningpo and Shanghai where the winters were cooler. In fact, Fortune was well aware of this overwhelming advantage in his favour. Unlike any of his predecessors he could collect temperate plants in the wild.

The first trees and other plants introduced into Britain from China – like the delightful yulan (*Magnolia denudata*) imported by Sir Joseph Banks in 1790 – were northern plants brought south and sold in the shops of Canton. The same was true of the shrubs introduced by William Kerr, the first full-time collector in China, who had been stuck in the tropics at Canton and Macao throughout the eight years he spent in China. Banned from the north, he could collect nothing in the wild that would grow in Britain. His acquisitions – shrubs like *Pieris japonica* and the eponymous *Kerria japonica* – were garden stock originally imported from the north.

Fortune realised he now had China at his feet. At any rate he could travel where no European had been before him and collect new plants on a scale never possible before. But there were limits – somewhat shadowy limits – to his freedom. According to the Treaty of Nangking, European travellers were allowed access to the five treaty ports and their neighbourhoods. How far did this allow a traveller to go beyond these five cities? For one day's journey, it appeared. But no one could tell Fortune how strictly the Chinese authorities would enforce the rules.

From Fortune's Wanderings in China

After the ferocious dry heat of Hong Kong in summer, and the accompanying epidemics of malaria and cholera, Fortune looked forward to the cool of Ningpo and Shanghai. But he aimed to see as much of the southern coast as he could. He left Hong Kong on 23 August 1843 in a ship heading for Amoy. On the voyage he was struck down by a dangerous attack of malaria. There was no doctor on board, but the sea air soon restored him. The ship first anchored at Namoa Island, one of the centres for the opium trade, where he was surprised to find British merchants, without any authority from the Chinese, had built roads and a bazaar. He was assured that the Chinese turned a blind eye to this kind of development – and no doubt he took this as a good omen for his own travels.

Amoy, on the other hand, he found disgusting. A sprawling city of some 300,000, it was, he wrote later 'one of the filthiest towns which I have ever seen, either in China or elsewhere'.[3] The streets were covered with mats, to keep off the sun, and only a few feet wide, as wheeled traffic was unknown in this part of China. Fortune found the stink from bakeries and food shops quite suffocating.

Outside the city and its suburbs there was another China of rolling hills and small villages, and Fortune revelled in it. He could hunt for plants without hindrance. Indeed the 'natives' often seemed delighted to see him.

> When the day was hot I would sit down under the shade of a large banyan-tree... and then the whole village – men, women and children – would gather around, gazing at me with curiosity not unmixed with fear, as if I was a being from another world. Then one would begin to examine my clothes, another would peep into my pockets, while several others were examining my specimens.

Sometimes, it was true, the villagers would seem anxious to be rid of him. 'Wyloe-san-pan-Fokei', they shouted. 'Friend, be off to your boat'. But Fortune could play the charmer – even play the fool – when it was needed. Soon the children were collecting plants for his specimen cases, and the headman of the village was offering him tea and cakes.

I thanked him and began to eat. The hundreds who now surrounded me were perfectly delighted. 'He eats and drinks like ourselves,' said one. 'Look,' said two or three behind me who had been examining the back part of my head rather attentively, 'look here, the stranger has no tail.'[4]

Fortune offered to cut off the pigtail of one of the local dandies and wear it himself, and of course the offer was indignantly refused – amid peals of laughter.

Fortune sailed north from Amoy at the end of September and narrowly avoided disaster. The passage to Ningpo and Shanghai by way of the Formosa Channel was notorious for its storms, especially when, as happened in autumn, the south-west monsoon was replaced by the north-east monsoon. Fortune's ship was attacked by a storm so violent that a large fish, weighing at least thirty pounds, crashed through the skylight on the poop and landed on the cabin table. But worse was to come. After changing ships, Fortune found himself storm-tossed once again in the Formosa Channel. The crew of Lascars were huddled under the longboat. The newest and strongest sails of the little schooner were split to pieces; parts of the bulwarks were washed away. Fortune and the captain had gone below when they heard a crash which sounded as if the ship's sides had been driven in. At the same moment the glass of the skylight came down about their ears, and the sea forced its way into the cabin. Fortune thought the end had come. But somehow the lee bulwarks held fast and the ship survived.

After three days the storm relented. With tattered sails the schooner crept into the harbour of Chimoo Bay, far to the south of their starting point a week before. No one had drowned, but the glazed Wardian cases had been dashed to pieces, and their contents scattered to the winds. These were Fortune's precious specimens, collected with the help of the local peasants, including the kindly villagers outside Amoy who had supplied him with tea and cakes.

Resilient as always, Fortune arranged a botanical ramble on the island of Chimoo. He was warned by his Chinese servant that the local people were well known to be thieves and robbers. But he brushed aside these warnings in the belief that his servant was feeling lazy. Fortune decided the man needed a long walk to cure his laziness. So he hired a boat and landed on the island. Once again he was warned – this time by the boatmen – not to proceed inland. But he now felt committed. He would put a bold face on the matter and proceed.

The two men set off into the hills, heading for a pagoda which crowned the summit. Soon they were surrounded by hundreds of the local Chinese who treated him, he later explained, as a 'natural curiosity'. The place teemed with people, barren as it was. 'I almost thought the very stones were changing into Chinamen, so rapidly did the crowd accumulate.'[5] Fortune did however manage to collect some interesting new plants to send to the Horticultural Society: an *Abelia* and a *Campanula*. He shook off the crowd and began to climb up to the pagoda. It proved very dilapidated – almost ruinous – and the wind howled through the broken balconies. But there was a fine view from the summit of the hill. Fortune realised for the first time why the crowds had been so thick. The whole island was covered with large villages and towns. It was now getting late, and time to return to the boat.

The crowds thickened again as the two men descended the hill. Fortune did his best to keep the crowd in good humour. They offered to show him some good plants for his collection. The next moment he felt a hand in his pocket, and saw the thief running off with a letter and some valuables. Fortune looked round for his servant. The terrified man had been attacked by eight or ten men carrying knives. They were about to strip him of anything of value when Fortune came running to his rescue. Of course, as he put it, 'my poor plants collected with so much care were flying about in all directions'.[6] But the attackers took to their heels, and the two men got safely to the beach where the boatmen were waiting anxiously, afraid that the two men had been robbed or murdered.

In forbidden territory

It was now low tide, with half a mile of raging surf between them and the ship that had brought them. Fortune was carried on the back of one of the boatmen 'who scampered like a racehorse across the wet sand' and then helped row him through the surf to the ship. Apart from being drenched to the skin, he was none the worse for his adventures. His immediate reaction was to say his opinion of the Chinese was now 'considerably lowered'.[7]

What he didn't care to admit was that many Chinese had good reason to feel hostile to the British. It was only two years since the First Opium War when the British army had stormed these coastal towns and killed many of the inhabitants. And he didn't add, but perhaps recognised, that he had been a fool to reject local advice. Next time he might not be so lucky.

By November 1843 Fortune had reached his principal goal at last: the Chusan islands and the treaty ports of Ningpo and Shanghai. This was temperate China and a welcome contrast to the barren hills of the south. Fortune was delighted by the richness of the soil and the wealth of unknown trees and plants. 'The first glance at the vegetation', he wrote, 'convinced me that this must be the field of my future operations, and I had then no doubt that my mission would end most successfully'.[8] One of the first new trees he spotted was a form of palm tree that later became well known as one of his namesakes: *Trachycarpus fortunei*, the Chusan Palm. The local Chinese used the fibre from the bracts of this tree to make ropes and cables. They also made hats and jackets from the leaves of the palm, which looked comical enough, but kept people snug against wind and rain. Fortune was so pleased with the palm that he insisted that one of the seedlings he sent home should be presented to the queen. (In due course the seedling was planted on the lower terrace at Osborne, where it flourished.)

Fortune was also dazzled by many new garden-worthy shrubs

Fortune's palm

from the glens of Chusan. His introductions included a new species of Daphne (*D. genkwa*), three kinds of azaleas (*A. squamata, A. sinensis* and *A. obtusa* – now known as rhododendrons) the paperbush (*Edgeworthia chrysantha*), an elegant white form of the Chinese wisteria (*W. sinensis 'Alba'*) and, what was to prove most popular of all, the winter-flowering jasmine (*J. nudiflorum*). As for trees, Fortune was the first person to introduce to Europe the olive-fruited plum yew (*Cephalotaxus fortunei*), similar to the common yew, but more decorative.

In the second half of November, Fortune sailed up the coast to Shanghai, the most northerly of the five treaty ports. He found it just opening for business. In fact the British consul, Captain George Balfour, had only arrived a fortnight earlier. It was a walled city of about 270,000 Chinese, and conditions were still somewhat primitive. Fortune shared a lodging with some of the twenty-five British merchants who had moved in. But the lodging was hardly more than a shed built on the side of a canal. The roof leaked, there was no proper stove for cooking, and snow blew in through the unglazed windows. Still, Fortune did not expect to be comfortable or fed luxurious meals. He forecast, with remarkable acumen, that Shanghai was going to be the giant that it has become today (the current population tops 26 million) and would soon make Canton look very small. Its port and canals were ideally placed to make it a hub: both for the export of tea and silk, and the import of factory-made goods from Europe and America. Meanwhile he found Shanghai a happy hunting ground for plants – not out in the rich black soil of the great plains beyond the city, but in the gardening shops of the narrow streets within.

Week by week he accumulated new plants, some of which had come from further north. He was hungry for 'moutans' (tree peonies) and their elegant yellow or lilac or purple varieties. Before he left Shanghai he had snapped up no fewer than thirty Chinese-bred varieties, ranging from 'Glory of Shanghai' to 'Bijou de Chusan'. All were securely replanted in Wardian cases, ready for dispatch to the Horticultural Society in London.

Ningpo he found even richer in ornamental plants than Shanghai, though few plants were for sale. The city was famous for its gardens. Many were the homes of merchants who had made their money in different parts of China and chosen to retire to Ningpo. Fortune was taken to meet an elderly mandarin called Dr Chang who had retired from trade many years before. His garden attracted numerous visitors, and was much admired. Like other grand houses in the city its central feature was a series of caverns built from rockwork – artificial but, as Fortune put it, 'the resemblance to nature is perfect'. These led from room to room with glimpses of small courtyards, planted with elegant dwarf trees and graceful creepers overhanging a series of small ponds.

Dr Chang welcomed Fortune to his home with a 'great many very low bows', entertained him with tea 'of the finest description',[9] and invited his particular friends to meet the distinguished foreigner. Fortune was carefully examined from head to foot. His watch proved especially fascinating, and Fortune was asked whether, as a special favour, he would allow people to put it to their ear and hear it ticking.

By the end of the year, Fortune was ready to return to Hong Kong with his newly discovered plants. They were packed in eighteen Wardian cases and duly dispatched to London. He returned in the spring and continued to search the three treaty ports – Chusan, Shanghai and Ningpo – for more rarities.

One excursion he made was to the celebrated Buddhist temple of Tein-tung ('Temple of the Heavenly Boys') in rich farmland about 20 miles from Ningpo. He travelled in a canal boat with the British consul and two other Englishmen. They were most hospitably received, although the monks couldn't hide their laughter when their English guests showed they were duffers at using chopsticks. Fortune himself had a narrow escape when searching for new plants. The monks grew bamboos whose delicate shoots were prized as vegetables for the table, but the bamboo groves were plagued by wild boars.

One night Fortune was invited to take his gun and shoot some of the marauders in a nearby ravine. But the night was too dark to see anything, and Fortune was afraid he might shoot a priest by mistake for a wild boar. In daylight he returned to the ravine to search for plants – and fell into a concealed pit dug by the monks to trap the boars. By good luck he was able to grab a small branch as the ground gave way beneath him. Otherwise, as he knew, he might have suffered a similar fate to that of David

Douglas, who fell into a bull pit in Hawaii and was apparently trampled to death by a wild bull.

None the worse for this experience, Fortune then made one of his most important discoveries. Near Tein-tung he collected seed from the Chinese version of the Japanese *Cryptomeria japonica*. Soon this was to be one of the star performers in the Horticultural Society's garden in Chiswick, and indeed in gardens and arboretums all over Europe.

But what of the mysterious interior, the vast, unknown China beyond the 30-mile limit imposed on European travellers by the Treaty of Nangking? Fortune must have been tormented by the thought of the botanical treasures which were just out of reach. At any rate in June 1844 he decided to push his luck and visit the city of Soo-chow-foo (Suzhou) which was about 50 miles north-west of Shanghai. This was the city famous throughout China for its works of art. 'If a stranger enters a shop in Hong Kong or Canton ... he is sure to be told, when he enquires for the price of any curiosity out of the common way, that it has been brought from this celebrated place ... fine pictures, fine carved work, fine silks, and fine ladies, all come from Soo-chow – it is the Chinaman's earthly paradise'.[10] And this paradise included, as he could have added, a number of famous gardens.

But how could Fortune elude the mandarins whose job was to stop him travelling beyond the 30-mile limit? He hired a small sailing boat, and at first all he would tell the crew was that they were 'going into the country in search of plants'. With the help of a pocket compass, he set off along the series of canals that led northwards towards Soo-chow. On the second day he told the crew where they were going – and offered them double money if they agreed to take the risk of being caught and punished. His offer was accepted. Fortune himself had had his head shaved, and wore a Chinese tunic, with a 'splendid' pigtail at the back of his

head ('upon the whole I believe I made a pretty fair Chinaman').[11]
The journey took several days, and brought them through several
somewhat dilapidated walled cities. They had moored the boat
under the ramparts in one of these cities called Cading, but
woke in the night to find the boat adrift in midstream. A thief
had stolen the entire contents of the cabin, including Fortune's
Chinese costume, before cutting the boat's moorings. Fortunately
he had slept with some dollars under his pillow, and he had
enough to buy himself a new costume in the morning.

The highlight of the journey was the day when the little boat
shot out into the grand canal, as broad as a big river and leading
ultimately to Peking. All round them were hundreds of boats
under sail, hurrying to their destinations, with 'pagodas here
and there... rearing their heads above the woods and Buddhist
temples... scattered over this wide and extensive plain'. Fortune
was particularly impressed by the rice fields which stretched as
far as the eye could see with 'everywhere the pleasing clatter
of the waterwheels... and hundreds of happy and contented
Chinese peasants'. He noted that ladies were employed driving
the waterwheels, four to each wheel, and these ladies had feet of
the natural size – unlike most peasant women whose feet were
too small, as they had been deformed by binding.[12]

Soo-chow itself was something of an anticlimax – at least the
gardens must have disappointed Fortune. He only discovered
three new plants: a new white form of the Chinese wisteria (*W.
sinensis* var. *glauca*), a 'fine, new double yellow rose' (now *Rosa x
odorata*) and a gardenia with 'large white blossoms like a camellia'[13]
(*G. jasminoides* var. *fortuneana*). All three plants were packed up
and sent back to London. But the city was the great emporium
for central China and a cheerful, flourishing place – unlike most
Chinese cities he had visited, except for Shanghai and Canton.
Fortune greatly admired the ladies in their elegant silk dresses,

despite their deformed feet and the unfortunate way they painted their faces with white powder. He also enjoyed strolling by the ancient walls, sporting his pigtail and Chinese tunic. The disguise was so convincing that even his English friends failed to recognise him when he returned to Shanghai a few days later.

After that year's collecting season was over, Fortune retired once again to Hong Kong. He needed a rest, and was hoping for a favourable reply to a letter which he had written to the Horticultural Society in August 1844. He was paid a mere £100 a year, and was asking for a modest increase. The humiliating reply finally reached him in the following March: they refused to give him the rise.

Swallowing his pride, Fortune set off in the spring to tidy up his collections in the north. He also hoped to visit the fifth treaty port, Foo-choo-foo (Fuzhou), half way between Canton and Chusan, and celebrated for the production of black tea.

In the event his visit was plagued with difficulties. The Min River, on whose banks the city was built, was bloated with floods. The mandarins in charge were uncooperative, and the public were openly hostile; they had suffered in the recent war. Fortune and his party were followed by crowds chanting 'Foreign devils, foreign devils'. Still, he made an important discovery which was to help shape his future career. He managed to visit the black tea plantations in the hills near the city, and found that the same species of tea plant, *Camellia viridis* (now *C. sinensis*) was used for the production of both black tea and green tea. What was different was the method of drying and processing the leaves.

On his return from Foo-choo-foo, Fortune was stricken with malaria, and had a series of encounters with pirates that nearly cost him his life.

He described these terrifying experiences in a long letter to his friend and patron, John Lindley:

On our way up the coast and when about 60 miles from the mouth of the Min, we were attacked by a fleet of Piratical Junks and I certainly thought then that my travels were to be brought to a premature conclusion. Our cowardly crew ran all below to save themselves from the shot which was flying about our heads in all directions and it was with great difficulty I could keep two of them at the helm to steer the junk. I knew quite well that if we were taken I at least had no chance of escape . . . I therefore loaded my gun and pistols with large charges and waited patiently until the nearest junk was within 30 yards of our stern. Our vessel had no guns and up to that time we received their fire without attempting to return it and now the pirates came on hooting and yelling in their usual savage manner apparently quite sure of their prize. Their decks were crowded with men and now I raised my gun and fired right amongst their heads . . .

The effect was wonderful and every man fell flat on his face on the deck as if a thunderbolt had struck them. Doubtedly I wounded a great number . . . and some were probably killed, however they required no more but instantly put the helm down and bore away. Another [junk] of larger dimension came down among us and was dispatched in the same manner when the rest of the fleet, luckily for us, decided it prudent not to attack us. On the second day after this we had another attack of the same kind, fortunately with the same results and I arrived at last in the safety of Chusan.[14]

Back in London the committee of the Horticultural Society eagerly awaited Fortune's return. Despite their rebuff to his letter asking for a rise, they were delighted with what they called 'the Chinese mission'. In May 1846 they listed some of the exciting new plants that he had already sent. These included twenty-two colourful new varieties of the 'moutan' or tree peony (*P. suf-fruticosa*), two new species of viburnums (*V. macrocephalum* and *V. plicatum*), a new weigela (*W. florida*) as well as the trees and other plants, like the cryptomeria and trachycarpus and azaleas already mentioned earlier in this chapter. But modern scholars, exploring Fortune's own records, have listed more than a hundred trees and plants introduced by Fortune from China in 1843–6. In addition he sent over a hundred dried specimens destined for the herbarium. It was these specimens that John Lindley used for identifying and naming the new plants. And he paid Fortune the well-deserved compliment of naming many species after him.

Of course some of Fortune's plants didn't survive the gruelling journey from China, snug as they were in their Wardian cases. Seeds survived better and were easier to distribute to the members of the Horticultural Society or to sell to commercial nurseries. By 1846 the society could boast it had distributed the tidy number of 42,584 plants and 308,371 packets of seeds – including some (perhaps many) from Fortune.

But Fortune himself had had his fill of the society and its ways. He was appointed to run the Apothecaries' Garden at Chelsea. Then he accepted a lucrative invitation from the East India Company: to return to China and use Chinese tea plants and Chinese expertise to help develop the tea industry in India.

Meanwhile, the commercial nurseries in Britain, eager to compete with the Horticultural Society, were enjoying a boom. Leading the pack was the Exeter firm of Messrs Veitch. Its ambitious owner and director, James Veitch, had decided that he could afford to send out his own plant collector and pay him generously. He would get an allowance of £400 a year, four times the salary paid to Robert Fortune. He chose William Lobb, a thirty-one-year-old gardener from Cornwall, whose brother Thomas worked for Veitch. William was to collect the seeds of temperate plants in the little-known parts of Argentina and Chile that spanned the southern spine of the Andes. Concentrate above all, he was told by James Veitch, on collecting the seeds of a mysterious freak: an extraordinary pine tree that looked like a spiky umbrella.

William Lobb sailed from Falmouth in November 1840 on board HM Packet *Seagull* bound for Rio de Janeiro. He had brought with him some seeds of a new hybrid rhododendron ('Cornish Early Red') to present to the emperor of Brazil, Pedro II, for planting in his garden in Rio. He made his presentation to the emperor, and set off to the south, to Argentina and Chile and the Andes. And then, for several months, there was silence.

CHAPTER 16

The Forgotten Explorer

Perhaps there was nothing mysterious about the so-called 'Chile pine' whose seeds James Veitch had sent William Lobb to collect. But it was certainly a freak. No other conifer looked quite so strange – and so pugnacious. Its upturned branches were covered in spikes, and its trunk was armoured like a dinosaur's skin. Veitch was certain that the British public would find its oddity irresistible. But where was this Jurassic beast of a tree to be found?

Forty-five years earlier, Archibald Menzies had explored the west coast of Chile on board Captain Vancouver's ship, *Discovery*. Menzies was the ship's surgeon and naturalist, and the voyage (as we saw) ended badly: with Menzies put under arrest for insubordination. He had blamed Vancouver for the loss of most of the trees and other plants he had collected on the west coast of North and South America. However, five small trees had survived the voyage, grown from some strange nuts given to Menzies at an official reception in Valparaiso. The five trees were called Chile pines (*Araucaria araucana*); three were then planted at Kew gardens. In the 1820s seeds from a later collection were sold in Loddiges's nursery. And it was then that James Veitch must have seen the tree and decided that it would make his fortune.

William Lobb, the young gardener to whom James Veitch had assigned the difficult and dangerous job of collecting the seeds, was the son of the estate carpenter at Pencarrow, the home of a dashing Cornish baronet, Sir Edward Molesworth. William had had no formal training as a botanist, but he was an enthusiast and a romantic. Employed as a gardener by the Williams family at Scorrier, near Falmouth, he had watched the packet boats setting out and returning from long voyages, and had made friends with their captains and heard their tales of trips to the Caribbean, Brazil and other exotic places. He longed to travel himself.

His younger brother, Thomas, happened to be employed as a gardener by James Veitch, and told Veitch about William and his romantic ambitions. Veitch duly summoned William to his office and was impressed. William had a 'keen manner'. He had even made a collection of dried specimens of British plants, including Cornish ferns. Veitch arranged with Sir William Hooker that William should collaborate with the experts at Kew and be shown the professional way to make specimens for the Kew herbarium. (It involved pressing plants between special papers, and was a tedious business that most collectors loathed.) By November 1840 William was primed for the journey, with maps, money, passports – and, for his spiritual comfort, a small leather-bound book, *Daily Food for Christians*.

After he landed at Rio, and presented the emperor of Brazil with Veitch's present of scarlet rhododendrons (apparently still growing in that garden in Rio today), William headed south to Buenos Aires and Argentina. He was aiming for Chile, but decided to avoid the dangerous passage around Cape Horn by taking a shortcut over the Andes. He hired mules and set off via the Upsallata Pass that led into Chile. He had not reckoned with the snow. In a letter to Hooker, James Veitch quoted William's account: 'On the fourth day from Upsallata... the snow was five feet deep, frozen so hard that the mules made no impression and the cold was intense'.[1] The party had to take shelter in crudely built huts, and William collapsed with fever. Eventually he reached Valparaiso on the west coast and took a boat south to Concepcion, from where he reached the region called La Araucana. The coastal strip was dotted with European-style farms and vineyards, and it was harvest time. Inland, between the sea and the snow-covered Andes, was a very different landscape: the gravelly foothills and the weird forests of Chile pine.

The local Araucano tribe made no objections to the arrival of William and his party, although they valued the trees as a source of food, eating the seeds from the pine cones, or grinding them up to make flour. William's job was to send home as many seeds as he could collect. But how was he to harvest them?

The pine cones were far out of reach, and the spiky trees impossible to climb. In the event William adopted the tactic used by David Douglas when hunting the sugar pine in the forests of north America: he used his gun. In Douglas's case, as we saw, this had provoked an alarming stand-off with the local Indians, but William was more fortunate. He took out his gun, loaded it with ball shot, then brought down a shower of spiky cones. Each cone contained more than a dozen large seeds, and soon William had collected a sackload of more than three thousand. This was duly sent off by a carrier down to the coast and shipped to London.

In May next year, a striking advertisement appeared in a number of horticultural papers:

> Messrs. Veitch and son, having raised many thousands of Araucaria imbricata from seed [i.e. *A. araucana*] are enabled to offer them in quantity at a very low price. Exeter May 18 1843.[2]

The price was £10 per hundred or 30s a dozen for seedling plants 3 to 4 inches high. Less than a decade earlier a reckless collector had had to pay £25 for a *single* small tree (£2,500 in today's money).

In fact it was this expensive rarity that gave the tree its unforgettable popular name: the monkey puzzle. The tree had been bought from a London nursery by Sir William Molesworth, the Cornish squire at Pencarrow where William Lobb's father had been estate carpenter. Molesworth arranged a suitable house party to celebrate the planting of his new acquisition. One of the guests, an eminent barrister called Charles Austin, picked up the tree – and soon regretted it. How should one handle this fearsome tree? 'That would be a puzzle for a monkey', he said, with feeling. And the name stuck.[3]

James Veitch, at any rate, had no reason to complain. A booming market for the monkey puzzle confirmed the success of his gamble in sending William Lobb to South America. Planting the tree became a fashionable cult among the great and the good. At Bicton, in Devon, Lady Rolle planted twenty-five pairs of monkey puzzles to form an avenue 500 yards long. James Veitch was her adviser (although he was sorry to say that she bought the trees from a different nursery who had larger trees than Veitch's seedlings). Other landowners followed suit: including Lady Louisa Tighe at Woodstock, County Kilkenny. The monkey puzzle theme was taken up in numerous pineta, including that of the pioneer of the genre, Lord Grenville at Dropmore. No one could then have foreseen the eventual fate of the species: to be mocked as the symbol of the suburban front garden. In its Victorian heyday the tree was almost universally admired. It was 'truly noble', as described by the arbiter of horticultural good taste, John Loudon. And as for its exotic form, Loudon claimed, its only rival was the celebrated cedar of Lebanon.

Back with his family in Cornwall after his exhausting trip in the wilds, William Lobb was congratulated by James Veitch.

William had sent back the seeds of about a hundred new or little-known trees and plants as well as the seeds of the monkey puzzle. Many of these novelties were now bursting with life in Veitch's numerous greenhouses. William had also packed up parallel sets of dried specimens to be examined – and identified – by professional botanists. This had been all part of the agreement when Veitch had picked the brains of Sir William Hooker at Kew before sending out William Lobb. And now the reports from Kew were most encouraging. William Lobb had introduced many new species. But perhaps his plant-hunting had only skimmed the surface. Should he return to South America? Like any gambler, James Veitch was prepared to double his money. And William was prepared to return to the wilds. After recuperating at home, he worked in Veitch's greenhouses, then sailed for Chile again in the spring of 1845.

William's second trip was even more successful than the first, judged by the number of saleable trees and other plants he sent back as seed. The British public, it was true, took time to recognise the value of some of them. And many of his introductions are more prized today than they were in his lifetime. William cast his net much wider on this second trip. His shortcut over the Andes had been a serious mistake. Now he followed the conventional route, sailing via Cape Horn and the south-west coast of Chile.

At Chiloe Island he found a large yellow-flowering shrub which is now the harbinger of spring in many British gardens: *Berberis darwinii*, discovered in 1835 by Charles Darwin during the voyage of the *Beagle*, but not introduced until spotted by William in the 1840s. Anther shrub William introduced was the Chilean lantern tree, *Crinodendon hookerianum*, an exotic creature with long, scarlet, tassel-like flowers. He brought back the seeds of what became the national flower of Chile: the Chilean bellflower, a spectacular evergreen climber, *Lapageria rosea* (named after Napoleon's first wife, the Empress Josephine, whose maiden name was de la Pagerie). Among the trees that he introduced were three that would in due course become celebrated.

The first was the Chilean firebush, *Embothrium coccineum*, that now forms a 40-foot-high pillar of scarlet in several favoured Irish gardens. The second was a southern beech, *Nothofagus antarctica*, with mottled bark and minute, crinkly leaves; it braves the winter close to the snowline in the Andes, and is one of the hardiest of its genus. The third was the most exotic, the alerce, alias *Fitzroya cupressoides*, named after the dashing Captain Robert Fitzroy who invited the young Charles Darwin to join him on the *Beagle*. Fitzroy's tree is the giant that straddles both sides of the Andes – Chilean and Argentinian –and, second only to the bristlecone pine of California, the longest-lived species in the world. But, sad to say, almost all the prodigious trees, over 200 feet tall and three thousand years old, were logged a century ago. Today it has found a refuge in Britain and Ireland, and the champion, at Ardkinglas in Argyll, is nearly 70 feet tall. But it's a thirsty tree, and finds even a wet Irish summer too dry for it. (I've planted four specimens in my arboretum and they are elegant, cypress-like creatures, all 6 feet high. So they have still some way to go.)

William's third trip was the most ambitious of all, judged by the number of important trees whose seeds he was told to collect. James Veitch, no doubt encouraged by Sir William Hooker, decided to send William to California and Oregon – the old hunting grounds of Menzies and, later, of David Douglas. William was not in good health. It appears that he had never fully recovered from the fevers he had contracted in South America. Veitch hoped the balmy climate of California would be more to his liking.

His ship sailed in 1849 and he reached San Francisco to find it transformed since the days of Menzies and Douglas. California had been an impoverished outpost of the Spanish empire from 1769 until 1821, and then part of an independent Mexico until 1848. By 1849 it had been grabbed by America, and was in the process of becoming the thirty-first state of the Union. It was also in the throes of the gold rush that had brought tens of thousands to seek their fortunes in the new-born state. When William's ship docked in San Francisco he found hundreds of ships in the harbour abandoned by their crews. The men had run off to the goldfields. William felt no temptation to follow. He headed south towards Monterey and Los Angeles, and soon struck gold of a different kind.

When James Veitch had planned this new trip for him, Veitch assumed that most of the important trees in this region had already been discovered by Menzies or Douglas. However some of these had only been sent to Europe as herbarium specimens. Others had been sent as seeds, but only in limited quantities. So this was William's main task: to track down the important species of trees already discovered, and to send back to James Veitch the seeds in commercial quantities. Was there a danger of flooding the market? The fact was that Douglas's introductions had merely whetted the appetites of British and European collectors. And perhaps William would also make new discoveries of his own. That would indeed be a bonus for Veitch.

In the event William achieved wonders. He hunted down and collected the seeds of five important pines, including the Monterey pine (*Pinus radiata*), soon to be the giant of the genus in Britain; the western yellow pine (*P. ponderosa*) not the biggest, but the most imposing of the genus; and the big-cone pine (*P. coulteri*) the pine with fir cones like huge pineapples. He tracked down the three prodigious silver firs: the grand fir (*Abies grandis*), the tallest; the noble fir (*A. procera*), the most handsome, as its name would suggest; and the Pacific silver fir (*A. amabilis*), a weeping giant whose branches sweep down to the ground. All these silver firs and pines had been introduced by David Douglas more than fifteen years earlier, but British collectors were still hungry for their seedlings.

William also sent seeds from an elegant silver fir, the Santa Lucia fir (*Abies bracteata*), which Douglas had discovered but never introduced.

Of course the seeds which most thrilled James Veitch (their seedlings would fetch the highest price in the market) were William's own discoveries. The most outstanding of these was the giant western red cedar, *Thuya plicata*, and by far the biggest and most impressive of all the thuyas. Somehow David Douglas had missed it, although it had actually been discovered (though not then introduced) by a late-eighteenth-century explorer called Tadaeus Haenkel. The species basks in the wetlands up the coast from Oregon to Canada. Its acrid-smelling wood is light but durable. It was the tree for Indian totem poles and war canoes. In Britain it was to have a more domestic role: it was perfect for garden huts.

Another all-important species of tree that William introduced was the coast redwood (*Sequoia sempervirens*). In 1795 it had been discovered, like so many west coast giants, by Archibald Menzies. But only a dried specimen had survived the voyage – and the row with Captain Vancouver. In due course the specimen was acquired by a leading botanist, Aylmer Bourke, and published in his sumptuous folios under the name *A description of the genus Pinus* (1803–24). The first introduction of the species into Britain – shortly before 1843 – made little impact, as the seeds arrived, presumably in a small packet, via Russia. Even when William sent home a much bigger batch of seeds, Veitch and other nurserymen were slow to realise the tree's extraordinary qualities.

This was, and still remains, one of the vegetable wonders of the world: the tallest tree known to have survived anywhere, in fact the world's tallest living organism, and one of the oldest. The current champion, 'Hyperion', hidden away in the spongy, fog-bound soil of northern California, measures a fraction under 380 feet tall with a girth of about 45 feet, and it's believed to be little less than two thousand years year old.

At first botanists thought the coast redwood was an evergreen form of the deciduous swamp cypress. This explains the relatively prosaic name for the species – *sempervirens* – simply meaning 'evergreen'. In 1847 the giant was given an official genus, *Sequoia*, named in honour of the remarkable mixed-race trader, Sequoiah, son of a British immigrant and a Cherokee Indian woman. He invented an alphabet for the Cherokee language, thanks to which his tribe quickly learnt to read and write. However he died in 1843, four years too soon to learn of the honour he was paid. In fact he was doubly honoured. His name was soon to be adopted for a second giant. And it was this second giant that was to make James Veitch lick his lips and bless the name of William Lobb.

By the summer of 1852 William had completed most of the tasks set him by Veitch. His consignments of seeds and living plants in Wardian cases had reached San Francisco, ready for shipping to Falmouth. He had agreed with James Veitch that he would spend one more year in Pacific America, but was now taking a well-earned rest on the balmy shores of California. One evening he was invited by Dr Albert Kellogg to attend the summer meeting of the Californian Academy of Science which Kellogg, a keen amateur botanist, had recently founded. Another guest was a professional hunter called Augustus Dowd, whom Kellogg introduced to the meeting. Dowd told them about his recent adventures, and his story was sensational. It certainly electrified William.

Earlier that year, Dowd had been chasing a large grizzly bear in Calaveras County in the foothills of the Sierra Nevada. The chase was long and hard, and brought him to a strange new part of the forested hills. Suddenly he found he had stumbled into a grove of gigantic trees. Forgetting the grizzly bear, he gazed in wonder at these colossal creatures. Back in his camp he told his companions about his extraordinary experience. Most of them were sceptical, and assumed that Dowd was drunk. But some believed him, and confirmed his story after being taken to see the monsters for themselves.

William didn't hesitate. There was not a moment to lose. He set off hotfoot for Calaveras County. He must be the first to collect seeds of the new giants and bring them in triumph back to England and James Veitch.

He found the grove easily enough, and collected the seeds and seedlings, with herbarium specimens to identify and name the discovery. Then he wrote to Veitch describing what he had found. William, romantic that he was, had never claimed to be eloquent. He was better at hunting trees than choosing words. His account of his discovery did the trees no honour: 'From 80 to 90 trees exist all within circuit of a mile, from 250ft to 320 feet in height, 10–20 ft in diameter'.[4] He might have been giving the measurements of a suburban housing estate, instead of describing one of the wonders of the world.

Of course William risked incurring James Veitch's displeasure by cutting short his trip and returning to England by the first boat, carrying with him the precious seeds and specimens. But he had gambled correctly. Veitch was ecstatic when he heard the news. His aim was to establish a monopoly in the sale of this new marvel, and time was short.

Already there was a report that William had been pipped at the post by a Perthshire laird called John Matthew, who had collected seeds in Calaveras County and returned with them four months before William. The report was true, but John Matthew had only distributed seeds to a few Scottish friends. Officially the credit of introducing the new giant would go to William and his employers, based on the herbarium specimens he had brought back.

But was this prodigy a new genus – or simply a new species of redwood? What name should it be given? And who should name it? In December 1853 an excited announcement appeared in the *Gardener's Chronicle*. Messrs Veitch had just received from their collector in California, William Lobb, foliage and seeds of a mysterious new tree. It turned out that Professor John Lindley, vice-secretary of the Horticultural Society, had been asked by Veitch to give it an official name according to international rules. The name chosen was *Wellingtonia gigantea*, creating a new genus in honour of Britain's war hero, the Duke of Wellington, who had died the previous year.

Not so fast, said a group of American botanists – for news of the new name reached the east coast with remarkable speed – not so fast. It's an American tree, and we shall call it an American name: *Washingtonia gigantea*, named after our own war hero, George Washington, who beat the British back in 1783.

The controversy rumbled on for several years, and only ended when *both* the proposed names were found to be invalid, according to international rules. It turned out that they had already been used for other plants. But the sequel, as we saw earlier, was a happy one: to name the tree first *Sequoia gigantea* (and then to create the new genus of *Sequoiadendron*) after a man of colour, and a hero in his own way – the mixed-race trader, Sequoiah, who had enriched the life of the Cherokee people with a brilliant new alphabet.

Meanwhile James Veitch lost no time in selling the offspring of the new discovery at hugely inflated prices. In June 1854, only six months since William's return to England, Veitch was offering seedlings at £3 2s 0d a piece, with a reduction to a guinea if the buyer bought 12 pairs – enough to plant an avenue.

There was no shortage of buyers at these exorbitant prices. In fact the craze for the 'Wellingtonia' (as it would continue to be called) could only be compared with the craze for the monkey puzzle, whose seeds had been brought back by William Lobb a decade earlier. And the Wellingtonia seemed heaven-sent for British gardens and arboretums. Its roots gripped the ground like talons; its bright green foliage seemed impervious to frost and wind. Soon the first generation of Wellingtonias would puncture the British skylines like church spires. The tree exploded in girth as arboretums well as growing astonishingly tall. This was a swaggering monarch of a tree that would dominate a new kingdom of arboretums and pineta. And it formed great avenues running to the horizon – from Benmore in Scotland to Stratfield Saye in Hampshire (where it received a special welcome from the new Duke of Wellington).

It was a discovery that enriched Europe and made James Veitch and his firm a small fortune. But in California it brought only disaster. The newcomers to the place, in the hectic days of the gold rush, had no respect for the venerable trees of Calaveras Grove. They quite literally danced on the graves of the giants. There is a jaunty engraving of a party in Calaveras Grove – the gentlemen top-hatted and the ladies in their crinolines – dancing a quadrille on the stump of a giant tree felled by the loggers. Another tree was sawn up and made into a bowling alley. A third, 116 feet tall, was felled and stripped, and the upper section of its bark dispatched to a museum in Washington; the lower section ended in the Crystal Palace after the building was moved to Sydenham. And the loggers, of course, made a meal from the trees in Calaveras Grove, and various other groves discovered in the foothills of the high Sierra. Ironically, the wood proved too brittle for building work. It was fit only for shingles and fence posts. Many giants were felled and then abandoned where they lay smashed on the hillsides.

By the end of the century Calaveras Grove and the other groves were unrecognisable. Fortunately an eloquent Scottish immigrant, John Muir, took up their cause, and other conservationists came to the rescue. Two of the trees were given an iconic, human identity: the biggest named, after two heroes of the American Civil War, 'General Sherman' and 'General Grant'. The federal government responded by creating a series of national parks – Yosemite, Sequoia (including Calaveras Grove), King's Canyon – where the giants could live safe from the loggers, and safe from wildfires. But how safe are they today in this era of global warming? Wildfires are endemic in the region; in fact the giants, shielded by their own enormously thick bark, depended on the wildfires to suppress their competitors. But the climate of California is changing for the worse. In 2020 the flames, fiercer than ever, came perilously close to General Sherman and the heart of Calaveras Grove.

Meanwhile William Lobb had set off on a second trip to Pacific America, despite pleas from his family in Cornwall for him to take life easy. His health was poor, and there was something odd about his manner, 'a sort of excitability' as James Veitch described it,[5] which worried his friends. No one, not even David Douglas, had done more to introduce new trees and plants to Europe. But he still dreamt of making new discoveries. His hopes slowly faded. Nothing he now sent back to Veitch was new or special, but just a repetition of previous batches of conifer seeds. His contract with Veitch expired in 1858. That year, after many months of silence, he wrote to Sir William Hooker enclosing five cases of seeds and living plants and dried specimens destined for Kew.

The news infuriated James Veitch. A tight-lipped correspondence followed. James was determined to prevent the seeds and plants falling into the hands of competitors. He sent one of his sons to Kew and paid £250 for all five of William's cases. Nothing more was heard from William, and James Veitch wondered if he had joined the gold rush.

In fact no one has discovered how William spent his final years. He is thought to have contracted syphilis on one of his journeys. He died in St Mary's Hospital in San Francisco in May 1864 – William Lobb, one of the world's greatest plant hunters, forgotten by his employers, cut off from his family and friends, and buried in an unmarked grave.

CHAPTER 17

The Quest for the Golden Goddess

Meanwhile Robert Fortune was living up to his name. He had led a charmed life in his first trip to China: polishing off pirates with his double-barrelled shotgun, and even disguising himself in Chinese attire. And now, in 1848, on his second trip to China, he was proving a new kind of plant hunter, and enjoying astonishing success. He was not in the power of any one employer like the unfortunate William Lobb, sent out to America and then abandoned by the firm of Veitch. In fact Fortune could now choose where he sent his plants, working for himself as a freelance.

Five years earlier, he had been sent to China to collect plants and seeds for the London Horticultural Society. As we saw, he risked his life to introduce dozens of new trees and other plants. But his salary was meagre, almost an insult: a mere £100 a year plus expenses. Back in London in 1848, he was head-hunted by the East India Company, one of the richest (and most controversial) of all British companies; it had grabbed a monopoly of trade in India, and forced China to accept its export of opium. The directors had now decided to compete with China by expanding their production of tea, and needed an expert to advise them.

Fortune seemed an ideal candidate. He was energetic and articulate, and not afraid to take risks. He also had excellent contacts in China. His recent book on his travels, *Three Years'*

Wanderings in China, had earned him nothing but praise. (Unlike most plant hunters, he had a talent for writing up his adventures.) Fortune struck a deal with the directors of the East India Company. He would supply them with seeds and plants and implements to grow Chinese tea plants in Himalayan India. He would also arrange for Chinese labourers to travel to India to help set up the new plantations. In return he would be decently paid and could splash out on expenses. Crucially, he could also work as a freelance, exploring China in search of new plants, which he was free to sell to nurseries in Britain.

For three years – from 1848 to 1851 – Fortune worked as an adviser in China and India. The deal worked perfectly. Fortune decided he would need at least a dozen Chinese tea workers to help develop the new Indian plantations. There would be no problem with the Chinese government. The emperor's men had their hands full. In 1850 the Taiping Rebellion, led by a charismatic leader in the south, began to eat away at the power of the imperial authorities.

Fortune decided to devote much of these three years to exploring the Chinese tea plantations in the east of the country, south-west of the treaty port of Ningpo. China, he felt, had all the answers for producing both black tea and green tea. And by a happy co-incidence the plains and valleys beyond Ningpo might contain other treasures as well as tea – rare and as yet undiscovered trees and other plants whose seeds he could sell to British nurseries.

But there was one alarming problem, which could have led to Fortune's arrest and even imprisonment. In 1842, cock-a-hoop after their victory in the First Opium War, Britain and the Western powers had bullied the emperor into accepting the terms of the Treaty of Nangking: Britain grabbed Hong Kong, and foreigners in general were given access to the five treaty ports, including Ningpo. Access to the rest of China was still forbidden

– apart from about 30 miles in the immediate neighbourhood of each treaty port. How then could Fortune explore the famous tea plantations, most of which lay more than 100 miles beyond Ningpo? And how could he pursue his other task: hunting for rare trees and plants in the great plains and hidden valleys unseen by any earlier European explorer?

Despite the risk of exposure, Fortune decided to don Chinese attire. It had worked before for a few weeks during his first trip to China. Now he told one of his two servants to shave off his hair and dress him in the flowing robes of a mandarin. In mid-October 1848 the party set off from Shanghai, heading for the black tea plantations at Mount Sunglo. At first they travelled by barge through the network of local canals and small rivers leading south. This brought them to a walled city, Hangzhou, which had been the imperial capital during the Song dynasty. Now it was the boisterous heart of the silk industry. White mulberry trees (*Morus alba*), whose leaves are food for silkworms, crowded the local gardens and even the pavements. Fortune had a nerve-racking experience when he was carried in a sedan chair, by mistake, into the main square of the ancient city. And there he was dumped while his bearers argued about the fee for their services. Luckily, his disguise, and his talent for speaking Chinese, proved sufficient. He passed as a mandarin from a different part of China – beyond the Great Wall.

Next day they continued upriver. At Waeping, about ninety miles from Hangzhou, they came to a wooded gorge full of rare trees and shrubs. For the first time Fortune saw some of the plants in the wild that he had known only from gardens – and in due course introduced to Britain. These included *Edgeworthia chrysantha*, the dazzling Chinese paperbush, with its cowslip-yellow flowers, and twigs so flexible that they can be knotted like string. Fortune also discovered a new species of cypress that delighted him.

But the most beautiful tree found in this district is a species of weeping cypress, which I had never met with in any other part of China. It was during one of my daily rambles that I saw the first specimen ... a noble-looking fir-tree, about sixty feet in height, having a stem as straight as the Norfolk Island pine, and weeping branches like the willow of St Helena [planted on Napoleon's grave] ... It reminded me of some of those large and gorgeous chandeliers ... in theatres and public halls in Europe.[1]

Fortune's weeping cypress, *Cupressus funebris*, one of the most elegant of all conifers, was soon to be a much admired specimen in the milder British gardens, especially those in Ireland.

Another of his discoveries in this district was to enjoy an even wider appeal, as it could brave any British winter, however low the thermometer sank. This was a new species of winter-flowering evergreen with spiky leaves and whiskery yellow flowers. He christened it *Mahonia bealei* after the merchant prince, and his own close friend, Thomas Beale, who kept open house for the British in his luxurious villa in Shanghai.[2]

Fortune spent much of the next year, 1850, browsing the plants in the gardens of Shanghai. He also found time to send a long, chatty letter to Sir William Hooker. He was sorry to hear that Joseph Hooker, Sir William's son, had been arrested in Sikkim. He trusted that Joseph would be released very soon; and he planned to meet him when he travelled to India next year. Meanwhile he was flattered to hear that Sir William admired the small plants of the weeping cypress which he had sent to the firm of Standish in Surrey, and were already on sale to the public. But he was sorry that Sir William was not impressed by the palm tree (the eponymous *Trachycarpus fortunei*) that Fortune had discovered on his first trip to China. As we saw, he had arranged for a specimen to be sent to Queen Victoria and it was duly honoured with a place on the lawn at Osborne.

Meanwhile he was busy preparing for his visit to the tea plantations of India. He filled sixteen Wardian cases with seedling tea plants, and seeds that would germinate on the voyage. As for the tea workers themselves, his friend Thomas Beale's agent had done a good job luring a team from the neighbourhood. The team included seven expert tea-makers, specialists in the production of green tea, and two men who could make tin canisters for packing the tea. Fortune and his party sailed for India from Hong Kong in the spring of 1851. After landing at Calcutta, where Fortune stayed with the director of the botanic garden, Hugh Falconer, they proceeded upcountry, first by boat up the Ganges, and then by carriage to the north-west – and into the foothills of the Himalayas. Fortune visited five Indian tea plantations north of Delhi, but was not impressed. The tea bushes were over exploited by plucking too many leaves when the bushes were young, Worse, the authorities had chosen the wrong terrain for many of these plantations. Some were too dry, others too wet for comfort. In his report to his employers Fortune pulled no punches. But history would show that the north-west of India was the wrong place to grow tea. The best place in India was the province of Assam, several thousand miles to the east. And the local Indian variety of tea plant, *Camellia sinensis var. assamica*, was actually more suitable for making black tea than the Chinese tea plant. Luckily, perhaps, this was yet to be discovered – and Fortune returned to England with his head held high, the most admired plant hunter, and tea expert, of the period.

Next year, 1853, the directors of the East India Company decided to offer Fortune a contract for a further three years helping to organise the Indian tea industry. They were delighted with progress, but realised that they needed thousands more tea plants and a second team of Chinese tea-makers. Fortune jumped at the chance. He would continue his double life: working as a freelance plant hunter, making money for himself, as well as collecting tea plants and tea-makers for the directors. The truth was he had fallen in love with China, and its people, despite the increasing dangers of travel in the eastern and central regions of the country.

He arrived in Shanghai in May 1853 to be greeted by an earthquake – a small one, but enough to knock down a few buildings near the house of Thomas Beale, where he was staying. It was a timely warning of the political earthquake which was starting to shake the Chinese empire to its foundations. In March of that year the Taiping rebels, who had been advancing eastwards up the Yangtse, captured the walled city of Nanking, killing many of the Manchu inhabitants of what had once been the imperial capital. The Europeans in Shanghai, less than 200 miles to the east, were understandably alarmed. The rebel armies were believed to number more than a hundred thousand men, including many forcibly recruited. Nothing was known for certain about the rebels' intentions. Messages reached Shanghai assuring the Europeans that they had no quarrel with them. But could the rebels be trusted? The chief magistrate in Shanghai, the taoutae, begged the British, French and American diplomats to intervene on the Chinese government's behalf. Western gunboats, powered by steam and armoured with steel, were already hammering the local pirates. Why not send the HMS *Styx* and HMS *Rattler* – or the French war steamer *Cassini* – to crush the rebels in Nanking?

The dilemma was sharpened by the bizarre character of the rebellion. Ten years earlier the Western powers had had no scruples in massacring Chinese in the First Opium War. Their own aim then was brutally self-serving and commercial: to force the Chinese to buy opium and other Western products in exchange for selling silk and tea. But was it now sensible for the Western powers to become involved in a Chinese civil war? These rebels claimed the moral high ground. They were Christians, they said, fighting a holy war against Buddhists, Taoists and other idolaters. And they sang hymns and circulated Christian scriptures in the ranks. Their charismatic leader, Hong Xiuquan, was a Christian convert – of a sort.

In fact the letter he sent the British plenipotentiary, Sir George Bonham, did not inspire confidence. Hong called himself 'the Celestial King', and claimed he was a younger brother of Jesus Christ. He astonished Sir George by telling him he was delighted that 'you English have not deemed myriads of miles too far to come and *acknowledge our sovereignty*'.[3]

Was the rebellion the first stirring of an attempt to convert millions of Chinese peasants to Christianity? Many of the more credulous Europeans thought so. Others, including level-headed men like Robert Fortune, thought the rebels' religious claims were a sham. But did this mean that Britain, France and America should intervene? Fortune was at a loss for an answer. What was clear was that neutrality seemed the least bad policy to all the Western powers – for the moment at least.

Fortune, at any rate, had no difficulty in continuing the hunt for the seeds of the best Chinese tea plants. He set up his headquarters in a Buddhist temple at Asoka near Ningpo. The local farmers sent in hundreds of packets of seeds that had ripened the previous year.

Later that summer Fortune hired a boat and set off once again up the small rivers west of Ningpo. He found many rare species of plants which excited him. He collected a specimen of the lacquer tree, *Toxicodendron verniciluum*, the tree that makes the varnish for the finest lacquerwork (but can poison a man with the fumes from its sap – and did very nearly kill the American consul in Shanghai, Mr Jones, when he rashly brought one home). Fortune collected hundreds of nuts of the Chinese sweet chestnut (*Castanea mollissima*) which he packed up for dispatch to India. These, he told his employers, would suit the Himalayas better than the European species. At any rate the experiment was worth trying.

And, best of all, close by a small temple in the mountains at Tsan-tsin, he stumbled on a dazzling new species of conifer. This was the conifer, he predicted, that would come to rival the cedars of Lebanon in magnificence, and come to be prized in all the finest British arboretums. It was a deciduous prodigy that seemed halfway between a larch and a cedar, later christened *Pseudolarix amabilis*, the 'lovely false larch'.

Fortune was captivated by this new monotypic species (that is, unique to its genus), but he found very few cones with viable seeds. For the next two years he was tormented by the thought: could he discover enough seeds to do justice to his discovery (dare one say it – to make Fortune's fortune), or would his golden goddess elude him?

Meanwhile he returned to Shanghai glowing with a discovery of a different sort. He had realised on this third trip to China why he had fallen in love with the country. It was because he identified it with his own happy childhood in the rich plains of rural Scotland. A respectable Chinese farmer had less land and was less wealthy than his Scottish equivalent. But each farmhouse

is a little colony, consisting of some three generations, namely, the grandfather, his children and his children's children. There they live in peace and harmony together; all who are able work on the farm . . . they live well, dress plainly, and are industrious, without being in any way oppressed. I doubt if there is a happier race anywhere than the Chinese farmer and peasantry.[4]

And of course Fortune revelled in the hospitality they offered. At first the ladies would rise hurriedly 'and disappear like a flock of partridges' when Fortune entered the courtyard unannounced. But soon they came to see he was 'a civilised being like themselves'. So he would be asked to sit down, and a chair would be set for him, and the lady of the house would bring him a cup of tea 'with their own fair hands'; and, while he was drinking it, they would be chatting and laughing as though he was one of the family.[5]

Fortune was delighted to sample the hospitality of farmers' markets and local Buddhist monasteries. And everywhere the villagers would flock to greet this mysterious stranger from another world, and beg him to stop and sit down and drink a cup of tea.

Everywhere in the countryside he was made welcome. But this only made more shocking what he encountered when he returned to Shanghai in early September, 1855.

The ancient walled city, enclosing a population of about 200,000, was now beset by rumours that a rising was imminent. The insurgents, it was claimed, were men from the southern provinces, and were linked with the Taiping rebels in Nanking. In the ensuing panic the imperial authorities in Shanghai prepared a reckless counterstroke. They hired a body of lawless men belonging to a secret society called the 'Small Sword Society', and armed them to defend the city.

The Europeans and Americans – diplomats, merchants, missionaries and others – all lived *outside* the walls in the leafy new town, created ten years earlier when Shanghai was chosen as one of the treaty ports. Naturally they found the rumours most alarming. But, despite their guns and their gunboats, they saw no reason to intervene – or even to take adequate measures to protect their own lives and property in the new town.

By chance Fortune had chosen the morning of 7 September

to pay a visit to the walled city, and entered by the north gate soon after daybreak. He was appalled by what he found. The bedding in the guardroom was saturated with human blood. He was told that the city's guards had been cut down by members of the Small Sword Society, who were now on their way to confront the two chief mandarins in charge of the city, the che-heen and the taoutae.

Despite the danger, Fortune could not resist following the trail to the che-heen's house. The old man had been abandoned by his forty guards, who were thought to have been in league with the rebels. He came out into the street, and tried to pacify the mob with fair words and promises for the future. He was told it was now too late for that. Then he was hacked to death, and his body exposed to view on a mat in a small courtyard, decorated with wisteria. Fortune was sickened by the sight. But he found that at least the rebels had spared the taoutae, the senior of the two chief mandarins. The taoutae was told to hand over his seals of office, and take an oath not to obstruct the new masters of the city. He was pleased to comply, and retired while the government buildings were wrecked by what Fortune called 'a set of respectable . . . looters'.[6]

It was this that shocked Fortune most of all. A city of two hundred thousand had surrendered to a motley band of barely five hundred rebels armed with old pistols, short swords and rusty-looking spears of various kinds. Shanghai had accepted its fate with apparent indifference. And the people who ransacked the government buildings, taking down the doors and windows and anything else of value – this was not 'a mob of lawless vagabonds', but the 'sober and industrious people of the neighbourhood'.

Fortune left Shanghai baffled by European indifference as well as by the Chinese variety. The rebels were besieged by government troops, but remained in full control of the walled city.

International trade with Shanghai collapsed – or was diverted to other ports. Yet the Great Powers sat on their hands, as if the rebellion did not concern them. And many European merchants made tidy sums by smuggling gunpowder and other vital supplies to the rebels.

Glad to be back in the countryside, where people behaved as if nothing had happened, Fortune returned to the tea districts where the tea harvest was in full swing. By the winter of 1853 he was ready to return to Hong Kong with more Wardian cases stuffed full of tea plants bound for India, and ornamental plants for the English market. To insure them against disaster, he spread the consignments over four different ships. And several months later he was relieved to learn that all the Indian consignments had arrived safely in Calcutta: no fewer than 23,892 tea plants (many of the seeds must have germinated on the voyage) as well as more that 300 sweet chestnut plants destined for the Himalayas.

By midsummer in 1854 he was ready to resume the hunt for the quarry which had haunted him for so long – the elusive golden larch, *Pseudolarix amabilis*.

His plan was to return to the temple at Tsan-tsin and collect a hoard of fir cones which would supply enough seeds to satisfy the hunger of even the most addicted British tree collectors.

After a day's comfortable travel by mountain chair through a series of romantic valleys west of Ningkang-jou, he found himself back at the temple of Tsan-tsin. The priests of the adjoining monastery were astonished. No other foreigner, it appeared, had been there before. But they were happy to honour him with a room next to that of the chief priest. The news of his arrival 'seemed to fly in all directions', as he later explained. While Fortune was eating his dinner, followed by a well-earned cigar, hundreds of villagers crept up to inspect the 'white devil'. In fact the 'doors and windows were completely besieged with people. Every little hole and crevice had a number of eager eyes peeping through it, each anxious to see the foreigner feed'. The chief priest himself seemed obsessed with Fortune, who became seriously alarmed; the old man followed Fortune with his eyes, whenever he moved, and Fortune began to fear the priest had lost his senses and might attack him in the night. One of Fortune's servants was sent to investigate, and reassured him with a laugh. The poor old priest was not mad. He only behaved like a madman partly 'through fear' and partly 'through curiosity'.[7]

Next day Fortune and his party began the hunt for fir cones of the golden larch. They found numerous giant specimens of the tree; many were more symmetrical – and ornamental – than the common larch of Europe. The finest of them swept up like flag poles for the first 50 feet, then threw out large branches parallel to the ground, ending with elegant leading shoots. Fortune reckoned the tallest trees were more than 120 or 130 feet. But the hunt for fir cones was deeply disappointing. Fortune strained his eyes for half an hour; he couldn't spot a single fir cone. Later he was taken to a temple at Quan-ting, in a wooded valley a day's journey from Tsan-tsin. The woods were richly furnished with timber trees: chestnuts and oaks and Japanese cedars and Chinese coffin-wood trees. And there were young golden larch closely planted high up in the mountains above the temple. What seemed to be the 'queen of the forest'[8] was a giant golden larch standing alone on the hillside. Fortune encircled the tree with his tape measure: its trunk was 8 feet in circumference, and he reckoned its height came to a full 130 feet. But once again the golden goddess eluded him. At any rate she was barren. Not a single fir cone could be found.

Back at Tsan-tsin, Fortune was assured by the monks that *next year* the trees would give birth to a healthy family of cones. They had a habit of only fruiting in alternate years. No doubt Fortune ground his teeth. But he would not have chosen a career as a plant hunter if he had not been able to cope with the occasional disappointment. Anyway he had a most successful second year supplying India with tea plants and tea manufacturers. And his hoard of new plant discoveries in 1854, for sale in England, was soon to delight the two nursery firms he supplied – Standish and Glendenning. His discoveries included several elegant camellias and the spectacular Chinese rice-paper plant, *Tetrapanax papyrifera*, which he had spotted on a one-day excursion to Formosa (now Taiwan). With his usual mixture of daring and good luck, he had hitched a lift in an American tug steamer, the *Confucius*. This had been hired by the Chinese authorities to take boxes of silver to supply the army facing a rebellion in Formosa. The rice-paper plant looks as if it belongs in the tropics, with palmate leaves at least 3 feet wide. In fact it proves tough enough to survive most British and Irish winters.

The following year, 1855, Fortune continued with his demanding task of buying still more tea seeds for India and hunting for rare trees and shrubs for England. He sailed to Shanghai full of hope early in the spring.

By now the siege of the walled city of Shanghai had reached a grim finale. The European merchants in the new town outside the walls had been persuaded to stop smuggling gunpowder and food to the rebels. The imperial troops sealed off the town with a new wall, and tightened the noose. The siege intensified. Even the rebels' European admirers began to lose faith. The French government sent a gunboat which battered a hole in the walls. The rebel commanders decided it was time to evacuate.

A fire and a massacre followed. When Fortune examined the smoking ruins, he found most of the city had been destroyed by the government troops. The trees which he had admired, including a huge, elegant ginkgo, were blackened stumps. In the plain to the west of the city, the government troops had made their camp. Now, as Fortune passed close by in a hired boat, he was overwhelmed by a sickening stench. They lay there, unburied or half buried, hundreds of headless corpses, the remains of the rebels who had been executed after failing to escape.

Fortune shuddered, then focused his mind on studying the silk industry and the mulberry trees on which it depended. He took a boat to the heart of the industry around Hoo-chow-foo and was understandably impressed. The variety of white mulberry in these silk districts produced a bigger, more striking and glossier leaf than the mulberries of south China and the Indian silk districts. All were in fact from the same superior clone, he was told, produced by grafting. Although other crops, like rice and vegetables, grew on the man-made embankments, it was the mulberry plantations that dominated these immense plains. From a distance the plains resembled one enormous mulberry garden.

Travelling on the intricate network of canals and rivers, through a landscape punctuated by ancient pagodas, suited Fortune perfectly. It was not only luxurious compared to travel by mountain chair. It was also relatively safe – so he thought. But later that summer he had an alarming experience, on his journey by canal back to Shanghai, which brought him close to disaster. While he and the crew were asleep one night, and the boat moored beside the canal, a party of thieves took out one of the windows from the cabin and stole the entire contents of his trunks and other boxes. One trunk contained all his money – 100 Shanghai dollars. Even more important, it had been stuffed with his botanical accounts, drawings, journals and other irreplaceable memoranda of three years in China. But as usual with Fortune, he led a charmed life. His name well suited him.

While it was still dark, the thieves brought back everything except the money – even the coat and trousers and necktie thrown on the table before he went to bed. They stood in the darkness on the opposite side of the canal and told his servants they had no use for the 'white devil's trunks and clothes'.[9]

Fortune was astonished, but could only feel grateful. 'What an extraordinary people the Chinese people are,' he wrote later, 'and how difficult to understand! . . . The thieves of any other nation would never have thought of bringing back what they did not want . . . Chinese thieves are much more considerate and civilized.'[10]

Civilised or not, the coastal pirates continued to make sea travel dangerous for Europeans. On his way back to Shanghai by P&O steamer, Fortune passed a small British gunboat, the *Bittern*, which had been sent to clean out a nest of pirates in the area. About twenty pirate junks were waiting in harbour for the *Bittern* to make a frontal attack. They had numerous guns ready to blow the British ship out of the water. They were shocked when the *Bittern* anchored just out of range, fired broadside after broadside, and then sent a party of marines to take the pirates in the rear. Hundreds of pirates were killed or drowned and their base destroyed. A similar fate awaited a pirate nest at Chusan. This was not 'fair fighting', Fortune was told by a Chinese friend, who shook his head disapprovingly. Fair or unfair, it certainly worked.

Back in Thomas Beale's luxurious villa in the new town of Shanghai, Fortune put the finishing touches to his plans for Indian tea. Two more teams of tea-makers were dispatched to Calcutta by way of Hong Kong, both consisting of men who specialised in black tea. A season's collection of plants for England was dispatched to the firms of Glendinning and Standish and Noble. But what about that elusive goddess, *Pseudolarix amabilis*, the golden larch?

In October of that year Fortune made a third visit to the

temple of Tsan-tsin and its 'imbecile' priests. He was told that this year he would find plenty of ripe seeds nearby in the Valley of the Nine Stones. It turned out that most of the small golden cones had already been harvested by an enterprising villager, who planned to sell them in Ningpo, after cleaning them. Fortune had arrived in the nick of time. He bought the seeds; and the villager arranged for the seeds to be delivered to him within a few days. So there was a happy ending to his three-year hunt for the elusive goddess. In a few years the seedling trees would be universally admired – and selling for an astonishing sum at Glendinning's nursery in Surrey. It was, he believed, the 'most important of all my Chinese introductions'.[11]

And there was a bonus attached to that happy ending. On the way up to the golden larch, in a romantic glen, Fortune stumbled on an unknown species of 'true' rhododendron. (It was strikingly different from the azaleas which represent the rest of the rhododendron genus in China according to modern taxonomy.) In due course it would honour Fortune's name – as *Rhododendron fortunei* – and provide one half of a hybrid called *Rhododendron x loderi*. This unusually fragrant hybrid is blessed with violet leaf stalks and a huge, lacy truss of flowers turning from pink to white. Many gardeners, myself included, regard it as the queen – or queen mother – of all rhododendrons.

Fortune finally sailed for Calcutta in the spring of 1856. His days as a wandering plant hunter were far from over. The dangerous East still beckoned. Japan, like China, was now open to daredevil travellers. And it was not only danger that sharpened Fortune's appetite. In Japan he would face competition from a trio of other plant hunters, including the delightful young son of the celebrated house of Veitch, and an ancient roué who had been expelled from Japan more than thirty years earlier.

CHAPTER 18

Beyond the Prison Island

Philipp Franz von Siebold was the much acclaimed author of *Flora Japonica*, published in Leiden when he was thirty-nine. He had been born in Wurzburg to a family of respected German doctors and professors. Now he was a man of sixty-four, honoured in Holland and Sweden, but battered by a series of scrapes and self-inflicted misfortunes. He had 'gone native', as people put it; which meant he was living with a Japanese mistress in a suburb of Nagasaki, the port city of southern Japan. He had fathered a child by her. But he was still as passionately committed to collecting – and identifying and selling – Japanese plants for the European market.

He had first sailed to Japan in 1823, as a physician and botanist employed by the Dutch government, and was lucky to escape with his life when the ship was struck by a typhoon. He then spent six years in the country, mainly on Deshima, a tiny man-made island, scooped out of the mud in the harbour of Nagasaki in the early seventeenth century, when the rest of Japan was sealed off against foreigners.

It was from this claustrophobic Dutch trading post, a miniature prison island, that his two distinguished predecessors, Engelbert Kaempfer and Carl Thunberg, had sallied out to make their botanical discoveries.

Kaempfer was resident physician and botanist there from 1690 to 1692. In due course he made one of the great botanical discoveries of the century. He found and described and named the first living 'fossil tree' – the ginkgo, brought from China to Japan about 300 years earlier.

Thunberg, who lived on Deshima from 1775 to 1777, found many elegant trees and shrubs new to Europe, and described them in his own scholarly *Flora Japonica*. These included at least a dozen that are prized in European gardens today: two celebrated maples, the Japanese maple (*Acer palmatum*) whose innumerable varieties, in autumn, glow with all the colours of the rainbow, and the big, boisterous painted maple (*A. pictum*); two celebrated oaks, the Japanese oak (*Quercus acuta*) and the monstrous-leaved daimio oak (*Q. dentata*); and, the most majestic, the blue-flowered empress tree (*Paulownia tomentosa*). Thunberg was a disciple and friend of Linnaeus, who paid him the honour of naming the Japanese black pine after him. But Thunberg, unlike most plant hunters, was a scientist not a gardener. He returned to Sweden from Deshima with dried specimens for the herbarium, not living plants for the garden. It was to be many decades until these trees and shrubs were introduced into Europe.

Deshima itself had been created by Shogun Tokugawa Ieasyu early in the seventeenth century. By then the shoguns had held Japan in their steely grip for five hundred years. As military dictators they were the real rulers of the country; the emperors had only nominal authority. Shogun Tokugawa had expelled the Portuguese traders and missionaries, and closed Japan to foreigners. This slammed the door on Europe, its trade and its ideas. Deshima was a vital crack in the door – just wide enough for the Dutch East India Company to organise once-a-year shipments of European goods to Nagasaki. When the fleet of Dutch merchant ships anchored in the harbour in the autumn, the Japanese could learn about the West by buying books and scientific instruments in exchange for Japanese exports like copper, silver and sugar. And the Western men of science like Kaempfer, Thunberg and Siebold could learn about Japan. For once a year in spring they were invited to go in a delegation to Edo (now Tokyo) to make their homage to the shogun. So the prison door swung open, and the distinguished botanists, under close supervision, could hunt for plants all the 600 miles to Edo and back.

Siebold himself found it easy to find loopholes in the system, and bend the rules. He made friends with high-ranking officials and offered them medical treatment. He organised a small hospital in Nagasaki to educate medical students on Western lines. This meant that he needed even more opportunities to leave Deshima to search for medicinal plants – so he claimed.

And Siebold knew how to enjoy himself. He applied for a 'wife' from the 'pleasure district'[1] of Nagasaki. Permission was granted and he set up house with a sixteen-year-old prostitute called Kusumoto Taki. In 1827 she gave birth to a daughter named Ine. His downfall came when he acquired several maps of Japan from the emperor's librarian in Edo. It was a capital offence to be found with a map of the country, as the shoguns were morbidly afraid of invasion by the Russians or Western imperialists. Siebold was accused of being a Russian spy, put under house arrest for a year, and then formally expelled from Japan. The unfortunate librarian died in prison. Kusumoto Taki, however, was not abandoned. Siebold left money for her upkeep and paid for Ine's education.

On his return to Europe, Siebold bounced back with remarkable speed. He had been thrown out of Japan but his luggage had already been sent ahead of him: sixty crates of herbarium specimens and numerous other trophies. He married a German girl and fathered three sons and two daughters. But his heart must have stayed in Japan. This was his obsession: to tell the world about the trees and other plants in that mysterious country. In 1832–52 he published his own *Flora Japonica* as part of *Nippon*, a heavyweight seven-volume work on the botany and ethnography of Japan. His botanical research was mainly based on his personal collection of twelve thousand specimens of dried plants which he sold in due course to the Dutch government.

Siebold, like Thunberg, was the first to collect and name many Japanese trees and shrubs popular in Europe today. He, too, named some dazzling maples: the hornbeam maple (*Acer carpinifolium*) the mushroom-like *Acer cissifolium* and *Acer rufinerve* with its glaucous shoots and snakebark trunk. He was the first European to describe and name *Cercidiphyllum japonicum*, the tallest deciduous tree in Japan, and the tree that smells of burnt toffee. Best of all, perhaps, was his discovery of a tall, willow-like magnolia (*M. salicifolia*). But he introduced none of these plants to Europe. He found it hard to bring living plants halfway across the world, and the job was left to posterity. Ironically, one of the few plants which he succeeded in introducing was not to prove a welcome guest. It was *Fallopia japonica*, the infamous Japanese knotweed.

In due course Siebold made his home in Leiden in the Netherlands, where the university was famous for its Hortus Botanicus, founded in 1590. *Nippon* was much admired by European scholars, and the Dutch king, William II, paid Siebold a generous salary. In 1842 he was appointed 'adviser to the king for Japanese affairs',[2] and other honours followed. He became Philipp von Siebold, an esquire in the Dutch nobility. And the Russian government invited him to St Petersburg to advise them how to deal with the Japanese. Of course he remained obsessed by Japan. Would he ever be allowed to return to Taki and Ine? It seemed as unlikely as the idea of Lieutenant Pinkerton returning to be the husband of Madame Butterfly.

But then, in 1854, the door to Japan was kicked open by Commander Perry and the American fleet. At last the shogun's bluff was called. Two and half centuries of isolation ended, as foreign traders (and travellers) were given limited access to the country. By 1857 Siebold's expulsion was cancelled; he was hired as an adviser by the Dutch Trading Society, and next year allowed to return, provided he kept a low profile and avoided local politics.

No doubt he found there was much in which he could now take pride. His daughter Ine, whose education he had paid for, was on the way to becoming the first woman doctor in Japan. He himself was a famous international scientist, the pioneer of Western medicine, and the grand old man of Japanese studies – even though he chose to live with a new mistress (and father a new child) hidden away in a suburb of Nagasaki.

It was there that Robert Fortune encountered him soon after Fortune had stepped off the boat in Nagasaki in the autumn of 1860. Siebold could be charming when he chose. He took the younger man to his library, and showed him the current collection of rare and interesting plants in his garden. He claimed that he was now safer in his suburban home than he would have been in the city itself. 'It is not necessary for me to carry a revolver in my belt, like the good people in Desima and Nagasaki.'[3] But it is striking that Fortune, describing this visit, makes no mention of being given any plants. The truth was that the two men were rivals – competing to sell Japanese rarities to the same European market.

Fortune himself was dazzled by what he saw in the gardens of Japanese connoisseurs. When he arrived in Kanagawa, near Edo (Tokyo), he found new trees even in the most obvious places. Most impressive of all was the Japanese umbrella pine, alias the parasol fir (*Sciadopitys verticillata*), in the grounds of the ancient temple at Bukengee. This, like the ginkgo, is a monotypic survivor (from a genus with only one species) and well known from fossils. Its branches project like the ribs of an umbrella and it had already been described and named by both Thunberg and Siebold. But neither man had succeeded in sending viable seeds to Europe. This was Fortune's chance.

Delighted by everything he saw – the massive timbers of the temples, the mixed forests of pine and oak and bamboo, and snow-covered cone of Mount Fuji, 'the queen of mountain scenery'[4] – Fortune continued snapping up seeds and seedlings. Four trees, common in the countryside, particularly excited him: the Japanese false cypresses (*Chamaecyparis pisifera* and *C. obtusa*), the Japanese silver fir (*Abies firma*) and the Japanese sweet chestnut (*Castanea crenata*). In due course he sent back to England the seeds, or seedlings, of dozens of new plants, including what is surely the most beautiful of all lilies, the golden lily (*Lilium auratum*), and a handsome form of hosta which was later given Fortune's name. He also sent an exotic pine tree with a bark patterned like marble, which he had introduced earlier from China (*Pinus bungeana*), an oriental cork tree (*Quercus variabilis*) and an elegant new shrub with a golden flower (*Hypericum patulum*). Many of these he owed to the discoveries of Thunberg or Siebold – a debt he was happy to acknowledge.

He was less happy in his relations with a new rival who had arrived in Japan just before him. This was the twenty-one-year-old plant hunter from the great house of Veitch.

John Gould Veitch was the great-grandson of the John Veitch who had founded the family firm in the early 1780s. This had begun as a small business on land leased from Sir Thomas Acland's estate at Killerton in Devonshire. Then it had grown, by leaps and bounds, to become one of the largest and most successful nurseries in Britain – and indeed the world. James Veitch, John's grandfather, was the domineering head of the firm who had commissioned the unfortunate William Lobb to bring back a succession of treasures from the Pacific. These included monkey puzzles from Chile and redwoods from North America. In 1853 he had moved the firm's headquarters to the King's Road in London, where young John Gould had cut his teeth in the firm's vast greenhouses.

Now, with the door to Japan open at last, John Veitch had been told to go out there and, like Robert Fortune, exploit the discoveries of Thunberg and Siebold. But there was a crucial difference between the resources of the two new arrivals. Fortune, the expert, was on a tight budget because he was self-employed; this meant he had no time to wander about looking for wild plants in the mountains; most of his time had to be spent hunting for plants in private gardens and local nurseries. John Veitch, the beginner, had the money and muscle of the family firm behind him, and he could rely on the backing of the leading botanist in Britain, the director of Kew, Sir William Hooker.

In December Fortune slipped back across the sea to Shanghai with a first consignment of trees and shrubs bound for London. Had he encountered his rival, John Veitch? Strange to say, Fortune makes no mention of meeting him. Perhaps he took care *not* to meet John Veitch. And perhaps he felt sore that it was a beginner, John Veitch, not an expert like himself, who was chosen to be the botanical adviser to the British consul in Edo, Rutherford Alcock.

It was Alcock, himself an amateur plant hunter, who got permission for a team from the British legation to be the first foreigners to scale Mount Fuji. John Veitch was delighted to be invited to join. The 12,389-foot volcano is much the highest mountain in Japan and a national icon. Its snow-capped summit has captivated Japanese artists for centuries. And it proved full of botanical treasures. In September, Veitch returned to Edo, after singing 'Rule Britannia' on the summit, with an exciting haul of new trees and shrubs for dispatch to London. To these he added many others from the forests north of Edo. The majority had been originally discovered and named by Thunberg and Siebold; others were entirely new to science; others again were duplicates of Fortune's latest collection – which meant there was trouble in store for both men.

But Veitch, still a mere boy of twenty-two, had certainly pulled off a botanical coup. From Mount Fuji itself he brought back the seeds of four new pines, including *Pinus densiflora*, which combines a cinnamon-red bark with glaucous young shoots; the Japanese black pine (*P. thunbergii*), the pine which Linnaeus had named in honour of Thunberg; and the Japanese white pine (*P. parviflora*) with silvery lines on the underside of its leaves. Most important, economically, he collected seeds of a species that, in British commercial forestry, was to outshine the common larch of Europe: the Japanese larch, *Larix kaempferi*. It grows faster and can put up with poorer soils. Most decorative of all was a new silver fir; the underside of its leaves sparkled like hoar frost; later botanists were to name it *Abies veitchii* in honour of John Veitch. (Unfortunately he failed to send back viable seeds, and it fell to a later plant hunter sent by the firm, Charles Maries, to introduce it to Europe.)

And John Veitch had spotted a number of new varieties of well-known species. He discovered a delightful version of the ubiquitous Japanese cedar. Called *Cryptomeria japonica* 'Elegans', this develops into an enormous bush, trapped for ever in childhood. In fact the leaves remain in their *juvenile* state: larger, softer, more slender and wider apart, glaucous in spring and summer, and bronzed by frost and snow. Veitch also discovered a new variety of the small, bushy magnolias introduced from Japan to Europe in 1790, and now known as *Magnolia liliiflora*. This variety, called 'nigra', is a great improvement on the original: more of a tree than a bush with flowers an imperial purple. Today it has much to its credit as it has given its purple genes to numerous modern hybrids.

None of these new species and varieties had been collected by Fortune. But seven others featured in both men's collections. The first was that beguiling fossil tree, the Japanese umbrella pine. The second was the bright green variant of the thuja, *Thujopsis dolabrata*. Two others were imposing trees of the forest: the Hinoki cypress and the Sawara cypress. And there was one herbaceous plant of exceptional quality: the golden lily (*Lilium auratum*). Who would introduce them first, Fortune or Veitch? That was a question yet to be decided. But it added to the tensions of life in Edo.

Despite these tensions, John Veitch was in high spirits and a popular guest at the legation. In fact he revelled in his new role as adviser to the British consul. One of his jobs was to pack up cases of plants to be sent to Sir William Hooker at Kew and Queen Victoria at Osborne. He also worked hard in the legation's garden. Someone had told him that Japanese vegetables were insipid or worse. So he laid out a vegetable garden 'on English principles',[5] using seeds sent out from Exeter by his family's firm. The legation itself was somewhat claustrophobic, as travel in the city could prove dangerous. John Veitch responded by editing a satiric newspaper called the *Illustrated Fuji Yama Gazette* with a caricature of himself at the centre. And then a blow fell which could have brought the careers of both men, Veitch and Fortune, to a sudden and violent end.

It was 5 July 1861. Veitch was about to return from a new collecting trip. Fortune had hoped to be at the legation, but Alcock was away and Fortune had been rebuffed by the acting consul. That night, while the legation guards were asleep, fourteen men armed with swords broke into the legation. They were renegade 'ronin' – followers of one of the great feudal lords – and their aims were never made clear. Were they planning to assassinate Alcock? Or was this an act of terror designed to express their disgust with the opening up of Japan? The legation staff, half their number but armed with pistols, fought with great courage. Two of the defenders were seriously wounded, and several of the intruders were killed, before the legation guards came to the rescue. Blood spattered the walls of the legation when Veitch returned a few days later.

It was a gruesome end to happy days of plant-hunting. Fortune left Japan soon after – anxious, no doubt, to reach London with seeds and plants before John Veitch arrived. *The Times* duly published an account of Fortune's astonishing new collections. This provoked a bellow of rage from James Veitch, junior. It was a lie, he wrote to the editor. His son John had been sending new

John Gould Veitch

seeds and plants from Japan *before* Fortune had ever set foot in the country.

The controversy could never be resolved, trivial as it was. Many of the plants that both men discovered travelled back to England on the same ship. Let us say that, in the race to be the first man to bring these treasures back to Europe, Fortune and Veitch were joint winners.

More important was the sad fate that awaited Siebold. He and Thunberg had prepared the ground for most of the plants introduced by Fortune and Veitch. Yet in 1862 the Dutch government which had hired Siebold for his second trip to Japan asked the Japanese authorities to expel him from the country a second time. They had found him too arrogant and combative to work with. So once again he was booted out of the country he loved, leaving a mistress and a young child. He died in 1866, still fighting to be allowed to return.

Still more tragic was the fate of young John Veitch.

He had inherited great gifts from his family – without the drawbacks. He had huge energy, like his father and grandfather, but didn't fly off the handle when crossed. He was clever and charming and efficient. He seemed destined for a long and dazzling career in charge of the family firm. But his health began to fail soon after his return from Japan. By his late twenties he was seriously ill. He married and fathered two children. Aged no more than thirty, he died of TB.

CHAPTER 19

How to Spend a Cool Million

Robert Holford was a born collector. He was also unusually shy and reclusive. As a boy, no one had expected a great deal from him. He made no mark when he went up to Oriel College at Oxford. His mother was Irish: the daughter of an obscure Irish clergyman. The Holford family came from the ranks of the minor gentry, with a small manor house in Gloucestershire rented out, until the 1820s. They were not countrymen. They had a lucrative legal practice in London; for several generations they were masters in chancery. Their estate at Westonbirt was humble enough compared to that of their neighbours. And then in 1839, the year Robert was thirty-one, a vast fortune came his way: a cool million pounds in cash (equivalent to a hundred million today), free of all responsibilities, a free ticket for a lifetime of collecting, and a bonanza to make even the richest of neighbouring landowners green with envy.

The Holford family felt squeamish about revealing the real source of this vast fortune. What they did say was that, in the eighteenth century, they had bought three shares in the New River Company, the company that supplied London with clean water from the aquifers it controlled. That was their story. The truth was that the cool million had been made by a bachelor uncle, an earlier Robert Holford, in speculating on foreign exchange. Young

Robert Holford

Robert, an only child, inherited every penny, and proceeded on a buying spree of heroic proportions.

His collection of pictures soon rivalled that of the newly created National Gallery in London. He had acquired many celebrated portraits, including a drawing of Isabella Brandt by her husband Rubens, a stunning portrait of the Abbé Scaglia by Van Dyck, and no fewer than five Rembrandts. But his strongest suit was in landscapes. He owned a pair of Claudes (*Les Bergers Musiciens* and the *Temple of Bacchus*) a pair of Lancrets (*Fêtes champêtres*) and others by Salvator Rosa, Gaspard Dughet, Claude-Joseph Vernet and Richard Wilson. He revelled in Italian bronzes and Chinese porcelain, not to speak of French furniture, French tapestries, early printed books and illuminated manuscripts. In due course he bought the site of the old Dorchester House with 100 yards of frontage in Park Lane, London, and commissioned

Lewis Vuillamy to build a huge Italian-style palazzo to house his treasures.

But he was much more than a connoisseur and collector of art. His most important collection, which was to prove a dazzling legacy for the future, was quite different. He was a passionate collector of trees. And he was spurred on by the competition with other landowners who suffered from the same obsession – like Lord Somers of Eastnor Castle or his versatile and eccentric neighbour, Henry Moreton, the 3rd Earl of Ducie.

The Ducie estate was blessed with 18,000 acres of wood and pasture, including an arcadian slice of the Severn valley. The family had dominated politics in Gloucestershire since the late seventeenth century. Henry's father, the 2nd Earl, was the first to indulge himself by building a large country house. He commissioned Samuel Teulon to do the job. The new Tortworth Court was a fashionable confection of Elizabethan gables and towers and turrets. But the 2nd Earl died in 1853, the year it was completed. It was his son, Henry, who began to make a collection of trees at Tortworth. He had tried big game hunting and shot an impressively large crocodile by the First Cataract in Egypt. But he found collecting trees more congenial – and a good deal safer.

Meanwhile Robert Holford had taken the lead with his own collection of trees. His appetite seemed to have no limits: that is, he planned to make an arboretum big enough to contain every tree that could survive the British winter. How should these trees be arranged? In other words, what form should he give to his new arboretum? That was the overwhelming question.

At first his ideas on landscape were dominated by those of the Gilpin family. William Gilpin, the late-eighteenth-century rector of the small village of Boldre in Hampshire, had launched the Picturesque movement in landscape design. His travel books, in search of romantic British landscapes in places like the Lake

District, proved to be bestsellers. In due course his ideas inspired two eloquent – and argumentative – country gentlemen: Sir Uvedale Price and Richard Payne Knight. Although they disagreed on many things (Knight had a controversial obsession with what he called the 'worship of Priapus') all three men denounced the sheer monotony of the late eighteenth-century taste in the design of parks and gardens. This was the 'naturalistic' style made fashionable by Lancelot 'Capability' Brown. These pioneers of the Picturesque style were joined by a fourth man, William Sawrey Gilpin. A nephew of the rector of Boldre, he had taken up landscape design in middle age after an earlier career as a landscape painter and drawing master. Variety and intricacy and contrast were the buzzwords of the new Picturesque style, and they became the keys to Holford's extraordinarily ambitious plans for Westonbirt.

Holford had inherited the family estate in 1839. His first plantings were conventional enough – indeed somewhat old-fashioned. He planted clumps of common oaks in the park, and a grove of Scots pines in the pleasure grounds by the house, a Gothic villa recently built by his father, George Holford. What about some exotics, too?

In 1831 an elegant, more pendulous species of cedar was discovered, and introduced to Britain, to add to the celebrated cedar of Lebanon. This was the Himalayan cedar, *Cedrus deodara*, which forms immense forests north of the plains of north-west India. Robert spotted the seedling tree in one of the fashionable nurseries – perhaps in Veitch's or Glendenning's. He planted the one-year-old tree in the pleasure grounds next to the house. Five years later he enriched the park with two giant-leaved maples (*Acer macrophyllum*) – the spectacular species that David Douglas had brought back from the north-west of America. But he seems to have felt it was premature to add many more kinds of exotics, either in the gardens by the house or in the park.

The truth was that, for the first twenty years, he was up to his eyes in a mass of other expensive projects. He studied the minutiae of Renaissance architecture; he spent a quarter of a million pounds on the vast Italianate palace he had commissioned from Lewis Vuillamy to replace old Dorchester House in Park Lane. He stood for Parliament and was elected the MP for East Gloucestershire. He acquired that astonishing collection of pictures and other works of art. And in 1850 he married and started a family; his wife was Mary Anne Lindsay, a daughter of the well-known Scottish connoisseur, Lord Crawford. No wonder that collecting trees was put on the long finger (as we say in Ireland). True, he built an Italian garden at Westonbirt incongruously close to his father's Gothic villa. And he had great plans for an arboretum.

But this was still to come. First he would transform the local landscape – which soon looked as if it had been hit by an avalanche. He was obsessed with the idea that both his garden and park were too small. To double their size, he decided to move the whole village of Westonbirt – ten cottages and a vicarage – lock, stock and barrel, half a mile to the west. (History does not record what the villagers thought about the move, but no doubt the plumbing in the new village, designed by Vuillamy, was an improvement on the plumbing in the old one.) The main road to Bath had run through the village. So the main road was moved half a mile to the north, and the local inn, the Hare and Hounds, was moved with it. Only the medieval church, and an elderly yew tree which accompanied it, survived these convulsions.

Bereft of its village, the Gothic church now dominated the lawn below the house, and marked the meeting place of two opposite styles. To the east stretched the formal Italian garden, with its stone kerbs, mannerist cupolas and balustrades. To the west informality ruled supreme, with a small lake and irregular groups of trees and shrubs planted on the site of the original village.

Formal or informal? Which style owed more to the ideas of the Picturesque school, led by William Sawrey Gilpin? In fact Gilpin had died in 1843, only four years after Robert had inherited Westonbirt, and Gilpin probably never visited the place. But his ideas were eloquently expressed in his book, *Practical Hints on Landscape Gardening*, published in 1832, denouncing the work of Capability Brown. One of Brown's most controversial ideas was to abolish the formal garden and bring the park, and its cattle, right up close to the windows of the house. What madness, claimed William Sawrey Gilpin. He insisted that a country house should be 'framed'' by a formal garden with axial terraces and geometric plantings. The 'Picturesque' elements, with varied and irregular groupings of trees and shrubs, were to be left for the outer section of the pleasure grounds and the park. In other words, his designs combined both styles, formal and informal. And Westonbirt owed a great deal to the posthumous influence of Gilpin.

In one respect, however, Robert Holford struck out on his own: in the design of the great arboretum he began to create as soon as he had completed moving the village.

He had set himself the task of collecting examples of every *temperate* species of tree (and many shrubs, too); in other words, every one that could brave the rigours of the British winter without the shelter of a glasshouse. That was his starting point, and of course Robert was not the first to aim at this ambitious target.

From the seventeenth century onwards, from the days of the Tradescants and the Bishop of London, enthusiasts had been haunted by the idea of a 'complete' collection of trees. The trouble was that the list could never be complete. Every year new trees were discovered in remote parts of the world and then introduced by plant hunters to Britain and Europe. Even if collectors had the time and energy, and other resources, to keep up with the ever-expanding list of new trees, it seemed inevitable that the collection would ultimately run out of space.

This was that fate of all the first wave of arboretums promoted by John Loudon and his *Gardener's Magazine*; not only the comparatively small arboretums like Loudon's one in Derby, but even the giants like the Duke of Devonshire's at Chatsworth and the Duke of Bedford's at Woburn Abbey. Of course this first wave suffered from an extra handicap. The trees were arranged in 'scientific'² order, that is in a fixed sequence of genera and families. This meant that there would be little room for newcomers, once the first trees had been planted.

Robert's ideas for an arboretum were entirely different. Like Lord Ducie and Earl Somers, he had no time for so-called 'scientific' order, which was anyway the subject of endless dispute among botanists. A private arboretum, he thought, should not ape the manners of a botanical garden. It must owe more to the art of landscape gardening than to the science of botany – as required by the students of the Picturesque. The arrangement of trees on a large scale demanded nothing more than a painter's eye, and an arboretum could be extended indefinitely, presenting a series of scenes, as new species were discovered.

But how did he hope to avoid running out of space? The answer was simple. He would appropriate a vast swathe of farmland beyond the park – no fewer than 600 acres – in order to make his arboretum the largest in Britain.

By 1856 he had taken the first steps. He had built a pair of baroque lodges at the entrance to the estate on the new main road to Bath. Opposite these lodges he built a formidable pair of iron gates to keep out unauthorised visitors from the new arboretum. The first specimen trees followed swiftly: two Wellingtonias, a foot high, apparently bought from the masterful firm of Veitch a year before. It was Veitch who had sent their plant hunter, William Lobb, to California in the previous decade, and Lobb had returned in 1854 with the precious seeds of the Wellingtonia. So Robert must have been one of the first connoisseurs to plant seedlings of this 300-feet giant, *Sequoiadendron giganteum* (named the 'big tree' or 'giant redwood' in America, but in Britain proudly celebrating the national hero, the Duke of Wellington, who had died a year earlier).

A few years later Robert planted three more Wellingtonias that were to play an even more dominant role in the design of the arboretum.

Planted by his three eldest children, the Three Sisters, as they were called, crowned the central avenue like three green obelisks. Beyond them were other newly discovered pines and spruce and other conifers from the north-west coast of America. They included David Douglas's now famous quartet of giants – the Sitka spruce, the grand fir, the noble fir and the eponymous Douglas fir. These newcomers were carefully contrasted with smaller deciduous trees like the red oaks and white oaks introduced by Bishop Compton from the east coast of America more than a century earlier. And smaller still were the dozens of exotic maples, including the recent introductions by the young James Veitch, the intrepid plant hunter sent out to Japan by the family firm.

Was there a master plan for this exciting new kind of arboretum? Strange to say, no plan – nor even a simple catalogue of the trees and shrubs planted by Robert Holford – has been so far discovered. Perhaps Robert was afraid of visitors. Give them a plan and a catalogue and they might make off with the jewels of his collection. But fortunately for the history of the arboretum this was not the view of Robert's only son, George Holford, who succeeded to the family estate when Robert died in 1892. George was a courtier, and man about town, who served as an equerry to a succession of British princes. After retiring with a knighthood, he spent more time at Westonbirt, and in 1826, just before he died, Sir George commissioned a very full catalogue of the collection, including the trees and shrubs in the arboretum. Using this catalogue it is possible to reconstruct the design of the arboretum as it must have appeared at the time of Robert's death.

The main arboretum (now called 'the old arboretum') was arranged in a half-circle around a large meadow known as the Downs. The layout took the form of a series of curved tracks, the upper one called the Circular Drive, leading to the Loop Walk, the lower one called the Main Drive and leading to Specimen Avenue. This might sound complicated. But the endless curves produced an endless series of glades, to the left and right of the track, each presenting a different scene. It was the perfect layout for Robert's theatrical version of the Picturesque.

At the back of most glades was a backdrop of evergreens: clumps of box and yew and rhododendrons and other evergreen shrubs, with perhaps the towering column of a pine or spruce in dramatic contrast. In the centre of the glade – at centre stage, so to speak – were the star performers, perhaps a rare American oak and a Chinese magnolia. And up close to the track – in the footlights – were the smaller trees and shrubs, Japanese maples perhaps, and snowbell trees, all carefully sited to produce a brilliant contrast in colour and form. It was a far cry from the conventional arboretum of the previous period, with its 'scientific' grouping of oaks and ash and pine by species and genera. And of course it was prodigal in the space it required. But of space

– and the money to buy more of it – there was no shortage at Westonbirt.

When Robert died aged eighty-four in 1892 he left his son George with what must have been the most complete collection of rare trees in the country. Even his rival Lord Ducie could only claim that his collection at Tortworth was a good second to Westonbirt's. How did the two collections compare in 1892? An exact comparison is impossible, as neither collection had been catalogued at that date. Judged from later reports, Robert Holford had a larger number of species in four major genera: silver fir (eight *Abies* at Westonbirt compared with only three at Tortworth), maples (nine *Acer* compared with three), cypress (four *Cupressus* compared with two) and pines (sixteen compared with two). But in one major genus Lord Ducie had beaten Robert hollow. He had no fewer than eighteen species of oaks, including rarities like *Quercus lobata* and *Q. kelloggii*, compared to only eight species of oaks at Westonbirt.

Still, what are mere numbers? There is a whiff of magic about the arboretum at Tortworth which hangs in the air today, despite all the wounds inflicted by time. The turreted Tortworth Court is now a brassy hotel, and the arboretum is shared between three oddly assorted owners – the hotel, an open prison and a private trust run by volunteers. Armed only with handsaws and slashers, these volunteers have been engaged in a ten-year war against an army of brambles. Some of Lord Ducie's champion trees have now emerged unscathed from the Dell: a huge Hungarian oak, a narrow-leaved ash and a Californian chestnut. Most alluring of all is an ancient Japanese maple whose roots are even more artistically arranged than its branches.

Clearly a posthumous triumph for Lord Ducie. But not enough, I fear, to make Robert Holford jealous.

CHAPTER 20

Treasures from China

One day in the summer of 1885, Sir Joseph Hooker received an intriguing letter from the heart of China. The letter was posted in Ichang – a booming new treaty port where the irrepressible River Yangtse, after rising in the Himalayas, at last breaks free from the mountains, and begins its 1,100 mile journey to the sea.

Hooker, one of the most distinguished botanists in Europe, was in his final year as the director of the Royal Botanic Gardens at Kew. In fact Kew owed a great deal – even its survival – to the Hooker family. In 1841 his father, Sir William, had snatched the royal gardens from the clutches of the Treasury; those mean-minded officials had planned to close down the gardens and sell off the site. In the next forty years Sir William, and his son, Sir Joseph, had transformed the place from a down-at-heel royal retreat into a great national enterprise. They had commissioned the Irish ironmaster, Richard Turner, to build an ultra-modern palm house. They had persuaded the architect Decimus Burton to design a sprawling, classical Temperate House. They had hugely extended the arboretum. Its rare trees and other plants were now an education and a delight for the visitor. It was also the botanical hub of the British Empire, specialising in economic botany.

Based on research at Kew, plants for crops and plantations, and a vital source of new raw materials, could be moved from one part of the world to another. It was Kew that was to give Malaya its lucrative new rubber industry, taking the rubber seeds (some would say, stealing them) from the wilds of South America, and growing the small plants at Kew before shipping them to Kuala Lumpa.

All this was achieved, not without controversy, by these masterful Hookers. And the third generation of the dynasty, in the shape of Sir Joseph's accomplished son-in-law, forty-two-year-old William Thiselton-Dyer, was now poised to take the helm.

But we must return to that intriguing letter from Ichang. It was signed 'Augustine Henry' – a name that must have meant nothing to Sir Joseph Hooker. Henry had written:

> I beg to forward to you a packet of seeds of the Chinese varnish tree... in the hope of their proving interesting... I hope to be able to obtain the flower and leaf this year. I have not seen the tree growing, as I have not made a sufficiently long excursion into the mountains.
>
> A good number of medicines are grown about here, and there seems to be a fair number of interesting plants; and, as this part of China is not very well known to botanists... interesting specimens might be obtained. I know very little of botany and have scarcely any books of reference. However, I should be very glad to collect specimens and forward them to you if you think they would prove useful. In this case any hints would be very acceptable.[1]

It turned out that Henry was one of about seven hundred British and other European expats who now worked in the treaty ports – Shanghai, Ningpo, Ichang and so on – as employees of the Chinese Imperial Customs Service. He came from Cookstown in the north of Ireland, the son of a local grocer and flax merchant.

But he had distinguished himself at school and university. He was awarded a first at Queen's College, Galway, and a master's at Queen's Belfast. Then he had been head-hunted by Sir Robert Hart, the all-powerful Ulsterman in charge of the Chinese Imperial Customs Service. After a crash course in medicine, Henry had been posted to Shanghai, and in due course sent upriver to Ichang. But after a couple of years he found the usual hobbies for expats – playing tennis or bridge – no longer attracted him. So he planned a new pastime to entertain him at weekends and holidays: plant collecting. And he asked for Hooker's 'hints'.

Augustine Henry

Of course Hooker, a Himalayan plant hunter himself when he was young, sent Henry an encouraging reply. Hooker followed this up with a letter explaining in detail the complicated techniques for drying, packing, numbering and dispatching plant specimens ready for study in the Kew herbarium. But what could Hooker expect from this newcomer Henry? The man apparently knew little or nothing about either horticulture or botany. He was an amateur and, worse, already employed by the customs service. Anyway Ichang and its surroundings were not thought to offer much in the shape of new plants.

Six years earlier, the enterprising firm of Veitch had sent out a professional collector, Charles Maries, to search central China for novelties. Maries spent several months at Ichang, where he was taken under the wing of the British consul, Thomas Watters, an amateur botanist and authority on Chinese Buddhism. But Maries was sorry to say that he had drawn almost a blank at Ichang. And the locals, he said, had no love for Europeans; he was often threatened, and his baggage was stolen on several occasions.

Henry's first consignment from Ichang was all the more of a surprise – and all the more dazzling. The boxes of dried plants reached Hooker at Kew in the spring of 1886: 1,073 dried specimens of plants and 183 dried fruits and seeds. And with each numbered plant came a neat little dossier: the date of collection, the place where it grew, its habit and its habitat, complete with its economic role and its Chinese name. Henry was a magician!

Hooker's team of taxonomists at Kew now had the excitement of sorting and identifying the numbered collection. Many plants, it proved, were new to science, and needed to be christened with appropriate botanical names in Latin. For some of the newly discovered species '*augustinii*' and '*henryi*' and '*henryanus*' and so on were obvious choices. Other names were borrowed, somewhat narcissistically, from the Kew team itself: '*oliveri*' from Professor Daniel Oliver and '*helmsleyi*' from William Hemsley and of course '*hookerianum*' from Sir Joseph Hooker.

Henry's collections had arrived at a particularly opportune moment. That year, 1886, the Linnean Society of London was to publish the inaugural volume in its pioneering *Index Florae Sinensis* – the first-ever index of Chinese plants. But the most recent contributions to this roll of honour were not from British plant hunters. It was the French who were now leading the field.

The pioneers of plant-hunting in central and western China had been a handful of long-suffering French missionaries posted there since 1860. Père Armand David was to be the most famous. But little attention had been given until recently to Père David's botanical discoveries. His ornithological and zoological discoveries had certainly startled the world's scientists. In the twelve years from 1862 to 1874 he had discovered hundreds of new kinds of birds and animals, culminating in the 'White Bear' – now known as the giant panda. (He had found, and accidentally killed, this exotic creature in 1869 in the mountainous borderland east of

Père Armand David

Tibet.) But it was many years before Père David's *botanical* discoveries were revealed to the world.

Despite the fact that his neatly packed botanical specimens, sent from China to the Musée d'Histoire Naturelle in Paris, had been subsidised by the French government, they were put on the shelf – and virtually forgotten for more than a decade. It was claimed that some of his specimens were actually lost. In 1880 an energetic newcomer, Adrien Franchet, took over the job of sorting, analysing and naming Père David's dried plants. By 1884 he was ready with the first volume of *Plantae Davidianae ex Sinarum Imperio* (*David's Plants from the Chinese Empire*). The results must have shocked international botanists, including Sir Joseph Hooker at Kew.

It had been assumed from Hooker's own discoveries in Sikkim in the 1840s that Sikkim was a botanical hub – that the Himalayas were the place where the world's rhododendrons were centred. Now it became clear from Père David's travels that China, too, was a centre for the world's plants. The opulence of the newly discovered rhododendrons was astonishing: *Rh. calophytum* with small white or pink flowers, *Rh. decorum* with large pink flowers, *Rh. strigillosum* with scarlet flowers, and many more. And Père David had found hundreds of new species as well as rhododendrons. There was a hungry new species of buddleia (*B. davidii*) a small tree with long, conical purple flowers; a vigorous new maple with bark like a snake's skin (*Acer davidii*); a new deutzia with jewel-like, purple flowers (*D. longifolia*); and a new evergreen viburnum with blue fruits on red stalks (*V. davidii*). Most striking of all was the dove tree or handkerchief tree (*Davidia involucrata*) which Père David discovered at Baoxing in 1869. One day this tree would be famous, and draw plant hunters like a magnet. But that day was still some years ahead.

All these discoveries had been made by Père David near

Baoxing, in the remote mountainous valleys of north-west China, close to the border with Tibet. No doubt Sir Joseph looked them up on his map of the region. Perhaps he even corresponded with Père David, who was living in retirement in Paris. But what must have fascinated Sir Joseph, and other international botanists, were rumours about the latest discoveries by a protégé of Père David's, a forty-seven-year-old French missionary-explorer called Père Jean Marie Delavay.

Like all Catholic priests who had volunteered to serve in China, Père Delavay had found life on the missions demanded continual self-sacrifice. Of course he had chosen it. The missionaries dressed like their parishioners, enduring the dirt and squalor and wretched food of subsidence farmers. They were despised by Chinese officials, who regarded them as agents of France – 'foreign devils' forced on them by the much resented treaty of 1860, which ended the 2nd Opium War. They were loathed by the Buddhist lamas who were the leaders of the local communities. Riots, inspired by the lamas, were alarmingly common. When Père Delavay had just arrived in his first parish in China – in the southern province of Guangdong – the parish church was attacked and burnt by rioters. Several parishioners were murdered and Delavay was lucky to escape with his life. And apart from the ever-present threat of violence, malaria and exhaustion took their toll. After thirteen years in the tropics, Père Delavay was a broken man. In 1880 he was told to return to France to recuperate.

There was, it must be said, one redeeming feature of life for a Catholic missionary in China. Beyond the squalid huts and straggling villages there might be a hidden Garden of Eden. To an amateur botanist, China was an unexplored corner of heaven. And Père Delavay had dabbled with botany since he was a boy.

The climate in the tropical plains of Guangdong was unsuitable for a plant hunter searching for plants to grow in temperate Europe. But much of central and western China was mountainous, and therefore a rich source of temperate plants. It was also a great deal healthier than the tropical south. For both reasons Père Delavay had applied for a new post in Yunnan, in the south-west; his request was granted. And before returning to China he made two momentous visits. Père David, whom he saw in Paris, was full of encouragement. New discoveries revealed the richness of Creation. Plant-hunting was a way of serving God. But to be effective he must talk to Adrien Franchet and the professional botanists at the Musée d'Histoire Naturelle. Franchet and the team were delighted to meet him, and explained the secrets of preparing dried plants.

By 1884 – two years before Hooker received Henry's first specimens from Ichang – Franchet had received a first consignment sent from Yunnan by Père Delavay. And it was no disappointment. In fact, although Franchet didn't publish Delavay's discoveries till later in the decade, they were quite as sensational as Père David's collections.

Delavay made most of his discoveries on the Cangshan, the mountain range facing the walled city of Tali (now Dali). The mountains boasted snow-capped summits reaching over 13,000 feet, with the treeline a mere thousand feet lower. From this alpine paradise Delavay added many sumptuous new rhododendrons to Père David's list: yellow-flowered *Rh. lacteum*, blood-red *Rh. haematodes* and pink or white *Rh. yunnanense*. He found a new crab apple (*Malus yunnanensis*) with brilliant scarlet fruit, and a new summer-flowering evergreen magnolia (*M. delavayi*) with sea-green leaves. (This upstaged the well-known American species, *M. grandiflora*.) He found an elegant new pink-berried rowan (*Sorbus vilmorinii*), a huge sweet-smelling philadelphus (*P. delavayi*) and a new deutzia (*D. purpurascens*) with flowers even more jewel-like than those of *D. longifolial*, the deutzia discovered by Père Armand.

Most alluring of all was Delavay's new silver fir (*Abies delavayi*) which he found in 1884 near the summit of the Cangshan, exposed to the storm winds of the monsoon. Nonetheless it is the handsomest of all its genus – more elegant even that the noble fir, *Abies procera*, discovered by David Douglas in the wilds of north-west America. Delavay's fir is dressed like a queen, its fir cones royal blue or violet-purple, and the undersides of its dark green needles splashed with silver.

* * *

What was Hooker's reaction to these astonishing discoveries by the two French missionaries? The uncomfortable truth was that the two international centres for botanical research – the Royal Botanic Garden at Kew and the Musée d'Histoire Naturelle in Paris – found it difficult to share information. France and Britain were traditional rivals. Small wonder that there was little sense of partnership in exploring the natural world, and a strong urge to compete. So the arrival of Henry's boxes of new specimens was a godsend for Kew. Still, in 1886 Hooker can have had no idea of how big a bonanza those boxes were to prove. Botanically speaking, Henry was a beginner. He was a shy twenty-nine-year-old son of an Ulster grocer. Who would have guessed that, judged by the huge number of his discoveries, he would prove to be the most successful plant hunter in the history of Kew?

His first problem might have seemed overwhelming. He was a full-time official of the customs service, with only weekends and other holidays to spare for plant-hunting. There was only one way to deal with that handicap. He must hire local Chinese to serve as plant hunters. Of course they would need to be trained, but the cost of hiring them would be minimal – about thirty shillings a month for a full-time assistant – and perhaps Kew would offer to pay. Henry himself could only spare the time for plant-hunting in the glens immediately west of Ichang. But his assistant (or assistants) could make more ambitious journeys, weeks or even months at a time, covering quite unexplored country north and south of the three great gorges of the Yangtse.

Henry's first season, in 1885, developed much as he must have hoped. At weekends Henry ransacked the wooded glens that plunged down to the Yangste west of Ichang. He found more than a dozen plants that were later deemed new to science. The first plant that caught his eye was a new clematis (*C. henryi*) coiling itself like a snake in a tree. There was a new deciduous viburnum (*V. ichangense*) which grows 10 feet high with creamy flowers arranged in fragrant clusters. There was a boisterous anemone (*A. hupehense*) that has now become a favourite in European gardens. And, most dramatic, a tall evergreen shrub (*Itea ilicifolia*) with leaves like a holly's, and racemes of elegant greenish-white flowers hanging down in summer.

The most exciting specimens, however, were collected by Henry's Chinese plant hunter 'Man Yang'. He spent weeks combing the hillsides at Patung (now Badung) 200 miles upriver from Ichang. He found a large new species of crab apple (*Malus hupehensis*) which is fertile but 'apomictic'. (This means that it reproduces itself without any need for sex, and therefore comes true from seed.) The tree can grow up to 40 feet high. In spring it explodes with white and pink flowers; in autumn its leaves make 'red tea', a local substitute for the real thing. He also discovered a new variety of maple (*Acer cappadocicum var. sinicum f. tricaudatum*) which has elegant pointed leaves, and a pushy new evergreen species of viburnum (*V. rhyditiphyllum*) with long puckered, leathery leaves, white flowers in spring and blue-black fruits in autumn.

Man Yang's most important discovery was a striking new magnolia tree (*M. officinalis*). This is now one of the rarest Chinese magnolias that survive in the wild. Often mistaken for the very similar Japanese magnolia (*M. hypoleuca*), the large, fragrant, late-flowering *Magnolia officinalis*, with its white flowers and huge leaves, make it one of the most noble and monumental of the genus. Unfortunately the Chinese have long valued it for the medicinal drug derived from its bark and flower buds. So the tree is now highly endangered in the wild, even if now cultivated for a commercial market.

Henry's next two seasons, in 1886 and 1887, were no less successful than the first. As before, he was unable to stray far from Ichang. But on a hillside known as the 'Dome', only a mile or two across the river from the port of Ichang, he made an astonishing discovery. He found an orange Turks cap lily which, unlike most of the genus, revelled in limestone. It grew up to 8 feet high and was as hardy as a brick. As Henry's lily (*Lilium henryi*) it has now proved irresistible for gardeners in both Europe and America. An even more spectacular plant, resembling a giant lily, and growing over 10 feet tall, was a Chinese variety of the Himalayan cardiocrinum (*C. giganteum var. yunnanense*) which Henry found in 1886. Other discoveries in the vicinity of Ichang were a new species of beautyberry (*Callicarpa bodinieri*) glowing with metallic pink or purple fruit in autumn, and a summer-flowering philadelphus (*P. incanus*) blessed with the fragrance of hawthorn.

Meanwhile Henry's assistant, the redoubtable Man Yang, had continued to comb the hillsides several hundred miles to the west. In 1886 he found a new species of rhododendron which has become famous as *Rh. augustinii*. In its finest forms, the flowers can be as blue as a sky in summer. Man Yang also found an unusually rampant honeysuckle, *Lonicera henryi*, with dusky red flowers and black fruits, and a ghostly whitebeam, *Sorbus folgneri*, whose leaves in autumn turn orange above and silver below.

Next year, 1887, Man Yang excelled himself. He found a luxuriant Chinese strawberry tree, *Cornus kousa chinensis*, which has proved even better suited to Europe than its Japanese sister, *Cornus kousa*. He also discovered a strange new genus of tree which was believed to be monotypic – meaning that it contained only one species, and one that was perhaps the only survivor from a genus once rich in species.

Emmenopterys henryi, as it was later named, is an elegant, grey-barked tree that can grow to a height of 80 feet. Its leaves, fleshy in texture, are long and pointed; in some forms they are a seductive pink. Its most striking feature is the long, white lobe, a kind of bract, that develops from some of the flowers. Unfortunately the climate of Britain and Ireland does not encourage the tree to flower. The large *Emmenopterys* adjoining the River Tolka in Dublin, the pride and joy of the National Botanic Garden, did succeed in flowering on a single occasion. Soon afterwards the river broke its banks and the *Emmenopterys* was swept away.

In these three short years, 1885 to 1887, Henry (and Man Yang) had triumphed where Charles Maries had failed. Maries was the plant hunter sent out by the powerful firm of Veitch in 1879. He had turned his back on central China; there was little there of interest, so he claimed. Now Henry – and Man Yang – had proved that Maries had made the greatest mistake in his life. Hubei province in central China was a natural garden, a treasure chest brimming over with exotic plants. But success had its price. Henry felt increasingly frustrated by his life as a full-time doctor employed by the imperial customs service. True, he could train a team of Chinese plant collectors – men as tough and intelligent as Man Yang, paid a mere 30 shillings a month. He could send them hundreds of miles into the unknown. But he could only join them on weekends, as if plant-hunting was only a weekend sport like bridge or tennis.

By 1888 Henry had made up his mind. He wrote to William Thiselton-Dyer, the new director of Kew Gardens, to ask his help in getting a year's leave of absence from the customs service. He wanted permission to explore three of the vast unknown provinces south of Hubei – Hunan, Kuangsi and Kueichow. He hoped that his mentor, Sir Robert Hart, all-powerful in the customs service, would be agreeable to the plan, if the proposal came from Kew. But Hart was not to be persuaded. All Henry could obtain was permission to take six months' leave exploring the mountains in Hubei and Sichuan, north and south of the Yangtse and the Three Gorges.

In April 1888 Henry's party set off upriver from Ichang. Then they struck out for four days to the south. Rolling hills were soon replaced by mountains, and deep gorges, coated with virgin forest. Henry had now brought with him as collectors about half a dozen Chinese associates of Man Yang. He was also accompanied by Antwerp Pratt, a cheerful English naturalist and explorer on his way to Tibet. The two men shared a mud hut in the market town of Changyang. The mountainous landscape was intensely exciting after the monotonous plain around Ichang. Antwerp Pratt recorded that 'in May and June the cuckoo may be heard, reminding one of home'. But this was also the home of golden pheasants, woodcock, deer, porcupines, wild pigs, leopards and tigers. Pratt revelled in the strangeness of it all. 'I remember', he later wrote, 'on one particular moonlit night the black forest standing out against the horizon, the loneliness, isolation and wildness of the scene'.[2]

For three months Henry, riding his pony or carried in his sedan chair, explored that threatened wildness: mountains and valleys, only too soon to be stripped of their forests by land-hungry peasants. New discoveries came thick and fast. He found a new whitebeam (*Sorbus hemsleyi*) sparkling with silver and a couple of stunning maples (*Acer oliverianum* and *Acer henryi*). 'Henry's maple', appropriately enough, was to be one of the most elegant of all the maples he discovered in China. Its young shoots emerge scarlet in the spring, and the leaves turn a glossy red and yellow in autumn, upstaging even some of the finest maples from Japan. He also found a strange new genus in the maple family, which came to be called *Dipteronia*. In the autumn the seeds of *D. sinensis*, embossed in a circular membrane, resemble a cluster of scarlet coins. (Hence its modern name 'the Chinese money maple'.)

And on 17 May he made the strangest discovery of all. He had crossed the provincial boundary between Hubei and Sichuan, and was riding his pony through a river valley near the village of Mahuang-po, when he spotted a single tree in bloom at the foot of a cliff. The sight was surreal. These were not flowers. The tree seemed to be draped with thousands of ghostly handkerchiefs.

What Henry had found was the 'Ghost Tree' or 'Handkerchief Tree' (*Davidia involucrata*) discovered at Baoxing in western Sichuan in 1869 by the French missionary-explorer, Père David. But Henry had stumbled on a new variety of the tree: *Davidia involucrata vilmoriana*. And no one had yet introduced either variety of the tree to Europe or America. The 'handkerchiefs' were in fact cream-coloured bracts which drape the tree like weird petals. Later that year Henry was to send some of his men to collect seeds from the tree, which were duly dispatched to Kew (By a strange mischance the Kew staff then pickled them by mistake.) But ten years later it was this surreal tree that would give a dramatic new impetus to plant-hunting – as we shall see in due course.

By midsummer Henry and his Chinese collectors had recrossed the Yangtse and headed for northern Sichuan. They found many new wonders, including two new genera, both of which were monotypic. The first was the spur leaf tree, *Tetracentron sinense*, whose short, stubby branches are covered with small flowers in spring and long tassels in autumn. The effect is so stylised that you might mistake the tree for a well-pruned espalier. Yet the tree grows to an enormous size in China. The second wonder was a tall deciduous tree named, in due course, *Poliothyrsis sinense*. Still rare in European gardens, it gives a sumptuous display of creamy-yellow flowers in late summer. Other discoveries included one of the most delicate and garden-friendly bamboos, *Sinarundinaria nitida*, and the most decorative of all lime trees, *Tilia henryana*. The leaves, which emerge pink in the spring, edged with sharp bristles, are like so many claws.

Back in Ichang that autumn Henry counted the number of dried specimens he could send to Kew and other botanical gardens. In the previous six months of gruelling travel, Henry and his team had collected no fewer than 27,300 herbarium specimens. Each one had had to be dried, pressed and tagged in the field, and then mounted on paper and crated in Ichang ready for the long voyage to Europe. And for Henry it was all a labour of love – a labour to which he could only devote Sundays and other spare time.

How he must have been thrilled by the sight of those crates! But then, in February 1889, he was shocked to receive new orders from Sir Robert Hart and the customs service. He was to leave Ichang, and proceed to the treaty port of Haikou in Hainan, a large tropical island a thousand miles to the south. The island was notoriously unhealthy; cholera and malaria were rampant. And there would be no prospect of collecting plants suitable for the British climate. The nearest mountains with a temperate climate were far from Hainan.

Predictably, Henry found life at Haikou frustrating, to put it mildly. It was a place for officials banished from Peking – and for Henry, too, it became a place of exile. After four months his health broke down and he felt utterly demoralised. He retired to convalesce in Hong Kong. and wrote to a friend at Kew:

> I can scarcely bear to speak of Hainan. I suffered from heat, home-sickness, got very ill, and the last blow has been the death of a dear friend from cholera on Sunday last. It is a perfect inferno.[3]

Fortunately Sir Robert Hart then took pity on his protégé, and Henry was given two years' leave which he could spend in Europe. Henry was back home in Ireland by mid-October, and later that year, when he came to London, the director and staff at Kew gave him a hero's welcome. It must have been an emotional moment. He, the untrained amateur and part-time botanist, had collected more specimens for Kew than any professional collector in its history. And for the first time he met the men who had unpacked the crates and identified his treasures and given them a name. In fact they had done more. They had given hundreds of plants Henry's own name – 'henryi', 'henryana' – and with that gift came a kind of immortality.

Henry made the most of his two years' leave by working on his specimens in the Kew herbarium. He also fell in love with a talented young artist called Caroline Orridge, the daughter of a London jeweller. They married in 1891, and sailed for China immediately after their honeymoon. But the marriage was to be cut short – tragically short. Caroline was suffering from incurable TB. Henry's next posting was to Formosa (now Taiwan) where the climate was quite unsuitable for an invalid. In desperation Caroline moved first to Japan, then to Colorado, and Henry planned to throw up his job with the customs service and follow her there. But she died before he could join her.

Botanically speaking, Henry's second decade in China could not compare with the first. True he collected thousands more dried specimens and sent them to Kew. But his two next postings – to Mengtze and Simao in southern Yunnan – were close to the border with French-controlled Vietnam and Laos, and too warm for temperate flora. By 1899 Henry had realised that his days as a plant hunter would soon be coming to an end. Already he had written to Thiselton-Dyer recommending that Kew should send out a full-time collector to temperate China. A vigorous young gardener would be the man for the job.

In May he was told by Thiselton-Dyer that Kew could not afford such a luxury. But the British firm of Veitch had decided to take on the job. Sir Harry Veitch, the domineering manager, was sending out a twenty-three-year-old gardener from Kew called Ernest Wilson. His first and principal job was to be kept secret from business rivals – especially the French. He was to collect thousands of seeds from the extraordinary 'handkerchief tree' (*Davidia involucrata*) spotted first by Père David in 1869 and more recently by Henry himself. Where would Wilson find a suitable tree in fruit? He would go first to Simao to see if Henry had the answer.

The two men met in Simao later that year, Henry exhausted after twenty years in the wilds, Wilson no doubt panting to make his name in his first venture abroad. Henry gave Wilson every assistance. He drew a sketch map of where he had seen the tree hundreds of miles away in southern Hubei. Months later Wilson reached the spot.

For Wilson it was start of a glittering career as a plant hunter. He was fortunate to be Henry's protégé. But, unlike Henry, Wilson was collecting fertile seeds for a plant-hungry commercial

Ernest Wilson

market, not dried specimens for the benefit of academic botanists. So it was natural that Wilson exploited Henry's discoveries and they became, in turn, his own introductions. Wilson was also to make hundreds of discoveries of his own.

The golden age of plant-hunting in China was now approaching its climax. A dozen plant hunters competed for first place, their triumphs a last hurrah before the world succumbed to the miseries of the First World War.

CHAPTER 21

The Triumphs of Ernest Wilson

Wilson had come 13,000 miles in search of this prize. And now it seemed within his grasp. Ahead was the solitary handkerchief tree discovered by Augustine Henry.

After saying farewell to Henry at Hekou in the autumn of 1899, Wilson had taken passage on a series of ships by way of Hong Kong and Shanghai. In early spring the Yangtse steamer had brought him to Henry's old base, Ichang, the treaty port a thousand miles upriver. In Ichang he had bought a houseboat big enough to take his new team of Chinese collectors and his mountains of gear. There were crates of paper and presses for dried specimens, boxes for seeds, several large plate cameras, a barometer, pedometer, medicine chest, and two sedan chairs to give him the status of a travelling mandarin. (The chairs, according to Wilson were 'more useful than a passport'.)

In early April 1900 the houseboat was dragged upriver through the treacherous Yangtse gorges and brought the party safely to Badung. But in Badung he was warned that it would be dangerous to continue by river. There had been anti-Christian riots in the vicinity, and a Catholic priest had been brutally murdered. Wilson decided to take no chances. Yes, it would be safer to leave the river and follow little-known tracks used by salt smugglers.

On 24 April he reached the village of Mahuang-po and met

the villagers who had guided Henry to the handkerchief tree more than ten years earlier. One of them told Wilson he would take him there. But Wilson was quite unprepared for what he saw. A new house built of wood occupied the site of the clearing, and beside it was the stump of the handkerchief tree. So this was the end of his 13,000 mile journey from England. Wilson must have been stunned. 'One more little cup of bitterness to drain', he wrote in his journal 'I did not sleep during the night of April 25th'.[1]

What on earth could he tell the Veitch family who had invested so much in this expedition? Should he now head for the Tibetan borderlands where Père David had found the first specimen of the tree? But fortune smiled. After his return to Ichang in the houseboat, Wilson was exploring a small wood south-west of the port when he stumbled on a astonishing sight. He was face to face with a handkerchief tree, 50 feet high – much higher than Henry's tree – and its bracts were in full bloom.

Wilson climbed into its branches to photograph it. He was entranced. 'Handkerchief' was too prosaic a word. These snow-white bracts fluttered in the slightest breeze like 'huge butterflies or small doves hovering among the branches'.[2] And there were about a dozen other trees of the same species nearby.

To collect healthy seed-bearing nuts from these trees meant he would have to return in the autumn. Meanwhile he could add to his collection of seeds from other trees and plants. Henry had collected thousands of dried specimens in central China. So had the French missionaries, Père David, Père Delavay and (more recently) Père Farges. But none of the four men had sent viable seeds in any quantity. As we saw, Wilson had been instructed to exploit these men's discoveries in order to introduce these new species to Europe, and now was his chance.

First came a dazzling new trio of maples. All three species were perfect for gardens in Britain and even the east coast of America: hardy enough to stand 15 °F of frost in winter, and decorative enough to satisfy the most exacting owner of an arboretum. The first was *Acer davidii* – Père David's maple. This is the biggest of the so-called 'snakebarks': the oriental maples with thin white stripes along their mottled bark. The second was *Acer pictum tricaudatum*, an elegant version of the painted maple discovered by Henry. The third was another of Henry's prizes and the most spectacular: *Acer griseum*. The trunk and branches are cinnamon-red and the bark flakes off like a birch tree's. The leaves are bright green and divided into three.

Three exotic trees followed. The first was *Magnolia delavayi*, a new kind of evergreen magnolia. Its jade-green leaves exude a whiff of magic missing from the well-known American evergreen, *Magnolia grandiflora*. But it resents cold winters, and in most British gardens needs a wall to protect it. The second was a Chinese version of the tulip tree, *Liriodendron chinensis*. Henry had discovered it in western Hubei and it was clearly a winner. Its leaves, cutaway and glaucous at the back, are even more bizarre than those of its American counterpart, even if its flowers are less colourful and tulip-like.

The third was perhaps the most remarkable, *Tetracentron sinense*, the spur leaf tree. Henry had found some gigantic specimens of this engaging creature. Its heart-shaped leaves sprout from a series of short horizontal branches, as if it had been an espalier; its delicate catkins hang down like necklaces. Perhaps Wilson introduced it more as a botanical curiosity than as a tree for gardeners. But this is a most elegant tree. It has proved perfectly hardy in the British climate, and certainly deserves to be better known.

As well as introducing so many trees and shrubs first recorded either by Henry or by the French missionaries, Wilson made many important discoveries of his own. He found a superior variety of the common clematis, a new climber which was in due course named *Clematis montana var. rubens*. The flowers are stunning; a beautiful rosy red. In W. J. Bean's monumental work, *Trees and Shrubs Hardy in the British Isles*, this new variety of clematis is given the well-merited accolade as 'probably the most beautiful and useful climber distributed in the twentieth century'.[3]

Another of Wilson's own discoveries was the beauty bush, *Kolkwitzia amabilis*. This deciduous bush, a sprawling mass of pink-and-yellow flowers up to 12 feet high, grew 10,000 feet up in the rocky gorges of the Yangtse. Wilson's seeds duly germinated in Veitch's greenhouses, but the plants didn't flower until 1910. Even then the beauty bush had to wait another fifty years before its charms were fully appreciated in Britain. (American gardeners were more discerning.)

Back in Britain early in 1902, Wilson was congratulated by his employers at the firm of Veitch: Sir Harry, always suave and diplomatic, but now semi-retired, and the new managing director, his temperamental nephew, James Herbert Veitch. Wilson had achieved the task they had set him – and a great deal more. Early in 1901 he had sent back to Britain a vast number of seeds of *Davidia*, the handkerchief tree. In fact the total number probably exceeded twenty thousand, as no fewer than thirteen thousand small plants were now poking their heads through the soil in Veitch's greenhouses. These small plants were destined to make the firm's fortune, when they were ready for sale. *Davidias* would soon be all the rage; every serious gardener in Britain and Ireland would be determined to possess one. And Wilson's other seeds would make good profits, too, despite the high cost of his trip to China – at least £2,000.

There was only one fly in the ointment, something to take the shine off Wilson's triumph. The Veitch family had concealed it from him for fear of 'dampening his enthusiasm'[4] before he set out. Now he was told. He was not the first plant hunter to claim the honour of sending seeds of the *Davidia* from China. In 1897 one of the French missionaries, Père Farges, had sent a packet of thirty-seven *Davidia* seeds to Maurice de Vilmorin, the French dendrologist. Only one seed had germinated, but it grew and cuttings were taken. Père Farges had sent further parcels of seed a few years later. This proved a different, less hairy variety of the species – named *Davidia involucrata var. vilmoriana*. But one thing was only too clear. The French had beaten the firm of Veitch in the race to introduce the new prodigy into Europe.

Wilson was allowed a brief holiday, largely spent in getting married to his girlfriend, Helen (Nellie) Ganderton. He was then employed for some months sorting out his seeds and specimens in the Veitch nurseries. But by the spring of 1903 he was back in China and heading up the Yangtse to his old hunting grounds. No doubt he was glad to leave the Veitch offices in Chelsea. His immediate boss, James Herbert Veitch was becoming increasingly excitable – the first signs of the unmentionable disease known as 'paralysis' but in fact an incurable case of syphilis. James Veitch was obsessed with secrecy. He warned Wilson against writing to his friends about his adventures, and forbade him to send anyone spare seeds of interesting plants. But even the excitable James Veitch found it hard to find fault with Wilson. Of all the firm's numerous collectors – totalling twenty-two since William Lobb had sailed for South America in 1840 – Ernest Wilson was proving the most professional and the most successful.

He was now in his element, with a new houseboat called the *Ellena* to carry him safely through the infamous gorges of the Yangtse. In fact the *Ellena* was nearly overturned twice in the boulder-strewn Mitsang Gorge, where many boats had come to grief. Wilson cheerfully recorded the frantic efforts of his crew to appease the water gods. 'My captain chin-chinned, joss sticks were exploded, a little rice and wine was thrown over the bow, joss sticks were burnt, together with candles and some paper trash – in short, every rite necessary to appease the terrible water-dragon was strictly observed.'[5]

The gods duly relented. Wilson, standing on deck, was lost in admiration for the surreal scenery of the gorge: towering cliffs one mass of pink and purple *Primula obconica*, every mossy cleft a niche for yellow *Corydalis thalictrifolia*; a waterfall drenching a bank of pale blue *Iris japonica;* and even the crags alive with roses and wisteria.

In the next months Wilson collected the seeds of hundreds of rare trees and shrubs, many originally collected by Henry, others new to science. His route eventually took him far beyond the parts of Hubei and Sichuan explored by Henry. He left the Yangtse and headed north-west, across unexplored mountains and valleys, towards Tibet. It was Tibet that he had been told was the home of one mysterious plant with which James Veitch had become obsessed – *Meconopsis integrifolia*, the yellow Himalayan poppy. Wilson was told to give the highest priority to finding the yellow poppy and bringing back its seeds. He had no permission to enter Tibet, but there was nothing to stop him. He crossed by the Ya-chia pass and took the road to Lhasa. At 12,000 feet he found an alpine meadow awash with yellow poppies. And, despite the altitude sickness that affected his whole team, there was a bonus. On a mountain close to the town of Sungpan, he found three other species of poppy – a red one (*Meconopsis punicea*), a prickly blue one (*M. horridula*) and a violet-blue one (*M. henrici*).

Back in Ichang in time for Christmas 1903, spent on board his houseboat *Ellena*, Wilson had plenty to celebrate. By pushing himself to the limits, he had achieved far more than his contract with Veitch required. In due course he received the welcome news from one of Veitch's staff that the yellow poppy had now germinated in their greenhouses. Less welcome was the news that a rival in the nursery business – Arthur Bulley of Bee's Nursery in Chester – was claiming that his firm had beaten Veitch in the race to produce the first flowering specimens of the yellow poppy. The story had been published in the *Gardener's Chronicle*. Of course James Veitch had scotched the story. What impertinence! He wired the *Chronicle* to point out that Veitch's yellow poppies had flowered at *precisely* the same time. But Wilson heard other news which was more serious than a trade war about poppies. Veitch's near monopoly in the sale of Chinese plants seemed to be ending. Arthur Bulley had commissioned a young gardener to go out to China to hunt for new plants. His name was George Forrest, and the world would soon hear of his discoveries – and his terrifying ordeal when pursued by lamas from Tibet.

George Forrest

Meanwhile Wilson continued to lead a charmed life and revel in the wilderness. In November he had climbed the sacred staircase to Mount Omei (Emei Shan) and its monastery; he was one of the first plant explorers to tap its rich seam of maples, viburnums and silver firs. Now he returned to the Tibetan borderlands and collected thousands more seeds. When he made his triumphant return to Britain early in 1906, his new introductions included the most decorative of all poplars, the necklace poplar (*Populus lasiocarpa*). Its green catkins hang down in chains among huge, red-veined leaves. He also brought seeds of one of the largest and noblest of all the rhododendron species, *Rh. calophytum*.

But Wilson's relations with the firm of Veitch were becoming strained. James Veitch's illness made him increasingly 'fiery' – which antagonised both the staff and their clients. James had a complete nervous breakdown in the autumn of 1906, and died of syphilis the next year. Meanwhile it was decided by Sir Harry that Wilson would be honoured by the firm with the presentation of a gold-and-diamond tie pin in the form of a yellow poppy. But Wilsons's contract, by mutual agreement, was not to be renewed. He had left China for good – or so he believed.

At this period the leading arboretum in America was the Arnold Arboretum in the suburbs of Boston. Its director and creator, under the aegis of Harvard University, was sixty-six-year-old Professor Sprague Sargent. Son of a rich banker, he had chosen botany and dendrology as his profession. His manner was intimidating – cool, even by the chilly standards of Boston society. He was a workaholic with no small talk, and no interest in social issues. He was seized with two dendrological obsessions: first, to save the wild trees in the Catskills and the Adirondacks, trees now threatened by the loggers; second, to make the Arnold Arboretum the finest in the world. And for the second he needed the help of plant hunters from England. He had tried and failed to persuade Augustine Henry to lead a new expedition to China. He hoped to have better luck with a protégé of Henry's, the English explorer working for the firm of Veitch – Ernest Wilson.

It's not clear exactly when the two men first met. But Sargent had been a client of the firm of Veitch for many years. In 1892 he had joined James Veitch on a trip to Japan, hunting for silver firs (*Abies maries*) and Japanese magnolias (*M. hypoleuca*). The two men had to share a straw hut on the icy flanks of Mount Hakkoda, but got on surprisingly well. Sargent had then proposed a joint expedition to China. At the time nothing came of that idea. Instead Sargent relied on donations of seeds from plant hunters in Europe and Asia, including Augustine Henry. Many European nurseries were flattered to sell him seeds for his arboretum, and Veitch had provided the lion's share after Ernest Wilson's two trips to China.

In the summer of 1906 he heard the startling news: Wilson was leaving Veitch and taking up a job as a botanist. Here was Sargent's chance to grab Wilson. At first Wilson dug in his toes. He and his long-suffering wife Helen were settling down in London with a newborn daughter (appropriately called Primrose). Sargent brushed aside Wilson's objections. 'So you have captured me after all' was Wilson's comment, as if he could hardly credit the news of his own surrender. He sailed for China early the following year.

Wilson's third and fourth expeditions, both financed by Sargent, were no disappointment. Wilson had already introduced four new maples from China, most of which had been originally discovered by Henry. All were exceedingly decorative. Wilson now added a fifth maple to his haul, a tree which Sargent generously christened *Acer wilsonii*. It's a winsome, slender tree which blushes prettily when young. Wilson also sent Sargent the acorns of two towering Chinese oaks which Henry had missed: *Quercus aliena*, whose large, coarsely toothed leaves resemble those of the

American chestnut, and *Q. variabilis*, whose bark is so spongy that it can be used to make corks, like the bark of the European cork tree.

The most important of Wilson's new introductions, however, were the giant magnolias. There are five magnolia species in China which can grow to the size of a large forest tree, like a beech or an oak. (In my recent book, *The Company of Trees*, I have called them the Big Five.) It was Wilson who both discovered and introduced three of these five. The first, predictably, added lustre to the name of Wilson's masterful employer. It became *Magnolia sargentiana*. The tree, more than 50 feet tall, bursts into blossom with huge pink flowers composed of up to sixteen tepals. The best pink and the most vigorous trees are found in a variety called *robusta*. Its chief advantage, compared with its rival, *Magnolia campbellii*, is that it flowers later in the season. In fact it usually escapes the frost in March which turns the latter's flowers to a bunch of brown rags. The second of Wilson's discoveries was equally elegant, with the same advantage; its white flowers, streaked with purple, normally wait until April to burst into life. This magnolia, too, honoured Sargent's world – christened *Magnolia dawsonia* after Sargent's chief assistant, Jackson Dawson.

Wilson's third discovery was the most striking of all – although, ironically enough, he was unaware he had made it. In 1900, and again in 1908, he found the magnolia which was eventually named *Magnolia sprengeri diva*. Wilson mistook it for a variety of the common yulan magnolia, brought to Europe more than a century earlier. But later botanists have agreed that it was a new, delightful species. You have only to visit Kew gardens in April to see how 'Primavera' would have served as an alternative name. A trio of these pink magnolias perform a dance beside the azalea garden, and there's more than a hint of the Three Graces in Botticelli's painting.

Wilson made two trips to China for Sargent, completing the second in 1913, after a landslide smashed his right leg and nearly killed him. Sargent then persuaded Wilson to join him in America and work in the Arnold Arboretum. After Sargent's death in 1925, Wilson was proud to be appointed director. Sad to say, his tenure was cut short. In China he had led a charmed life, dodging death in so many forms – including death from the landslide. But his luck finally ran out one afternoon in 1930. Driving back to Boston with his wife Helen he skidded on a greasy road, lost control of the car, smashed through a fence and rolled down a 40-foot embankment. Neither he nor his wife Helen survived the crash.

Meanwhile the world of plant collecting had changed in numerous ways. The family firm of Veitch, which had dominated the market for rare plants since the 1840s, had finally run out of suitable heirs. Sir Harry Veitch had then wound up the firm, and sold its acres of stock, shortly before the First World War erupted in 1914. The sale proved a theatrical end to an era. But already the rich landowners who had been clients of the firm had begun to rely less on buying exotic trees and shrubs from nurseries. Instead they hired plant hunters themselves. This meant the search for rare plants could better suit their own requirements. It also better suited the plant hunters.

Wilson, hired by Sargent, was the first to benefit. He was followed by a young Scotsman whom he was quick to identify, and resent, as a rival – although it would appear that the two men never met. The rival was George Forrest. Like Wilson, Forrest began his career hunting plants in China as the employee of a nurseryman; later he was commissioned by a series of private syndicates. And it was on the first of these trips that he only escaped death by a miracle.

CHAPTER 22

Last of the Great Plant Hunters

In 1904 George Forrest had been hired by Arthur Bulley, a Liverpool cotton merchant and recent founder of a small nursery firm called Bees. Bulley had commissioned Forrest to collect plants for himself and his firm in China. Bulley was rich – cotton broking was a successful family business – and somewhat eccentric. He was a socialist, a teetotaller and a philanthropist; later he stood for Parliament (with notable lack of success) as a champion of women's suffrage. He was now making a 60-acre garden for himself at Ness, outside Liverpool, and decided he needed a personal plant hunter who could supply him with Chinese plants unknown to the rest of the world. He asked the advice of the Regius Professor of Botany at Liverpool, Sir Isaac Bayley Balfour, and Balfour recommended Forrest, who then had a modest job in the herbarium, pressing, sorting and mounting rare plants.

Forrest was a Scot and some people found him touchy and stubborn. It was true he had a passion for independence and did not suffer fools gladly. By origin a country boy from Kilmarnock, he had been happy in his own company, roaming the woods and fields in pursuit of rare plants and birds. After leaving the local academy, he took a job in a chemist shop and learnt the basics of pharmacy. But before he was eighteen he sailed for Australia and tried his luck as a prospector – Australia was then in the grip of gold fever – and later worked as a hired hand on a sheep station. Now he was thirty-one, with a shell as tough as a coconut's, although he knew how to make friends and how to keep them.

Bulley had hired him to collect rare plants in the little-explored north-west corner of Yunnan which bordered on Burma and Tibet. It was here, in the wild borderland, that a group of French missionaries had built their churches and established their missions; their converts now numbered several hundred Chinese. Forrest spent the winter of 1904–5 a hundred miles to the east, in the security of the walled city of Tali (Dali). Then he headed for the borderland, and was invited to stay at the mission post of Tseku (Cigu). His host was a sixty-four-year-old priest, Père Jules Dubernard, who had devoted years to evangelising the local farmers and villagers.

Forrest, burdened with the usual plant hunter's equipment, busied himself with assembling a team of porters, and training other men as collectors. It was now the spring of 1905, and in April the region seemed free from disturbance – perfect for plant-hunting. That autumn Forrest could expect a rich harvest of seeds. The valleys around them were teeming with new trees and other plants. Already Forrest had sent the cones of a new silver fir back to Bulley at Ness – a variant of Delavay's fir with dazzling white markings under its leaves.

Unknown, however, to Forrest and Père Dubernard, a murderous revolt had broken out at Patang (Batang), a mere 100 miles to the north, and the frontier post on the main road to Lhasa. The local Tibetan lamas had long hated the way their Chinese overlords imposed their rule, forcing the lamas to accept both Chinese immigrants and the missionaries of an alien religion.

Two events now precipitated the revolt. First, there was the British expedition to Lhasa, led by Colonel Younghusband in 1903–4. Although this 'invasion' was unauthorised by the Indian government (Younghusband was actually supposed to be leading a boundary commission) the lamas felt threatened. Was this the first step in a British plan to take over their sacred motherland, Tibet? Second, the lamas were enraged by the sight of a newly created Chinese garrison at Patang.

In late March the lamas murdered several Chinese officials in the town, then seized the local French missionary, fifty-four-year-old Père Mussot, and took him to their lamasery, where he was chained up and later shot. The revolt spread southwards to the town of Yaragong (Cakalho), on the east bank of the upper Mekong River, where French missionaries had built a church and a small school. The priest in charge, forty-five-year-old Père Jean Soulie, had worked in the missions in China for nineteen years. Like many of the French priests, he had taken to plant-hunting as a hobby, and had sent back to Paris a total of seven thousand dried plants, including an elegant, glaucous rose that came to bear his name. He had also introduced to Europe the seeds of some important plants, including *Buddleja davidii*, the Butterfly Bush. Now he was trapped in Yaragong, surrounded by rebel lamas and their tenants.

Just before sunset on 3 April they broke into his house, and launched a frenzied attack on him and his parishioners. Wounded in the side by a sword thrust, he was chained to the staircase and tormented for more than week before being marched out, tied to a tree and shot in the head.

Garbled news of the murders began to reach Forrest at Tsekou that summer. But he was relieved to hear that in April the Chinese authorities had sent extra troops to defend Atuntze (Dequin), a small trading town two and a half days north of Tsekou. Forrest was still confident that the Chinese authorities could deal with the revolt. Nothing could stop him plant-hunting. In May he sent out two collectors, and in June he sent out four men to scour the mountains. He wrote a cheerful letter to his old employer, Sir Isaac Bailey Balfour. 'I have now nearly 300 species for you, and have located some fairly good things for Mr. Bulley'.[1]

July came and Forrest remained defiant. There was no news of the lamas, no reliable news at any rate. He wrote home: 'We are all rather humpy with the continued strain we have undergone for the last two months... Whatever happens we mean to stick here to the last... even supposing... I have to take to the hills'. In another letter he explained why he was taking the risk of staying: 'I might as well be scuppered as go home a failure'.[2]

Then, after days of rumour and counter-rumour, the unthinkable happened. At 5 p.m. on 19 July a runner reached the mission with the news that the Chinese garrison at Atuntze had fallen, and a tsunami of bloodthirsty lamas was sweeping down the east bank of the Mekong towards Tsekou.

Where could Forrest and the two elderly French priests now turn for help? Yetse, the nearest safe village – if safe it was – was three days' march to the south.

The mission at Tsekou and all Forrest's collections of seeds and dry specimens had to be abandoned. At 7 p.m. the moon rose and the priests, both heavily armed, set off on mules surrounded by about eighty of their Chinese parishioners. Forrest led them on foot. Even now the priests dithered. They stopped by the road sipping a cup of tea. Forrest told them that their only chance of eluding the lamas was to take a track through the mountains. At this the priests seem to give up hope. At any rate Forrest then decided to push on without them.

Next day he reached a ridge from which he could see Tsekou. A great column of smoke rose from the village in the still morning air. The church, the school, the mission house, Forrest's collections – they were all on fire. Meanwhile the lamas had crossed the Mekong at the next village to the south, cutting off the escape of Forrest and the others. Suddenly a large number of armed men appeared running at great speed down the track towards them. Forrest gave the alarm and his followers scattered in every direction. Later he described how their little band was picked off one by one, or captured; only fourteen escaped. Of his own seventeen collectors and servants, only one escaped. Both the priests were hideously tortured before they were killed.

As for Forrest, he avoided death by the narrowest of margins.

When I saw all was lost I fled east down a breakneck path, in places formed along the faces of beetling cliffs by rude brackets of wood and slippery logs. On I went down towards the main river, only to find myself, at one of the sharpest turns, confronted by a band of hostile and well-armed Tibetans... I turned back, and after a desperate run, succeeded in covering my tracks by leaping off the path... I fell into dense jungle, through which I rolled down a steep slope for a distance of two hundred feet before stopping, tearing my clothes to ribbons, and bruising myself horribly in the process... Fortunately, however, they did not find me... and rushed past my hiding place. There I lay till night fell, when I attempted to escape south, but after toiling up 3,000 feet of rock and through forest and jungle, I found a cordon of Lamas with watch fires and Tibetan mastiffs, which precluded all hope of escape in that direction.[3]

For eight days and eight nights the same desperate pattern was repeated. Forrest hid during the day and tried, with no success, to break out from the valley at night. He had virtually nothing to eat: a mere handful of dried peas and some ears of wheat left behind by a traveller. He had to discard – and bury – his boots to avoid making tracks in the mud. Twice he was nearly discovered;

asleep under a log, he woke to see a party of Tibetans, in full warpaint, cross the stream a few yards from him.

After eight days he had ceased to care whether he lived or died. His feet 'were swollen out of all shape, my hands and face torn with thorns, my whole person caked with mire'.[4] He decided to make a final, desperate bid for life. In the valley were two small groups of huts which belonged to a Tibetan sub-tribe called Lissoos. Forrest planned a violent hold-up; at gunpoint he would force the villagers to give him food. But the Lissoo villagers turned out to be friendly. In fact their headman, according to Forrest, 'proved one of the best friends I ever had'.[5] Despite the risks to himself and his villagers, he made immediate arrangements to smuggle Forrest out of the country.

To escape from the noose set by the lamas around the valley, Forrest was told they would have to climb to the snow-covered summit of the neighbouring mountains. It took them the best part of a week and, as he put it, 'the misery of it all is beyond my powers of description'. They had no covering at night, and next to no food – apart from a few mouthfuls of dried barley. The rain fell in torrents; to light a fire was impossible.

Up and up they climbed through miles of rhododendrons, tramping over primulas, gentians and lilies, until they reached the summit. Here they turned south, walking for six days over glaciers, snow and ice, and tip-tilted limestone strata which tore his feet to ribbons. At last they had passed the main danger zone, but even now the misery was not complete. As they were descending towards Yetche and the villages by the Mekong, Forrest trod on a hidden bamboo spike, protecting one of the maize fields. The spike pierced his foot and protruded a couple of inches above it. Forrest suffered 'excruciating agony for many days, and it was months before the wound healed completely'. [6]

Fortunately Forrest had visited Yetche earlier that year. The headman now proved a loyal friend. Bands of lamas were still reported to be prowling about in the district. So it was arranged that Forrest, disguised as a Tibetan, should be escorted along the road to Tali.

Forrest finally reached safety on 25 August – to find that his friends had given him up for dead. In fact a week earlier his former employer, Sir Isaac Bayley Balfour, had received a telegram from the Foreign Office to say that the British consul at Tengyueh had reported that there was 'unfortunately little doubt that an Englishman, named Forrest, was murdered on July 21 . . .'[7] Balfour then broke the news of the catastrophe to Forrest's fiancé, Clementina, to his family and to his new employer, Arthur Bulley. The news shocked them all, including Bulley, who felt personally responsible. 'I feel very sick', he told Balfour. 'The vile feeling is that this fine young fellow was working for pay for me . . . that he lost his life in the endeavour to earn my beastly money'.[8]

Thirty-six hours later a second telegram reached the Foreign Office from Tengyueh; 'Forrest is alive and safe'.[9] The news was quickly spread by Balfour, and brought joy and relief to everyone, although Bulley sent a firm letter to Forrest warning him against taking risks in future. Only after safety was assured 'are you to trouble your head about flowers'.[10]

Back in Tali, Forrest recovered from his ordeal with astonishing speed. After such a close encounter with death, most people would have been eager to shake the dust of China off their feet. Not George Forrest. He had always prided himself on his stamina. He planned a winter expedition with his friend George Litton, the British consul at Tengyueh. He had lost a season's work – a season that his rival far to the north, Ernest Wilson, had presumably put to good use. But Yunnan was more or less peaceful again. He would continue to collect seeds and dried specimens as if nothing had happened.

He returned to Britain in 1907 with a haul that delighted both Arthur Bulley and Sir Isaac Bayley Balfour. (In fact it was as rich, in its own way, as the haul that Ernest Wilson was to send to Messrs Veitch the following year.) The most elegant new plant was a snakebark maple, duly christened *Acer forrestii*, with graceful pointed leaves sprouting from red leaf stalks. Forrest also collected a stunning group of new primulas: including yellow and orange versions of *P. bulleyana* (in honour of his employer), *P. vialii* (the 'orchid primula') and P. *secundiflora* (a cowslip with clusters of purple flowers up to 3 feet high). The most striking tree was a silver fir, *Acer delavayi var. forrestii*. This was a variant of a tree discovered by Père Delavay in the 1880s, but only introduced recently to Europe by Ernest Wilson. Forrest's form was even more elegant – with more conspicuous silver stripes under its leaves – than the variant Wilson had introduced.

Forrest made two trips to China as Bulley's personal plant hunter, and then decided against renewing the contract. He found Bulley 'stingy' and insensitive, and longed for a more appreciative employer. In 1912 he found one: a Cornish millionaire, whose family had made their fortune from copper mining. J. C. Williams, as he was called, was creating a vast new garden at Caerhays Castle, tucked away in a romantic cove in south-west Cornwall. By now Robert Holford's concept of the arboretum had been subtly remodelled, as new plant collectors appeared on the scene. The Holfords' original arboretum at Westonbirt consisted of specimen trees and shrubs arranged in irregular glades. By contrast the Williams' new garden at Caerhays was to borrow many ideas from the woodland garden, ideas that were now becoming fashionable. The most daring of these was to let loose on a hillside an avalanche of multicoloured rhododendrons.

It was here, above all, that George Forrest saw his chance to beat Ernest Wilson at his own game. Wilson had introduced about a dozen species of rhododendrons, some of which had originally been discovered by the French missionaries. Forrest introduced at least twenty-five important new species. In 1910, his final season working for Bulley, he sent back seeds that Bulley sold to Williams: *Rh. lacteum* (with flowers the colour of a canary), *Rh. fictolacteum* (with huge leathery leaves and cream-coloured trusses) and *Rh. haematodes* (pillar-box scarlet). His haul in 1912–15, when working for Williams, was just as spectacular: *Rh. scintillans* (an elegant moorland species with lavender-blue leaves), *Rh. clementinae* (named after his wife, Clementina, as loyal and long-suffering as Wilson's wife, Helen) and, best of all, the great *Rh. sinogrande*. This is the species which Gulliver might have met in the land of Bromdingnag. Its leaves were the largest in the genus: they were often more than 2 feet long, and formed astonishing silver plumes as the buds burst open. In fact these leaves were so impressive that the celebrated author W. J. Bean called it 'the most splendid and remarkable of all rhododendrons or indeed of all woody plants hardy in this country.'

As for giant magnolias, Wilson's speciality, Forrest could claim to have discovered the finest of the Big Five. At any rate it proved the giant magnolia most suitable for British arboretums and large gardens. Discovered in 1914, and christened *mollicomata*, it was an eastern subspecies of *M. campbellii*, with two important advantages. It was hardier than the main species, as its huge pink flowers appeared a fortnight later in the spring. It also flowered years earlier in its own life cycle. You could enjoy its first flowers before it was ten years old, instead of having to wait more than twenty.

George Forrest made these discoveries despite a series of mutinies and revolts, and the declaration of a republic to replace the child emperor. Living in China at that time, according to Forrest, was like camping beside an active volcano. In 1912 he began his first trip as a plant hunter working for J. C. Williams. Tengyueh, close to the border with Upper Burma, had proved a safe base in the past. But now, as the Manchu empire tottered and fell, there were revolutionary mobs in the streets.

Summary executions were common. Forrest reckoned that in Tengyueh alone 250 people had been beheaded without trial. Somehow he organised his team of collectors and began to scour the mountains for trees and other plants. But in August he was told that Tengyueh was about to be attacked and his escape route to Burma was blocked. With the greatest difficulty he found an alternative road across the mountains to the south. The journey to the frontier was even more miserable than expected. 'Rain poured in solid sheets . . . the mountains [were] swathed in heavy mists and the streams continually rose.'[11] For five days and five nights they were hammered by the rain, with mules falling, loads slipping and five mountain streams to cross by temporary bamboo bridges. Still, Forrest was used to discomfort. In Burma he waited until calm returned to China. He was back in Yunnan early in 1913, and divided his team of collectors into four groups spread over more than 200 miles of mountains and valleys.

But worse was to come. In November he had written to J. C. Williams an unusually cheerful letter. Collecting was going well. 'I have seed enough to sow all Cornwall.' He loved this alpine landscape at Lichiang: the snow-powdered mountains set against a sapphire sky and the frosty meadows glowing with blue gentians. Of course he missed Clementina – missed her desperately. 'Nothing', as he told Williams, 'will ever compensate me for the separation from my wife and children'. But he promised Williams he would do 'my utmost for you at all times'.[12]

Confident that the political disturbances were now over, he reached Tali on 8 December – only to hear the sound of heavy gunfire. People fleeing from the city gates told him that the army garrison of three regiments had mutinied that morning. Fortunately he was friends with a doctor called Hanna who ran the China Inland Mission. He found him in the schoolhouse made into a temporary hospital, and joined him in tending the wounded and dying. A fortnight's reign of terror followed. No one dared go on the streets. When the mutineers were defeated, and the city rescued by regular troops. Forrest felt he was lucky to be alive. But his escape had been by 'too narrow a squeak to joke of'.[13]

In the next seventeen years Forrest made five more plant-hunting trips to China. The sponsors varied but J. C. Williams paid for a significant share in all of the trips. None were as traumatic as the first. But Forrest continued to be irritated by competition from other plant hunters. He called them 'poachers' who had no right to be in his 'territory'. Ernest Wilson was soon followed by a young Englishman: Reginald Farrer. In turn they were followed by Frank Kingdon-Ward. But Forrest outlasted them all except Ward. In 1930 he planned one last trip to China. Already he must have achieved his goal of introducing more species – and contributing more to British gardens – than anyone except for Ernest Wilson. With Wilson he had to admit he had shared the honours.

By January 1032 he could congratulate himself that this final trip was one of his best. He was sending home 300lb of seed representing four to five hundred species of lilies, primulas, poppies and so on. 'If all goes well,' he wrote home, 'I shall have made a rather glorious and satisfactory finish to all my past years of labour'.[14] He might have added that at last he could claim the reward of a happy retirement, and a life shared with Clementina.

But there was to be no happy retirement for Forrest. On the morning of 6 January he had gone out to shoot game about four miles from his base at Tengyueh. He suddenly felt faint, and called out to two of his men who were nearby. They tried to support him, but he died within a minute or two – apparently of a heart attack. He was buried next day in the small foreign cemetery on a hillock outside the town. His coffin was covered with a large Union Jack, and a small wreath of white roses from his Chinese servant put in the place of honour.

TWIGS

EPILOGUE

Ghosts

Today the arboretums and tree collections of Britain and Ireland are peopled by the ghosts of the men (and women) who created them. I am afraid most of these ghosts must be disappointed.

The centuries have not been kind to the legacy these collectors have left us. The Tradescants' garden in Lambeth vanished under a tidal wave of bricks and mortar more than three hundred years ago. Nothing remains of the original trees planted by Bishop Compton at Fulham Palace (although, as we shall see, the bishop has been honoured by new planting there). I can find no trace of the trees planted by John Evelyn after the great storm of 3 November 1703. It is possible that a cedar of Lebanon from Peter Collinson's collection has survived at Mill Hill; his garden was later incorporated in the public school of that name. Other cedars from the eighteenth century survive at Goodwood, planted by the Duke of Richmond, and at Croome, planted by the Earl of Coventry. But their ghosts must be dissatisfied. The cedars are now merely the remnants of the landscapes created by Capability Brown and no longer part of an exotic collection.

By contrast the ghosts of Princess Augusta and her mentor, Lord Bute, must be delighted when they return to visit Kew. As the creators of Britain's first arboretum, they must recognise Kew's four remarkable survivors, now called the 'Old Lions': the pagoda tree (*Styphnolobium japonicum*) the black locust (*Robinia pseudoacacia*), the sweet chestnut (*Castanea sativa*) and the famous ginkgo. And they can take comfort in the progress since their deaths.

Kew can now boast one of the most comprehensive of arboretums, rescued and reborn thanks to three generations of the masterful Hooker dynasty. Other cheerful ghosts well pleased with progress on their former estates must include the two ducal pioneers, Bedford and Devonshire. Both estates include large remnants of their original arboretums. If only the same could be said of the estate of the third, the Duke of Marlborough, alias Duke Micawber. Nothing now remains of Whiteknights except one or two old oaks that survived after the site was swallowed by Reading University.

This brings us to the ghost who must have suffered the sharpest disappointment: the high priest of the arboretum movement, John Claudius Loudon. He had driven himself to the edge of bankruptcy – and into the grave – in order to create what he called a 'paradise' in Britain. All the nation's finest parks, like Hyde Park, Regent's Park, Greenwich Park and many others, would become arboretums. Old-style planting, with monotonous clumps of oak and planes, would cease forthwith. Instead the public would be dazzled by the richness of arboretums whose trees came from all over the temperate world – dazzled and instructed. But what has been done by the authorities in the last two centuries to make this happen? Little or nothing.

Poor Loudon. He was a social reformer, intoxicated with a vision of an arboretum as a source of improvement as well as delight. It was to bridge the gap between horticulture and botany, and between the rich and the working class, but proved a bridge too far.

And a visit to the Derby Arboretum, the only one Loudon

personally designed, rubbed in the message. Today it's a public park near the centre of the city of Derby with few exotic trees to show it was once a magnet for thousands of excited visitors.

Still, Loudon's ghost must take comfort from one dazzling success. The largest, and most spectacular, arboretum in Europe was the heir to Loudon's most extravagant ideas. At Westonbirt Robert Holford and his family had acres enough – and millions enough – to make a truly comprehensive arboretum. It was here that every species of tree tough enough to survive the British winter could find a home. And today Westonbirt is the favourite child of the Forestry Commission and the nearest to what Loudon's ghost would call 'paradise'.

One other ghost would take comfort from a visit: Bishop Compton's. As we saw, none of the trees he planted in his garden at Fulham Palace have survived today. But a catalogue of his collection has been lovingly reconstructed. And the bishop still has many admirers. About twenty-five years ago it was decided to replant a selection of his most inspiring introductions.

In June 2023 I followed the winding, grassy path, leading from his modest tomb by the east window of the church across to the walled garden and the lawn in front of the palace. Most of the newly planted trees here are exotics from America, like those originally sent by young John Banister at the cost of his life. By now the bishop's favourite trees, a black walnut, a black locust and a glaucous-leaved magnolia are adolescent – just as they were when he knew them.

One more tribute was paid to the bishop: a small American shrub was christened *Comptonia*. Would he have felt humiliated to lend his name to such an insignificant plant? Perhaps not. I think he would have accepted it with Christian humility.

ENDNOTES

Chapter 1

1 D. Defoe, *The Storm*, p. 57.
2 Ibid. p. 134.
3 Ibid. p. 135.
4 J. Evelyn, *Silva* (1776 edition), p. 482.
5 Ibid. p. 485.
6 Ibid. p. 646.
7 Ibid. p. 633.
8 Ibid. p. 645.

Chapter 2

1 E. Carpenter, *The Protestant Bishop*, 1956, p. 7.
2 G. Stirn, diary entry July 1638, quoted in P. Leith-Ross, *The John Tradescants*, pp. 152–3.
3 J. Evelyn, diary entry September 1657, *Diary* ed. E. S. De Beer, pp. 347–8.
4 J. Tradescant the Elder, *Journal*, quoted in P. Leith-Ross, op. cit., p. 62.
5 Ibid. p. 224.
6 E. Gent, quoted in P. Leith-Ross, op. cit., p. 110.
7 J. Banister to Bishop Compton, quoted in Jean O'Neill, *Country Life*, 17 November 1977, p. 1496.
8 Ibid.
9 Ibid.
10 J. Loudon, *Arboretum et Fruticetum Britannicum*, I. 44.
11 J. Ray, quoted in Jean O'Neill, *Country Life*, 8 December 1977, pp. 1712–13.

Chapter 3

1 P. Collinson in A. W. Armstrong (ed.), *'Forget Not Mee & My Garden...'* (2002).
2 P. Collinson to John Bartram, 17 January 1734, op. cit., p. 11.
3 *'Forget Not Mee & My Garden...'*, pp. 11–15.
4 Ibid. p. 26.
5 Ibid.
6 P. Collinson to J. Bartram, 4 April 1765, *The Correspondence of John Bartram*, p. 644.
7 P. Collinson to J. Bartram, September 1741, op. cit., p. 167.
8 P. Collinson, pp. 66–69.
9 P. Collinson to J. Bartram, 31 July 1742, J. O'Neill, *Peter Collinson*, p. 101.
10 Ibid. p. 101.
11 Ibid p. 101.
12 Duke of Richmond to P. Collinson, 17 December 1742, Add. MSS 28726 f 124.
13 W. J. Bean, *Trees and Shrubs Hardy in the British Isles*.
14 P. Kalm, *Visit to England*, pp. 66–70.
15 Collinson Memoranda, 20 August 1762.
16 Duke of Richmond, Add. MSS.
17 P. Collinson to Linnaeus, 16 March 1767, in J. O'Neill, *Peter Collinson*, pp. 271–2.
18 P. Collinson to C. Colden, 25 February 1764, in A. W. Armstrong (ed.), *'Forget Not Mee & My Garden...'* pp. 254–7.
19 P. Collinson to C. Colden, op. cit.
20 P. Collinson to C. Colden, op. cit.

Chapter 4

1 H. Walpole to E. of Strafford 5 July 1761 in *Letters of Horace Walpole* Vol. 3, pp. 409–10.
2 *Walpole Society* vol. 18 (1929–30) p. 13.
3 Ibid. vol. 3 (1955) p. 153.
4 Quoted in R. Desmond, *Kew*, p. 31.

Chapter 5

1 Duyker and Tingbrand (eds.), *Daniel Solander: Collected Correspondence*, p. 358.
2 P. Cibot, *Memoires*, quoted in R. Salisbury, *Paradisus Londinensis*, I. 38.

Chapter 6

1 Harcourt Papers IV, 21–23, quoted in A. Roberts, *George III*, p. 507.
2 RL RCIN 1047014, quoted in A. Roberts, op. cit., p. 527.
3 A. Menzies to Sir J. Banks 1–14 January 1793 in *The Indian and Pacific Correspondence of Sir Joseph Banks* vol. 4, document 13, p. 38.
4 Ibid. p. 39.
5 Ibid. p. 41.
6 A. Menzies to Sir J. Banks, 8 September 1794, op. cit., document 140, pp. 225–6.
7 A. Menzies to Sir J. Banks, 26 March 1795, op. cit., document 171, p. 273.
8 A. Menzies to Sir J. Banks, 28 April 1795, op. cit., document 178, p. 289.
9 Ibid.
10 A. Menzies to Sir J. Banks, 14 September 1795, op. cit., document 196, pp. 308–9.

Chapter 7

1 Banks, 'Hints on the Subject of Gardens' in *The Indian and Pacific Correspondence of Sir Joseph Banks* vol. 3, document 304, pp. 414–5.
2 Ibid.
3 Lord Macartney's journal, quoted in J. Goodman, *Planting the World*, pp. 231–2.
4 Cranmer-Byng (ed.), *An Embassy to China*, p. 125.
5 E. Backhouse and J. Bland, *Annals and Memoirs of the Court of Peking*.
6 G. Staunton to Sir J. Banks, 12 November 1793, *The Indian and Pacific Correspondence of Sir Joseph Banks* vol. 4, document 95.
7 Haxton's Journal, 14 October 1793 quoted in *The Indian and Pacific Correspondence of Sir Joseph Banks* vol. 4.

Chapter 8

1 Public Record office of Northern Ireland Foster/Massereene Papers D562/7829C.
2 Ibid.
3 J. Ellis to J. Foster, Sep 1770, quoted in A. Malcolmson, *John Foster*, p. 346.
4 C. Nelson and E. McCracken *The Brightest Jewel* pp. 48, 65, 68–9.
5 Ibid.
6 J. Swift, quoted in J. D'Alton *The History of County Dublin* (1838), pp. 174–5.
7 C. Nelson and McCracken, op. cit., p. 48.
8 C. Nelson and McCracken, op. cit., p. 49.
9 C. Nelson and McCracken, op. cit., p. 76.
10 C. Nelson and McCracken, op. cit., p. 75.

Chapter 9

1 D. Douglas, 6 August 1823, *Journal Kept by David Douglas During His Travels in North America 1823–1827*, pp. 4–5.
2 D. Douglas, 23 August 1823, op. cit., p. 8.
3 D. Douglas, 27 August 1823, op. cit., p. 9.
4 D. Douglas, 1 September 1823, op. cit., p. 9.
5 D. Douglas, 4 September 1823, op. cit., p. 10.
6 D. Douglas, 16 September 1823, op. cit., p. 12.
7 D. Douglas, 20 September 1823, op. cit., pp. 14–15.
8 D. Douglas, 30 September 1823, op. cit., p. 16.
9 D. Douglas, 1 October 1823, op. cit., p. 17.
10 D. Douglas, 10 October 1823, op. cit., p. 20.
11 D. Douglas, 3 November 1823, op. cit., p.25. D
12 D. Douglas, 8 April 1825, op. cit., p.102.
13 D. Douglas, 10 April 1825, op. cit., pp.102–3.
14 A. L. Mitchell and S. House *David Douglas, Explorer and Botanist*, (1999) p. 31.

Chapter 10

1 D. Douglas, 7 April 1825, op. cit., p. 102.

2 D. Douglas, 11 August 1824, op. cit., p. 84.
3 D. Douglas, 29 September 1824, op. cit., pp. 88–9.
4 D. Douglas, 5 November 1824, op. cit., p. 92.
5 Ibid.
6 D. Douglas, 14 December 1824, op. cit., pp. 93–4.
7 D. Douglas, 18 December 1824, op. cit., p. 95.
8 Ibid.
9 D. Douglas, 1 January 1825, op. cit., p. 100.
10 D. Douglas, 12 February 1825, op. cit., p. 101.
11 D. Douglas, 7 April 1825, op. cit., pp. 101–2.
12 D. Douglas, 8 April 1825, op. cit., p.102.
13 Ibid.
14 D. Douglas, 19 April 1825, op. cit., p. 106.
15 D. Douglas, 20 June 1825, op. cit., p. 129.
16 D. Douglas, 19 July 1825, op. cit., p. 138.
17 Ibid.
18 D. Douglas, 9 October 1826, op. cit., p. 218.
19 D. Douglas, 19 October 1826, op. cit., p. 225.
20 D. Douglas, 24–25 November 1826, op. cit., p. 229.
21 D. Douglas, 26 November 1826, op. cit., p. 230.
22 Ibid.
23 D. Douglas, 27 November 1826, op. cit., p. 231.

Chapter 11

1 RHS *Transactions* vol. 6 (1826) Preface, p. v.
2 RHS *Transactions* vol. 7 (1830) Preface, p. ii.
3 J. Loudon ('The Conductor') *Gardener's Magazine* vol. 5 (1829)
   pp. 344–8.
4 *The Times*, 15 January 1830.
5 *Gardener's Magazine* vol. 6 (1830) pp. 234–5.
6 Ibid. p. 241.
7 Ibid. p. 237.
8 Ibid. p. 239.
9 Ibid. p. 252.
10 D. Douglas to Sir W. Hooker in W. Hooker, 'A Brief Memoir to the
   life of Mr David Douglas', *Companion to Botanical Magazine* 2, 1836.
11 Ibid.

12 Ibid.
13 D. Douglas, *Journals* Appendix I, pp. 296–2.

Chapter 12

1 See the plan in H. Repton, *Fragments on the Theory and Practice of Landscape Gardening*, p. 527.
2 J. Loudon, *Gardener's Magazine* vol. 6 (1830) pp. 582, 719 and *Gardener's Magazine* vol. 7 (1831) p. 203.
3 J. Loudon *Gardener's Magazine* vol. 9 (1833) pp. 468–9.
4 Ibid. p. 469.
5 J. Loudon, *Gardener's Magazine* vol. 12 (1836) pp. 28–35.
6 Mrs Arbuthnot's *Journal*, 14 January 1821, vol. 1 (1950) p. 63.
7 Mary Mitford to her father, quoted in M. Soames *The Profligate Duke*, p. 125.
8 Ibid. p. 126.
9 Mary Mitford to Sir W. Elford, quoted in M. Soames, op. cit., p. 127.
10 J. Loudon, *Gardener's Magazine* vol. 9 (1833) pp. 664–9 and vol. 11 (1835) pp. 502–3.

Chapter 13

1 C. Greville, 20 January 1820, *The Greville Memoirs* I. 23.
2 J. Forbes, *Hortus Woburnensis*, p. xix.
3 Ibid. pp. 236–7.
4 Ibid. p. 238.
5 J. Loudon, *Gardener's Magazine* vol. 7 (1831) p. 395.
6 J. Paxton, *Horticultural Register* I (3) 1 September 1831.
7 K. Colquhoun, *A Thing in Disguise*, p. 57.
8 Ibid. p. 42.
9 J. Paxton to S. Paxton, quoted in K. Colquhoun, op. cit., p. 58.
10 Duke of Devonshire to J. Paxton, quoted in K. Colquhoun, op. cit., pp. 60–61.
11 Duke of Devonshire to J. Paxton, K. Colquhoun, op. cit., p. 62.
12 J. Loudon, *Gardener's Magazine* vol. 11 (1835) pp. 385–95.
13 J. Paxton to S. Paxton, K. Colquhoun op. cit., p. 57.
14 Duke of Devonshire Diary, 10 November 1836, quoted in K. Colquhoun, op. cit., p. 57.

15 J. Loudon, *Gardener's Magazine* vol. 16 (1840) pp. 521–45.
16 Ibid. p. 75.
17 Ibid. p. 535.
18 Ibid. p. 534.

Chapter 14

1 J. Hooker to G. Bentham, 1 April 1849, J. Hooker, *Indian Letters 1847–1851.*
2 J. Hooker, *Himalayan Journals*, p. 131.
3 J. Hooker, op. cit., vol. 2, pp. 202–3.
4 Ibid. p. 203.
5 B. Hodgson to Sir W. Hooker, 1 December 1850, *Indian Letters 1847–1851*, f 223.
6 J. Hooker, op. cit., vol. 2, pp. 219–20.

Chapter 15

1 RHS Fortune Volumes (1843) quoted in A. Watt *Robert Fortune* pp. 23, 370–3.
2 R. Fortune, *Three Years' Wanderings in the Northern Provinces of China*, pp. 1–2.
3 Ibid. p. 24.
4 Ibid p.26–28.
5 Ibid. pp. 42–3.
6 Ibid. p. 46.
7 Ibid. p. 47.
8 Ibid. p. 50.
9 Ibid. p. 88.
10 Ibid. pp. 253–4.
11 Ibid. p. 256.
12 Ibid. pp. 258–9.
13 Ibid. p. 263.
14 RHS Fortune Volumes, quoted in A. Watt, op. cit., pp. 83–4.

ENDNOTESENDNOTES

Chapter 16

1 J. Veitch quoting from a letter from W. Lobb to Sir W. Hooker in S. Shephard, *Seeds of Fortune*, p. 83.
2 Veitch's advertisement 18 May 1843 in S. Shephard, op. cit.
3 *Country Life.*
4 W. Lobb to J. Veitch in S. Shephard, op. cit., p. 115.
5 J. Veitch to Sir W. Hooker in S. Shephard, op. cit., p. 125.

Chapter 17

1 R. Fortune, *Journey to the Tea Districts of China*, pp. 61–62.
2 R. Fortune, op. cit., p. 214.
3 R. Fortune *Residence among the Chinese*, p. 14.
4 Ibid. pp. 98–99.
5 Ibid. p. 99.
6 Ibid. p. 121.
7 Ibid. p. 270.
8 Ibid. p. 286.
9 Ibid. p. 368.
10 Ibid. pp. 385–6.
11 Ibid. p. 415.

Chapter 18

1 Wikipedia.org/wiki/Philipp von Siebold, p. 3/13.
2 Ibid p. 5/13.
3 A. Watt, *Robert Fortune*, p. 199.
4 R. Fortune, *Yedo and Peking* (reprint 2005), p. 49.
5 S. Shephard, *Seeds of Fortune*, p. 144.

Chapter 19

1 W. S. Gilpin, *Practical Hints upon Landscape Gardening* (1832)
2 J. Loudon, *Arboretum et Fruticetum Britannicum*, I. 211–2. And see P. Elliot, C. Watkins and S. Daniels in *The British Arboretum* (2011) pp. 40–5.

Chapter 20

1 A. Henry to Sir J. Hooker, 20 March 1885, quoted in S. O'Brien, *In the Footsteps of Augustine Henry* pp. 31–2

2 A. Pratt, *To the Snows of Tibet through China* (1892) p. 49, quoted in S. O'Brien, op. cit., p.71.

3 A. Henry, quoted in S. O'Brien, op. cit., p. 190.

Chapter 21

1 E. Wilson Journal, quoted in T. Musgrave, C. Gardiner and W. Musgrave, *The Plant Hunters*, p. 158.

2 S. Shephard, op. cit., p. 244.

3 W. J. Bean, *Trees and Shrubs Hardy in the British Isles*, vol. I. p. 653.

4 S. Shephard, op. cit., p. 246.

5 Ibid. p. 257.

Chapter 22

1 G. Forrest to I. B. Balfour, 27 May 1905, Archives of the Royal Botanical Garden Edinburgh quoted in B. MacLean, *George Forrest: Plant Hunter*, p. 64.

2 G. Forrest to I. B. Balfour, 3 July 1905, op. cit., p. 66.

3 G. Forrest quoted in J. M. Cowan, *The Journeys and Plant Introductions of George Forrest*, pp. 12-13.

4 G. Forrest, ibid. p. 13.

5 G. Forrest, ibid. p. 13.

6 G. Forrest, ibid. p. 14.

7 Consul Litton to I. B. Balfour, 17 August 1905, Archives of the RBGE, op. cit., p. 67.

8 A. K. Bulley to I. B. Balfour, 19 August 1905, ibid.

9 A. K. Bulley to I. B. Balfour, 19 August 1905, ibid.

10 A. K. Bulley to G. Forrest, 21 August 1905, Forrest family papers quoted in B. MacLean, op. cit., p. 67.

11 B. MacLean, op. cit., p. 110.

12 G. Forrest to J. C. Williams, 10 October 1912, Archives of the RBGE, op. cit., p. 119.

13 G. Forrest quoted in B. MacLean, op cit., p. 120.

14 G. Forrest to his wife quoted in J. M. Cowan, op cit., p. 35.

BIBLIOGRAPHY

Aiton, W. T., *Hortus Kewensis: a Catalogue of the Plants Cultivated in the Royal Botanic Garden at Kew* (London, 2nd ed. 1813)

Annesley, A., *Beautiful and Rare Trees and Plants* (London 2003)

Arbuthnot, Mrs H., *Journal* vol. 1 (London 1821)

Armstrong, A. W. (ed.) *'Forget not Mee & My Garden...': Selected Letters, 1725–1768 of Peter Collinson, F.R.S.* (Philadelphia 2002)

Backhouse, E. and Bland, J., *Annals and Memoirs of the Court of Peking* (London 1914)

Bartram, J., *The Correspondence of John Bartram 1734–1777*, eds Berkeley, E. and Berkeley, D. (Florida 1992)

Bean, W. J., *Trees and Shrubs Hardy in the British Isles*, 4 vols (London, 1976–81)

Bretschneider, E., *History of European Botanical Discoveries in China*, 2 vols (London 1898)

Chambers, Neil, *The Indian and Pacific Correspondence of Sir Joseph Bank 1768–1821*, ed. Neil Chambers, vols 3–4 (London 2010)

Clarke, D. L., *Trees and Shrubs Hardy in the British Isles*, vol. 5 (London 1988)

Colquhoun, K., *A Thing in Disguise: The Visionary Life of Joseph Paxton* (London 2003)

Crane, P. R., *Ginkgo: The Tree that Time Forgot* (London 2013)

Cranmer-Byng, J. L., *An Embassy to China: Lord Macartney's Journal 1793–1794* (London 2004)

D'Alton, J., *The History of the County of Dublin* (Dublin 1838)

De Belder, J., *Het Arboretum van Kalmthout* (Belgium 1998)

Defoe, D., *The Storm* (London 1704; paperback edition, London 2005)

Desmond, R., *Kew: the History of the Royal Botanical Gardens* (London 1999)

Desmond, R., *Sir Joseph Dalton Hooker* (Suffolk 1999)

Douglas, D., *Journal Kept by David Douglas during his Travel in North America 1823–1827* (London 1914)

Duyker, E. and Tingbrand, P. (eds.), *Daniel Solander: Collected Correspondence 1753–1782* (Melbourne 1995)

Edwards, A., *The Plant Hunter's Atlas: A World Tour of Botanical Adventures, Chance Discoveries and Strange Specimens* (London 2021)

Elliott, P. A. Watkins, C. and Daniels, S., *The British Arboretum: Trees, Science and Culture in the Nineteenth Century* (London 2011)

Elwes, H. J. and Henry, A., *The Trees of Great Britain and Ireland*, 7 vols (Edinburgh 1906–13)

Evelyn, J., *Silva: or a Discourse of Forest-Trees, with notes by Dr A. Hunter* (York, 1776)

Evelyn, J., *The Diary of John Evelyn:* edited by E. S. de Beer (Oxford 2006)

Farjon, A., *A Handbook of the World's Conifers*, 2 vols (Leiden 2010)

Flanagan, M. and Kirkham, T., *Wilson's China a Century On* (London 2009)

Forbes, J., *Hortus Woburnensis. A Descriptive Catalogue* (London 1833)

Forrest, G., *Journeys and Plant Introductions* (Oxford 1952)

Fortune, R., *Three Years Wanderings in the Northern Provinces of China* (London 1847)

Fortune, R., *A Journey to the Tea Countries of China* (London 1852)

Fortune, R., *A Residence among the Chinese: Inland, on the Coast, and at Sea* (London 1857)

R. Fortune, *Yedo and Peking: A Journey to the Capitals of Japan and China* (London, 2005)

Fry, C., *The Plant Hunters: The Adventures of the World's Greatest Botanical Explorers* (London 2012)

Gardiner, J. M., *Magnolias* (Connecticut 1989)

Goodman, J., *Planting the World. Joseph Banks and His Collections – An Adventurous History of Botany* (London 2020)

Greville, G., *The Greville Diaries*, vol. 1 (London 1875)

Grimshaw, J. and Bayton, R., *New Trees: Recent Introductions to Cultivation* (Kew 2009)

Heseltine, M. and A., *Thenford. The Creation of an English Garden* (London 2016)

Hooker, J. D., *Himalayan Journals* (London 1854)

Hooker, J. D., *The Rhododendrons of Sikkim-Himalaya* (London 1849–51)

Hooker, W. J., *A Brief Memoir* (London 1836)

Hunt, D. R. (ed.), *Magnolias and Their Allies: Proceedings of an International Symposium* (London 1998)

Huxley, L., *Life and Letters of Sir Joseph Dalton Hooker* (London 1918)

Jackson, A. B., *Catalogue of the Trees and Shrubs [at Westonbirt] in the Collection of the Late Sir G. L. Holford* (Oxford 1927)

Kilpatrick, J., *Fathers of Botany. The Discovery of Chinese Plants by European Missionaries* (London 2014)

Kalm, P., *Visit to England* (London 2012)

King, A. and Clifford, S., *Trees Be Company. An Anthology of Poetry* (Bristol 1989)

Kingdon-Ward, F., *Berried Treasure: Shrubs for Autumn & Winter Colour in Your Garden* (London 1954)

Lamb, K. and Bowe, P., *A History of Gardening in Ireland* (Dublin, 1995)

Lear, M., *Oare House: Sir Henry and Lady Keswick's Collection of Trees and Shrubs* (Oxford 2016)

Lear, M., *Glenkiln Garden and Art. Sir Henry and Lady Keswick's Collection etc* (Oxford 2019)

Leith-Ross, P., *The John Tradescants: Gardeners to the Rose and Lily Queen* (London 1984)

Loudon, J. C., *An Encyclopaedia of Gardening etc* (London 1822)

Loudon, J. C., *An Encyclopaedia of Trees and Shrubs* (London 1842)

Loudon, J.C., *Arboretum et Fruticetum Britannicum*, 8 vols (London, 2nd edn 1844)

Malcolmson, A., *John Foster (1740–1828): The Politics of Improvement and Prosperity* (Dublin 2011)

McLean, B., *George Forrest – Plant Hunter* (Suffolk 2004)

Mitchell, A., *Trees of Britain and Northern Europe* (London 1982)

Musgrave, T., Gardner, C. and Musgrave, W., *The Plant Hunters* (London 1998)

Nelson, E. C. and McCracken E. M., *The Brightest Jewel. A History of the National Botanic Gardens Glasnevin, Dublin* (Kilkenny 1987)

O'Brien, S., *In the Footsteps of Augustine Henry* (Suffolk 2011)

O'Brien, S., *In the Footsteps of Joseph Dalton Hooker* (London 2018)

O'Neill, J. and Maclean, E., *Peter Collinson* (Philadelphia 2008)

Pakenham, T., *Meetings with Remarkable Trees* (London 1996)

Pakenham, T., *Remarkable Trees of the World* (London 2002)

Pakenham, T., *The Company of Trees* (London 2015)

Pim, S., *The Wood and the Trees: A Biography of Augustine Henry* (Kilkenny 1984)

Pratt, A. E., *To the Snows of Tibet through China* (London 1892)

Ray, J., *Historia Generalis Plantarum* (London 1686–1704)

Repton, H., *Fragments on the Theory and Practice of Landscape Gardening* (London 1816, republished by J. Loudon 1840)

Roberts, A., *George III: The Life and Reign of Britain's Most Misunderstood Monarch* (London 2021)

Rushforth, K., *Trees of Britain and Europe* (London 1999)

Salisbury, R. A., *Paradisus Londinensis* (London 1806)

Sargent, C. S., *Plantae Wilsonianae etc* (Cambridge 1913–17)

Shephard, S., *Seeds of Fortune: a Gardening Dynasty* (London 2003)

Soames, M., *The Profligate Duke: George Spencer-Churchill, Fifth Duke of Marlborough, and His Duchess* (London 1987)

Spongberg, S., *A Reunion of Trees* (Cambridge, Massachusetts, 1990)

Staunton, G., *An Authentic Account of an Embassy from the King of Great Britain to the Emperor of China*, 2 vols (London 1797)

Toomer, S., *Planting and Maintaining a Tree Collection* (Portland 2010)

Treseder, N. G., *Magnolias* (London 1978)

Van Hoey Smith, J., *Trompenburg Arboretum: Green Oasis in Rotterdam* (Rotterdam 2001)

Veitch, J. H., *Hortus Veitchii* (London 1906)

Walpole, H., *The Letters of Horace Walpole*, vol. 3 (London 1906)

Walpole Society 1929–30, vol. 18 (Oxford 1930)

Watt, A., *Robert Fortune. A Plant Hunter in the Orient* (London 2017)

Wilson, E. H., *A Naturalist in Western China with Vasculum, Camera and Gun* (London 1913)

Periodicals

Botanical Magazine
Gardener's Magazine
Gardener's Chronicle
Horticultural Register
International Dendrological Society Yearbook
RHS Transactions

Manuscripts

Duke of Devonshire in BM Add. MSS
J. D. Hooker Indian Letters and Journals at Kew
Duke of Richmond in BM Add. MSS

Digital

Jstor
Wikipedia

ACKNOWLEDGEMENTS

Once again I have relied on the generous advice of experts. Foremost among them was my godson, Matthew Jebb, Director of the National Botanic Garden at Glasnevin, and Seamus O'Brien, his deputy at Kilmacurragh. The head gardeners who advised me included Adam Whitbourn at Blarney Castle, and Neil Porteous, formerly at Mount Stewart. Among the botanists and dendrologists who helped me were Tom Christian, Tony Kirkham, Martyn Rix, Keith Rushforth, Simon Toomer, Alison Vry, Dan Crowley and Michael Lear.

I am most grateful to two of my friends – Terence Reeves-Smyth and Charles Horton – who read an early draft of this book. Their comments were invaluable.

I am much in the debt of the staff at the RBG at Kew Gardens, the RBG at Edinburgh, the RHS garden at Wisley and the National Arboretum at Westonbirt. All four institutions helped me in numerous ways.

I was also fortunate to enjoy the hospitality – and to be able to pick the brains – of the following collectors of trees: Mary Ballyedmund, Simon and Alice Boyd, Teddy Clive, David Davies, Stoker and Amanda Devonshire, the late Lindy Dufferin, Olda and Catherine Fitzgerald, Anthea Forde, Maurice Foster, Kathy Gilfillan, Tracy Hamilton, Michael and Anne Heseltine, Tom Hudson, Henry Keswick and the late Tessa Keswick, Brian Kingham, Allen and Lorena Krause, Julie and Paddy Mackie,

Daphne and Bill Montgomery, Maureen and Liam O'Flanagan, Alison and Brendan Rosse, Fergus Thompson, Aidan Walsh, Robert Wilson-Wright.

Most of the trees that I bought for my own arboretum came from the remarkable nursery run by Jan Ravensberg at Clara, County Offaly.

I must thank Ed Lake, Lucinda McNeile and all the staff of Orion who helped make this book a reality.

I must also acknowledge my debt to the following close friends who spurred me on: Jacky Ivimy, Jennie Bland, Neiti Gowrie, Kate Kavanagh, Barbara Bailey, Barbara FitzGerald, Octavia Tulloch, Margie Phillips and the late Mark Girouard, and the late Timothy and Patricia Daunt.

All my family have been most supportive, especially my son-in-law Alex Chisholm.

And I owe most of all to my wife Valerie who died in January 2023.

INDEX

Pandora, HMS 103–4
paperbush 244, 269
Parkinson, John 25, 27
Parkinson, Sydney 77
Paxton, Joseph 4, 201–7, 209, 212, 218, 219
Paxton, Sarah 205, 209
pea 219
pear 24
Peckham 51–2
Pedro II 252
Peel, Sir Robert 216
Peking 107, 111, 112
Pennsylvania 29, 134
penstemon 151
peony 108, 251
Pepys, Samuel 14
persimmon 28, 71
Petre, Lord 40, 42, 48, 49, 53, 64
Philadelphia 41, 135
philadelphus 311, 314
Phipps, Lieut Constantine 76
phlox 151
Physic Garden, Chelsea 39, 50, 51, 65, 68, 69, 139
Pigou, William 85
pine
  big-cone 173, 259
  black 127, 290
  bristlecone 258
  Chilean 101, 127–9, 140, 253–6
  digger 173
  foxtail 71
  gigantic 156, 158–9
  glaucous 187, 208
  Monterey 3, 97, 208, 259
  Norfolk Island 127–9
  P. bungeana 288
  P. densiflora 290
  P. radiata 172
  Scots 198
  species 13, 51, 208, 288, 302, 303
  sugar 185, 204, 255
  swamp 70
  umbrella 28, 190, 287–8, 291
  western yellow 204, 259
  Weymouth 50, 62, 70, 198
  white 290

Pitcairn Island 104
Pitt family 93
Pitt, William the Elder 72
Pitt, William the Younger 88, 89, 90–3, 104, 118, 127
Poliothyrsis sinense 318
poplar 329
poppy 225, 327–8, 329
ports, treaty 234, 237–8, 243–4, 246, 249, 268–9, 275, 304–5, 318, 322
Pottinger, Sir Henry 237
Potts, John 133
Powell, Thomas 12
Pratt, Antwerp 316
Price, Sir Uvedale 297
primula 225, 340
Primula obconica 327
protea 83
Providence, HMS 104–5
Prussia 72, 73

Qianlong emperor 106, *106*, 108–14
Quadra, Juan Francisco de la Bodega y 95–6, 97, 99
Quakers 37, 38, 41, 43, 55, 68

redwood 97, 173, 260–1
Regent's Park 4, 186, 216
Repton, Humphry 182, 187, 190, 198
Resolution, HMS 78, 83, 102
rhododendron 225–6, 231–2, 252, 254
  hybrids 45, 282
  species 45, 52, 191, 244, 309, 311, 314, 329, 341
rhubarb 225
Richmond, 2nd Duke of 40, 42, 49, 53
Richmond Lodge, London 61
Richmond, Thomas 77
Rio de Janeiro 142–3, 252, 254
Rolle, Lady 256
rose 114, 115, 219, 248
Ross, Sir John 221
rowan 311
Royal Family, British 3, 14, 21–2, 69
Royal Horticultural Society (RHS) 3, 215
Royal Society 14–15, 37–40, 75, 76, 78, 79, 115